Lev Shestov

Philosopher of the Sleepless Night

Matthew Beaumont

BLOOMSBURY ACADEMIC

LONDON · NEW YORK · OXFORD · NEW DELHI · SYDNEY

BLOOMSBURY ACADEMIC
Bloomsbury Publishing Plc
50 Bedford Square, London, WC1B 3DP, UK
1385 Broadway, New York, NY 10018, USA
29 Earlsfort Terrace, Dublin 2, Ireland

BLOOMSBURY, BLOOMSBURY ACADEMIC and the Diana logo
are trademarks of Bloomsbury Publishing Plc

First published in Great Britain 2021
This paperback edition published in 2022

For legal purposes the Acknowledgements on p. ix constitute an extension
of this copyright page.

Cover design by Charlotte Daniels
Cover image: Portrait of Lev Shestov (© Heritage Image Partnership Ltd /
Alamy Stock Photo)

A catalogue record for this book is available from the British Library.

Library of Congress Control Number: 2020941210.

ISBN: HB: 978-1-3501-5114-7
PB: 978-1-3502-0402-7
ePDF: 978-1-3501-5116-1
eBook: 978-1-3501-5117-8

Typeset by Deanta Global Publishing Services, Chennai, India *for Camilla, who came like a thief in the night*

Watchman, what of the night?

(Isa. 21: 11)

Take ye heed, watch and pray: for ye know not when the time is.

For the Son of Man is as a man taking a far journey, who left his house, and gave authority to his servants, and to every man his work, and commanded the porter to watch.

Watch ye therefore: for ye know not when the master of the house cometh, at even, or at midnight, or at the cockcrowing, or in the morning:

Lest coming suddenly he find you sleeping.

And what I say unto you I say unto all, Watch.

(Mark 13: 33–37)

Contents

Figures

Acknowledgements

For encouragement of various kinds, I'd like to thank Bruce Baugh, Tim Beasley-Murray, Steve Edwards, Linda Freedman, Leo Hollis, Josephine McDonagh, Andy Murray, Charlotte Robertson, Alberto Toscano, Michael Weingrad and Sarah Young. I am extremely grateful to the anonymous referees commissioned by Bloomsbury Academic for their generous and constructive comments. At Bloomsbury, in addition to the support of Lucy Russell, I have benefitted greatly from the commitment, above all, of Lisa Goodrum, whom I also sincerely thank. I am an interloper, in disciplinary terms, when it comes to the study of Lev Shestov's thought, so I'd here like to register my respect for the scholarship of those specialists in this and adjacent fields that I cite in this book, and in particular for Ramona Fotiade's tireless promotion of his intellectual importance.

I want to express my gratitude to Kate Rothko Prizel and Christopher Rothko for permission to reproduce an image of Mark Rothko's painting *Gethsemane* (1945) in Chapter 4; also to Henry Weinfield for permission to quote from his translation of Nerval's 'Christ at Gethsemane' and Faber and Faber Ltd. for permission to quote from T. S. Eliot's *The Waste Land*. Finally, my thanks to the Chambers Fund in the Department of English at UCL for providing generous financial assistance in the reproduction of images.

Introduction
Staying woke and staying awake

Stay woke!

What does it mean, politically speaking, to resist the temptation to sleep? To be awake? And to remain awake? The word 'woke', used in its colloquial sense as an adjective to signify 'alert to racial or social discrimination', was first included in the *Oxford English Dictionary* in 2017. The *OED* explains that, in this sense, the origin of 'woke', which it identifies as 'US regional and nonstandard', lies in an African-American usage from the late nineteenth century, meaning simply 'awake; not (or no longer) asleep'. Specifically, it traces this slang term, in print, back to the white American folklorist Joel Chandler Harris, whose Uncle Remus stories were both a record of African-American oral stories, if no doubt a partial and unreliable one, and an emblem of white Americans' unacceptable appropriation of African-American culture. In Harris's *Balaam and his Master and Other Sketches and Stories* (1891), Balaam himself, a former slave, whose ideological role is to reassure white readers of the timeless loyalty and respect of African-American people in the United States, describes another oppressed black man of his acquaintance as 'dreamin'', and comments, 'He ain't woke good yet!'[1]

The *OED* ascribes the more recent, figurative inflection of the word 'woke' to the Civil Rights movement, citing an article in the *New York Times Magazine* from 1962 that includes a short glossary of African-American slang. The glossary contains this entry: '*If you're woke, you dig it... Woke...*well-informed, up-to-date ("Man I'm woke")'.[2] The *OED* goes on to credit the African-

American singer Erykah Badu with reinitiating this trend by including the phrase 'I stay woke' as a refrain in her song 'Master Teacher'. First released in 2008, Badu's song takes aim at the narcotic temptations, especially religious ones, which neutralize or undermine the political struggle of African-American people: 'What if there was no niggas/ Only master teachers? / (I stay woke)'. More recently, and more pressingly, over the course of the last five or six years, the Black Lives Matter movement has revived and re-politicized this usage of the phrase. In the aftermath of the murder of Travyon Martin, an unarmed African-American teenager, in Florida in February 2012, activists set up a website called StayWoke.org in order to recruit people to their campaign against racist violence. Since then, increasingly detached from this movement, the phrase has proliferated and become evermore diffuse in its application – not least in the form of the Twitter hashtag #staywoke. Today, it is arguably little more than an algebraic slogan designed to signal a vague awareness that something, something or other, is wrong with the world. As Amanda Hess commented in a delightfully scornful piece for the *New York Times Magazine* in 2016, '"stay woke" is the new "plugged in"'.[3]

'Man I'm woke', then, is currently *le dernier cri* in liberal circles in the United Kingdom and the United States. Metropolitan hipsters, keen to indicate not simply a certain solidarity with oppressed minorities, especially black or African-American ones, but some more universal attitude that advertises the fact that they are conscious of their own comparative social privilege, have adopted it to the point where, on social media, it seems to have become a reflexive, perhaps instinctively defensive, response to the slightest hint of entitlement. This is the third in a series of appropriations by white people. The first is of course Harris's in the early 1890s. The second, dramatized in the *New York Times Magazine*'s glossary from the early 1960s, is that of white beatniks. 'If You're Woke, You Dig It', the article that contained the glossary, was by the young African-American novelist William Melvin Kelley. Three weeks after the opinion piece appeared in print, Kelley published his beguiling first novel, *A Different Drummer* (1962). Set in a fictional southern state that represents a kind of historical dead-end for African Americans, *A Different Drummer* describes the entire black population of one town mysteriously, wordlessly, migrating to the north. They leave behind them a white population that, used to appropriating or simply silencing black voices, is rendered speechless by this biblical exodus.[4] 'If You're Woke, You Dig It', for its part, was about white beatniks' use of 'today's Negro idiom' – another form of appropriating or silencing. 'I asked someone what they felt about white people trying to use "hip" language,' Kelley remarks at one point; 'He said: "Man, they blew the gig just by being gray."'[5]

The third appropriation, finally, is the one that has taken place in the last few years, in the course of which the militant emphasis it acquired once it had been re-functioned by the Black Lives Matter movement has faded because white liberals have adopted it as a code word for communicating little more than a modish awareness of social issues. It is the 'Open Sesame' that white liberals use to gain entry to black culture. It is the sign of the cross they automatically make in order to indicate both to themselves and others that, however crass their cultural appropriations, they do not intend to sin against the collective social conscience. As the sociolinguist Nicole Holliday has noted, the word 'woke' appeared in MTV's list of '10 words you should know in 2016', where it was defined simply as 'being aware – specifically in reference to current events and cultural issues'. '*Woke* has been racially sanitized for a mainstream audience', Holliday observes; '*Woke* has been removed from its ties to black communities as well as its reference to black consciousness and political movements.' 'The appropriation of *woke*', she concludes, 'has lulled it into a complacent, apolitical slumber where, ironically, it simply means "awake".'[6] White liberals, in other words, blew the gig just by being grey. But the term 'woke' has also fallen victim to the logic of commodification and co-optation that is characteristic of counter-cultural language in capitalist society, especially in the age of social media.

This book, *Lev Shestov: Philosopher of the Sleepless Night*, is not about 'staying woke', either in the properly militant or in the blandly triumphant inflection of the term. Nor is it about simply 'being awake', if this phrase necessarily entails passive connotations. It is, instead, about 'staying awake', in some active and even agonistic sense. And, to this extent, though it does not address questions of race, it deliberately situates the political discourse of wakefulness, the resonance of which it emphatically underlines, in a rather different, more fully philosophical context, thereby defamiliarizing and displacing it in an attempt to restore a sense of its persistent, and urgent, importance. It returns to the prophetic 'revelations', and the rhetoric, of the almost forgotten Jewish-Russian religious philosopher Lev Shestov (1866–1938). Between the two world wars, Shestov commandeered Judaeo-Christian, Pascalian, Kierkegaardian and Nietzschean influences in the name of an openly apocalyptic thought that pitted Faith against Reason, Anti-Necessity against Necessity. Like Plotinus, on whose 'ecstasies' he wrote an essay published in Paris in 1926, Shestov felt, as he put it, 'that he must not lull to sleep the unrest and spiritual tension within him, but goad it on to the highest degree, where sleep becomes impossible'.[7] He passionately believed in stimulating the restlessness and spiritual tension latent in other people, too, into sleeplessness; also, as I propose in this book, the restlessness and political tension within them. *Lev Shestov* thus argues for the sort of expanded, philosophically nuanced, but also polemically effective, form of wakefulness that its protagonist consistently sponsored in his writings from roughly a century ago. It insists, furthermore, that Shestov's powerful prose, aphoristic and essayistic by turns, itself delivers salutary jolts of what, in a different context, Gene Ray has recently called 'critical reflection and social and political wakefulness'.[8]

Affirming the spiritual and political imperative of sleepless vigilance, Shestov reconstructed and extended a counter-Enlightenment tradition that ran from the Hebrew and Christian prophets, through Pascal, to the anti-philosophical thinkers of the nineteenth and twentieth centuries. In so doing, he sought in a dual sense to alarm the intellectual complacencies of Enlightenment rationalism in its most somnambulistic forms. The Enlightenment, according to an irony of which Shestov was acutely conscious, is itself a source of darkness. 'Too much clarity darkens', as Pascal is supposed once to have remarked in criticizing Descartes.[9] Shestov was committed, according to a converse logic, to the darkness that illuminates, the night that is a source of light. In his critique of the perilously soporific influence of the Enlightenment, he consciously reclaimed the night – like one of those Counter-Reformation mystics such as St. John of the Cross – as a sacred time of eternal wakefulness and watchfulness.[10] In an era of social and political emergency, the first half of the twentieth century, he consecrated the night as a site of incessant openness to the sudden irruption of some transformative spiritual drama into the continuum of history; a drama either of damnation or, as he hoped, redemption.

Shestov's name, as Boris Groys has observed in a fine discussion of this philosopher, 'says relatively little to the Western reader today', in spite of his 'significant if hidden influence on some of the best representatives' of the period between the two world wars.[11] Over the course of the first four decades of the twentieth century, at a time of sustained political crisis in Europe, Shestov consistently and influentially explored the implications of his fundamental claim that, in the face of the horrors of contemporary history, and in opposition to the rationalist Enlightenment thought that had fatally failed to explain it, that had indeed justified and mandated it, we should develop a state of preternatural wakefulness and watchfulness in order to ensure that the prospect of human suffering ultimately becomes absolutely unacceptable. Ramona Fotiade, the scholar who has probably done most to foster and maintain interest in Shestov's thought in the twenty-first century, summarizes his position in these terms, ventriloquizing his voice:

> We are like sleepwalkers in a world whose logic and a priori principles seem unsurpassable and prevent us from seeing the incongruities and arbitrary connections which make up the fabric of our daily lives. It takes an extraordinary effort to break the spell of self-evident truths and awaken from the nightmare of one's powerless submission to misfortune, injustice, suffering, and death.[12]

It takes, so Shestov claims, a sort of spiritual insomnia. The trope of sleeplessness that, for this reason, reappears throughout my book is summed up in the imperative: No Sleep 'til the End of the World! This formulation, which in one iteration or another Shestov repeats and elaborates with the persistence of a musical motif, is adapted from 'The Mystery of Jesus', Pascal's fascinating, fragmentary discussion of Christ's sleeplessness during the episode in the Gospels that unfolded on the night before his arrest in the Garden of Gethsemane. There, Jesus confronted his tragic loneliness, and the apparent failure of his messianic project, as his closest disciples slept. 'Jesus will be in agony until the end of the world', Pascal wrote in what is surely his most apocalyptic sentence: 'There must be no sleeping during that time.'[13]

Shestov, who argued again and again, during the darkest and most benighted of times, against the somnolent effects of Enlightenment thinking, on the grounds that it fosters a fundamentally passive, quiescent relationship to the world, appropriated Pascal's statement as a slogan of spiritual and, implicitly, political empowerment. This book revisits Shestov's anti-rationalist philosophy, and specifically his reading of Pascal, both because of its intrinsic interest and because of its haunting insistence that, so as not to sleepwalk into a future that is even more oppressive and replete with suffering than the present, we need to remain intensely, perpetually alert to our political and spiritual responsibilities – in short, awake until the end of time. 'Christ's agony is not yet finished', Shestov writes in *Gethsemane Night* (1923), his inspiring book-length essay on Pascal; 'It is going on, it will last until the end of the world.'[14] This 'agony' means, among other things, the horror of human history, which in the 1920s was of course far from finished (some five months after this essay appeared, the so-called Beer Hall Putsch, Adolf Hitler's unsuccessful but profoundly ominous *coup d'état*, took place in Munich). Shestov cites his hero Pascal because of the French philosopher and scientist's brilliant critique of the Cartesian principles of the Enlightenment. These principles, the Russian claims, have over several centuries provided an ever more unassailable rationale for accommodating oneself to a universe the superficial inevitability of which should instead be systematically challenged. In a rampantly rationalist society, as *Gethsemane Night* makes evident, Pascal offered Shestov a decisively significant precedent for refusing Enlightenment logic. '"One must not sleep," Pascal tells us.' So Shestov repeats, before forcefully adding: 'No one must sleep. No one must seek security and certainty.'[15]

In excavating this forbidding imperative from Shestov's account of Pascal, *Lev Shestov: Philosopher of the Sleepless Night* seeks, as I have already implied, to activate or re-appropriate its semi-concealed politics. In order to do so, it frequently situates Shestov's thinking in relation to elements of the thinking of contemporaneous philosophers associated with the Frankfurt School such as Theodor Adorno and Walter Benjamin. For example, it implicitly associates Shestov's comparatively apolitical claim that the Enlightenment tradition, which according to him comprises a set of rationalistic and scientistic assumptions that collectively constitute a kind of modern myth, not only with Adorno and Horkheimer's critique of the Enlightenment but also with Benjamin's scattered assertions that, as he clearly put it in the preparatory stages of his *Arcades Project*, 'capitalism was a natural phenomenon with which a new dream-filled sleep came over Europe, and, through it, a reactivation of mythic forces'.[16] In quite different styles and vocabularies, Benjamin and Shestov both effectively argued that, as the latter once remarked in a discussion of his hero Dostoevsky, 'the painful convulsions of a doubtful awakening' are better than 'the grey, yawning torpidity of certain sleep'.[17] If philosophers have hitherto only interpreted the world, Shestov seemed to say, the point is to awake from its 'dream-filled sleep'. For this reason, Shestov was committed to making his readers, in some literal sense, restless; permanently, almost intolerably, alert and awake.

Lev Shestov: Philosopher of the Sleepless Night centres on Shestov's ethics, poetics and politics of awakening. Of remaining awake. Chapter 1, 'Athens and Jerusalem', sets the scene for the book's guiding arguments, sketching the elderly Jewish philosopher's visit to Jerusalem in the mid-1930s and outlining his investment in the pivotal spiritual drama that occurred at the start of the Passion narrative – when, in the form of sleeplessness, Christ was forced to confront his solitude and spiritual desperation in Gethsemane. This chapter offers a preliminary overview of Shestov's thought, which it explains in terms of its characteristic antinomies: Shestov sets Judaeo-Christian thought against Graeco-Roman thought, Faith against Reason, Revelation against Speculation. Chapter 2, 'Philosophy and anti-philosophy', reconstructs aspects of both Shestov's biography and, more fully, his existential philosophy. It explores the iteration and development of Shestov's ideas in his own writings, over many decades, but also illustrates them in relation to a contemporaneous Russian writer, Andrei Bely, and in particular his novel *Petersburg* (1913–14), which shares a comparable commitment to notions of contingency and Anti-Necessity.

This chapter claims that Shestov is most conveniently understood – here I use a term that, though it originated in the counter-Enlightenment rejection of the *philosophes* in France, before being revived by Jacques Lacan, has in our own time been productively promoted by commentators such as Alain Badiou and Boris Groys – as an 'anti-philosopher'. That is, to put it simply in the first instance, he is best grasped as a thinker who privileges being over thinking, the concrete particular over the abstract universal, the singularity of experience over metaphysical truth. And who does so with a certain uncompromising militancy. 'A true anti-philosophy', Badiou has observed, 'is always an apparatus of thought that is intended to tear someone away from the philosophers, to remove him from their influence'.[18] Shestov, profoundly invested in this rather violent intellectual enterprise, for all his pacifism, sought precisely to tear his readers from their affiliation to the rationalist tradition; to shock them out of their unthinking adherence to its thinking. He thus pitted Pascal, whom Badiou identifies as a classical anti-philosopher, against a line of descent running from Plato to Descartes and, in his own time, Husserl.

Chapter 3, 'Angels of history and death', outlines Shestov's connections to some of his more famous, largely younger contemporaries, especially those living in Paris between the wars. It outlines Shestov's reception in Britain, briefly sketching his impact on D. H. Lawrence and Hugh MacDiarmid, but focuses in particular, first, on the influence he had on the Surrealist philosopher Georges Bataille; and, second, rather more extensively and elaborately, on the affinities between his thinking and that of Benjamin, whose Marxism, as their mutual friend Gershom Scholem insisted, was inflected by a distinctive debt to Jewish mysticism. This chapter compares Benjamin's celebrated allegorical image of the 'angel of history', which it re-reads in terms of ideas of wakefulness, with Shestov's figure of the 'angel of death'. In Chapter 4, 'Garden and wasteland', I explore the crucial episode in the Gospels of the Agony in the Garden, which was of immense ethical and spiritual importance to Shestov because of its allegorical drama of wakefulness. This chapter offers an account of the mediation and representation of Christ's night in Gethsemane in various works of art and literature from the fifteenth to the early twentieth century, from Mantegna to Rothko, and from Thomas More to T. S. Eliot, in order more fully to understand its theological and political significance (oddly, there seems to have been little attempt so far, systematically at least, to trace the iconography of Gethsemane in the histories of art and literature). In the conflicted times in which Shestov lived, when for historical reasons it acquired new force, the scene functioned, I contend, as an emblem both of despair and possible hope in the face of the horrors of mass suffering.

Chapter 5, 'Sleep and the sleepless', building on this account of Christ's spiritual tragedy in Gethsemane, goes back to Shestov's remarkable interpretation of

Pascal, reading in close detail the former's book-length essay on the latter's fragment known as 'The Mystery of Jesus', so as to explore the apocalyptic potential of sleeplessness. It argues that this essay, Shestov's *Gethsemane Night*, is the basis for a powerful politics of wakefulness, one that ascribes to the philosophical or anti-philosophical tradition to which he himself adhered a prophetic role in awakening people from the somnambulistic condition that consigns them to a state of impotence in the face of oppression. Finally, the Conclusion titled 'Auschwitz and the end of the world' examines what it meant for Shestov and some of those directly influenced by him, in particular Gilles Deleuze and the Jewish Romanian philosopher and poet Benjamin Fondane, to bear witness, in a state of wakefulness and watchfulness, to extreme forms of barbaric suffering. Through Deleuze and Fondane, but also the thought of Adorno, it excavates the strain of optimism in Shestov's apocalypticism, identifying the 'hope against hope' that shapes his philosophy of tragedy. Here, I consolidate in fairly explicit terms a claim that is implicit throughout this book, namely, that Shestov's thought contains urgent and important political lessons for the times in which we currently live.

'Will men awake, or are they destined to a heavy slumber to the end of time?' Shestov demands at the end of 'Memento Mori' (1916), his lengthy critique of Edmund Husserl.[19] And once awake, we might add, will they remain awake? Will they be sleepless 'til the end of the world? At the present time, as in the past, it is not our political and spiritual duty simply to be 'woke'. For this is a phrase that, in its liberal appropriations, piously implies a state of enlightened consciousness; and, moreover, creates the complacent impression that this state of enlightened consciousness, even if it cannot be dismissed as completely empty, has already been accomplished. Instead, it is our political and spiritual duty – in some active, agonistic sense – to remain constantly awake, to remain ceaselessly vigilant, both in order to catalogue the crimes taking place before us on the stage of history and, potentially, in order to redeem and even reverse those tragedies. In an article entitled 'Standing Vigil for the Day to Come' (1963), Michel Foucault once suggested, in a luminous image, that 'one day we should ask ourselves what, in a culture like ours, might signify the prestige of the Vigil, of wide open eyes that admit yet ward off the night'.[20] A generation earlier, Shestov had consciously, strategically asserted just the 'prestige of the vigil' invoked by Foucault; the importance of 'wide open eyes'. He was, after all, the author of a collection of articles, still not translated into English, entitled *The Great Vigils* (1910). Today – as a thinker 'in dark times', to recall Hannah Arendt's minatory phrase[21] – Shestov can still teach us how to 'admit yet ward off the night'.

What will happen to us if we fall asleep? Or remain asleep? What if we fail to ward off the night? In Philip Roth's novel *The Plot Against America* (2004), the narrator, himself called Philip Roth, describes a fateful night in 1940 when he was only seven years old. While he and his brother slept, his mother and father listened to a live radio broadcast from the Republican National Convention. It is on this occasion, at 3:18 a.m., that the aviator Charles A. Lindbergh, an admirer of Hitler who is aggressively anti-Semitic, makes a surprise appearance at the convention hall. By 4 a.m. the Republicans have officially nominated him as their presidential candidate. In *The Plot Against America*, as J. M. Coetzee put it in his review of the novel, 'real history is the unpredictable';[22] or, in Shestovian terms, anti-Necessity. That night, at exactly the moment Lindbergh is nominated as the Republican candidate, which is the penultimate phase of his ascent to the nation's highest office, the narrator and his brother are abruptly woken, as if by an alarm: '"No!" was the word that awakened us, "No!" being shouted in a man's loud voice from every house on the block. It can't be. No. Not for president of the United States'.[23] Here is an instance of the sort of protest – I return to this politically suggestive concept in the Conclusion to this book – that Shestov's brilliant disciple Fondane, faced with the rise of fascism in Europe in the 1930s, designated 'irresignation'.[24]

'No!' is not enough, even if it emanates from every house on the block. Unless, that is, it is repeated 'til the end of the world. There must be no sleep 'til the end of the world! This is the imperative encoded in the anti-philosophy of Lev Shestov that I seek to reconstruct and (in Brechtian phrase) re-function in this book – for our times.

'These are our nights of Gethsemane', Albert Camus wrote with ominous solemnity in *The Myth of Sisyphus*, a philosophical essay influenced by Shestov, in the early 1940s.[25] These are our nights of Gethsemane.

Stay awake!

1

Athens and Jerusalem
Lev Shestov in Gethsemane

I

In 1936, the seventy-year-old Russian Jewish philosopher Lev Shestov, accompanied by his sister Elisabeth and her husband, German Lovtsky, travelled from his home in France to Palestine. There, at the invitation of the Cultural Department of the Histadrut, the Jewish trades-union organization, he delivered a series of lectures in the Zionist settlements – Haifa, Tel Aviv and, foremost among these cities, Jerusalem.

Although Shestov's 'inner biography remains unknown', as V. V. Zenkovsky observed in his monumental *History of Russian Philosophy* (1953), it can be surmised that his journey to Palestine entailed an implicit, perhaps semi-conscious attempt to come to terms with his Jewish origins.[1] His relationship to his familial and cultural heritage had been complicated, and had required some kind of reckoning, at least since the time when, as a young man engaged in a more or less Oedipal rejection of his merchant father's patronym, he first changed his name from Lev Isaakovich Schwarzmann to Lev Shestov.[2] But his attempt to escape his past, as this assumed name probably indicates, was incomplete. He remained profoundly shaped by his Jewish background. This might have included a debt, identified by the historian Sidney Monas, to the Hassidic movement 'which had an enormous influence in the Jews of the diaspora during the time of Shestov's childhood and early youth'.[3] Encouraging him to make the journey to Palestine in the mid-1930s, his friend Aaron Steinberg urged him 'to show the world once again the Jew beneath the Russian persona'.[4] And this does indeed seem to have been one of the consequences, intentional or unintentional, of Shestov's two-month trip. For according to one of his intellectual biographers, his appearances there 'evoked an enthusiastic response from audiences who recognized the aged Shestov as one of the great Jewish philosophers of the century'.[5]

Emmanuel Levinas, writing in the *Revue des Études Juives* in 1937, the year after Shestov's trip to Palestine, summarized him in these terms:

> M. Shestov, Jewish philosopher, but certainly not a philosopher of Judaism, in the heritage of Jerusalem he does not separate the Old Testament from the New. But he is a philosopher of religion. And under its existential form, religious philosophy returns to important problems of salvation, which is to say the essential message of Judaism. And he does this in a more radical fashion than ever, since existential philosophy – M. Shestov shows admirably and obstinately – explodes the synthesis of the Greek spirit and the Judeo-Christian, which the Middle Ages believed to have accomplished.[6]

As a thinker, Shestov identified equally, and equally idiosyncratically, with the Judaic and Christian theological traditions; and, at least after moving to Paris in the early 1920s, he demonstrated a consistent, if not relentless, commitment to excavating the relevant, revelatory truths, as he perceived them, buried in the Hebrew and Christian Bibles. In both, he celebrated what he called 'the "madness" of Scripture' – their scandalous refusal to conform to the protocols of reason.[7] Take, for example, the idea found in Mark's and Matthew's Gospels that faith might move a mountain. This notion, almost literally outlandish, is simply not susceptible, so Shestov claims, to some rationalist interpretation that, offering a 'uniform explanation' that 'exclude[s] contradictions', makes it conform 'to the common conceptions of the work and problems of life'. For Shestov, contradictions are the very condition of truth; and the idea that faith might move a mountain should be celebrated, like the Old and New Testaments themselves, for commending what he called 'the maddest and most perilous experiments', experiments that threaten to capsize reason in spite of its authority and apparent stability.[8] Shestov, in short, proclaimed the

possibility of impossibility. And he came to the Bible, as he said of his hero
Fyodor Dostoevsky, 'to be rid of the power of reason'.[9]

Because of its historic and symbolic importance for both the Jewish and
Christian faiths, Shestov regarded Jerusalem, the first city he visited during
the trip to Palestine, as a sacred city. 'Let my tongue cleave to the roof of my
mouth if I forget thee, O Jerusalem!', he repeated after the Psalmist (137: 5)
in 'A Thousand and One Nights' (1917), an essay whose title was intended
to transmit millenarian associations as well as merely literary ones.[10] For
Shestov, as Michael Finkenthal has commented, 'Jerusalem was not the city
of David only but also that of the crucifixion, of Christ'.[11] Far more than
that, though, its name delineated an entire matrix of philosophical ideas and
spiritual commitments that stood out against the Enlightenment tradition
he so doggedly attacked in his writings. Indeed, his final book, which he
completed in 1937, after stubbornly working on it for more than seven years,
was entitled *Athens and Jerusalem* (1938). This was his *chef d'oeuvre*, and its
title clearly signalled that here he was going to gather strength from what the
intellectual historian Adam Sutcliffe has categorized as 'the mythic resilience
of Judaism', which 'holds within it a unique power to call attention to the
limits of the Enlightenment'.[12] Shestov summarized his intellectual enterprise
in these terms in the Foreword: 'The task which I have set for myself in this
book, *Athens and Jerusalem*, consists in putting to proof the pretensions to the
possession of truth which human reason or speculative philosophy make'. In a
Kierkegaardian formulation, he added: 'Man wishes to think in the categories
in which he lives, and not to live in the categories in which he has become
accustomed to think: the tree of knowledge no longer chokes the tree of life'.[13]

Pointedly, Shestov gave the title 'Athens and Jerusalem' to one of the lectures
he delivered in the Holy City in 1936. On this occasion, the German-Jewish
philosopher and theologian Gershom Scholem, who had admired Shestov's
work for a long time, introduced him to the audience (though he remained
slightly bemused by the elderly Russian's performance, complaining that he
'read from the manuscript so badly that it was quite impossible to understand
anything of consequence, even for wholly favourably predisposed listeners
such as myself'). Concluding his brief account of the event in the course of
a letter to his old friend Walter Benjamin, Scholem exclaimed: 'The event

was a terrible fiasco!' Scholem nonetheless underlined his profound respect for Shestov, whose style he characterized as 'magnificent'.[14] And, certainly, when Shestov died in Paris in November 1938, this 'fiasco' didn't prevent a memorial service from taking place in Jerusalem, where the eminent Jewish philosopher and theologian Martin Buber, who had only recently settled in the city, delivered a speech for the occasion.

II

So, what precisely did Jerusalem signify for Shestov? It represented, as one commentator has noted, 'a kind of sensibility, a way of living based not on logic but on trusting in God, believing in miracles, paradox, contingency, and irrationality'.[15] In *Athens and Jerusalem*, and throughout his intellectual career, to put the case at its plainest and most Manichaean, Shestov pitted Judaeo-Christian thought against Graeco-Roman thought, Faith against Reason, Revelation against Speculation, Paul against Plato, the Particular against the Universal, Kierkegaard against Kant, Being against Thinking, the Tree of Life against the Tree of Knowledge – in short, Jerusalem against Athens. These are the terms of Shestov's Either/Or. In the tradition of the Church Father Tertullian, whom he profoundly admired, he effectively asked, *Quid ergo Athenis et Hierosolymis?* 'What indeed has Athens to do with Jerusalem?' Tertullian's point, as Shestov insisted, was that 'what for Athens is wisdom is for Jerusalem foolishness'.[16]

The rationalist philosophical tradition, as Shestov conceptualized it, did not have a monopoly on truth. Shestov did not reject rationalism *tout court*. He was emphatic, as he put it in an article on Kierkegaard in 1938, that 'reason is indeed necessary, very necessary for us' and that 'under the ordinary conditions of our existence it helps us to cope with the difficulties, even the very great difficulties, we run up against on our life-path'.[17] Furthermore, in spite of his Pascalian campaign against Cartesian philosophy, he praised Descartes' works for 'the extraordinary vigour, the uncommon passion and emotion which fills them'.[18] Notwithstanding his characteristically emphatic rhetoric, then, Shestov's objection was less to reason or science *tout court* than to the rationalist ideology of the Enlightenment and to scientism.[19] But he contended nonetheless that, in part so as to be able to help people cope with the irruption of extraordinary experience into their everyday existence, including death itself, revelation should not simply rival but should supersede both reason and scientific knowledge as the source of truth. The spiritual teaches us far more than the rational. As Shestov framed it in the stirring final paragraph of 'Memento Mori' (1916), the essay on Edmund Husserl that did so much to publicize the phenomenologist's thinking in France when it first appeared in translation in 1925, an 'obscure feeling' persists; namely, the conviction that 'the truth which our ancestors sought unsuccessfully in Paradise' can only be found 'beyond reason' and that 'it is impossible to discover it in the immobile and dead universe which is the only one over which rationalism can rule as sovereign'.[20]

Reason, Shestov declared in 'A Thousand and One Nights', at his most polemical, 'is completely incapable of creating anything whatsoever that is alive'. 'By its very nature', he added, 'reason hates life more than anything in the world, feeling it instinctively to be its irreconcilable enemy'.[21] Reason subordinates life to thought', he continued to argue more than twenty years later in *Athens and Jerusalem*; 'and the more we try to subordinate our life to our thought, the heavier our slumber becomes'.[22] Shestov took a certain pride in the fact that his repetitious pronouncements, which elicited Albert Camus's exasperated but admiring judgement – in *The Myth of Sisyphus* (1942) – that the Russian's writings were 'wonderfully monotonous', infuriated his critics.[23] His more or less apocalyptic enterprise demanded an insistent, iterative, even obsessive mode of speech that, like other prophetic forms, at times proved slightly deaf to other voices. He compared the irritation of his critics, in distinctly grandiose tones, with 'the Athenians' dissatisfaction with Socrates'.[24] In this spirit, in spite of his suspicion of the rationalist legacy of Socrates, he saw his role as that of someone who must help prevent people, in their ordinary lives, from remaining in the grip of the spiritual and intellectual stupor against which he fulminated.

The English surrealist poet David Gascoyne, a great admirer of Shestov, was correct to characterize him, with calculated literalness, as a 'profoundly disturbing' thinker. And to value Shestov's impassioned commitment to disrupting what, in a sentence that accelerates almost uncontrolledly in its intellectual excitement, Gascoyne described as 'the easily available, conventionally legitimized means whereby men commonly stupefy themselves so as to continue to be able to remain fast asleep even when wide awake and busily occupied in carrying on very competently their no doubt highly important and altogether worthwhile daily affairs'.[25] Shestov's calling was – calling. Or crying, groaning and lamenting – in short, all those activities that Spinoza prohibited, to Shestov's perpetual contempt, when he offered his influential advice to philosophers: *Non ridere, non lugere, neque detestari, sed intelligere*. Shestov, to the contrary, advocated laughing, weeping and screaming; everything except contemplative understanding.[26] All that profoundly matters, according to Shestov, exceeds the limits of language; instead, it must be voiced or emitted from some place deep within the diaphragm. Whereof one cannot speak, to frame it in Wittgenstein's terms, thereof one must make ... inarticulate noises. In essence, Shestov's thinking was informed by the belief that humanity's predicament was most profoundly articulated in the anguished cry of Christ on the cross: 'My God, My God, why hast thou forsaken me?' This expression of despair, the ultimate instance of seeking in lamentation, is both the opening of Psalm 22 (22: 1) and, in the Gospels of Mark and Matthew (15: 34; 27: 46), the culmination of Christ's misery, the moment at which he drinks the dregs of the cup of trembling and wrings them out: Eli, Eli, lama sabachthani.

Shestov's journey to Jerusalem, then, was something of an intellectual and spiritual pilgrimage. It was also of personal, genealogical importance, as I have implied; in the course of this trip, he ascended the Mount of Olives, whose peak is part of the ridge on the eastern edge of the Old City, in order to visit the ancient Jewish cemetery where his grandfather had been buried. At the same time, there can be little doubt that Shestov was acutely conscious of the specific theological significance of the Mount of Olives. It is mentioned several times in the Old Testament; for example, in 2 Samuel, where there is a poignant description of David escaping from Absalom and his spies: 'And David went up by the ascent of *mount* Olivet, and wept as he went up, and had his head covered, and he went barefoot' (15: 30). It is also crucially important, of course, in the New Testament, in part because Jesus preached and prophesied there, but above all because the Garden of Gethsemane lies at its foot. The Garden of Gethsemane is the place where, on the eve of his crucifixion, immediately prior to his betrayal and arrest, Jesus prays to God in desperation that his suffering will be relieved, or at least rendered manifestly meaningful: '[He] fell on his face, and prayed, saying, O my Father, if it be possible, let this cup pass from me: nevertheless not as I will, but as thou wilt' (Matt. 26: 39).

Immediately prior to this moment, Jesus has made a poignant request of his three closest disciples, Peter, James and John: 'My soul is exceeding sorrowful, even unto death: tarry ye here, and watch with me' (Matt. 26: 38). He needs them to keep watch because he expects to be betrayed and arrested. But as he discovers no less than three times, the disciples are incapable of remaining awake:

> And he cometh unto the disciples, and findeth them asleep, and saith unto Peter, What, could ye not watch with me one hour?
>
> Watch and pray, that ye enter not into temptation: the spirit indeed *is* willing, but the flesh *is* weak.
>
> (MATT. 26: 40–41)

Jesus thus conducts his vigil, which lasts throughout the night, utterly alone. In Gethsemane, the German theologian Jürgen Moltmann writes, 'Jesus wrestles with the dark side of God, and the stifling unconsciousness of sleep descends on the disciples until the night has passed and the day of Golgotha has begun.'[27] This is the scene of the Passion in which, cut off both from his own followers and from God the Father, Jesus is at his most psychologically and spiritually destitute – in short, his most human. As Shestov argued in a discussion of Dostoevsky, whom he regarded as a Christ-like figure, it is only 'in the dead of night, in complete silence' that one encounters truth. In this context, he wrote of 'modern man' that, 'when people abandon him, when he is left alone with himself, he automatically begins to tell himself the truth, and, my God, what a horrible truth it is!' In relation to Nietzsche in the same book, he calls this 'midnight reality'.[28]

Gethsemane is the site, it might be said, of Christ's subjective destitution; and it is the moment at which, instead of transcending history, he seems suddenly and ruinously to be situated inside it. Human, all too human; historical, all too historical. His sleeplessness, in the course of this fatal night during which his exhausted, spiritually inattentive comrades repeatedly fall into a bestial slumber, is the principal symptom of his humanity, a humanity that is a complicated admixture of weakness and strength. If sleeplessness, then, is a sign of self-doubt – and of what the phenomenologist Emmanuel Falque, in his recent commentary on the scene, calls 'the real solitude of anxiety and anguish'[29] – it is also a sign of supreme attentiveness. Karl Barth, writing in the aftermath of the Second World War, at one point compared Jesus at Gethsemane unfavourably not only to Socrates, and to 'many a Christian martyr', but also to 'many Communists – as we can see from their letters – who were under sentence of death in the time of Hitler'. Provocatively, he even compared him in this regard to the Nazi general Alfred Jodl at Nuremberg. Why? Because Jesus was susceptible, according to Barth, to a profound lack of self-belief; because his commitment to the cause for which he was fighting was compromised.[30] Shestov, in an attempt to redeem Jesus's insomniac doubt, offered a more positive interpretation. He identified the traumatic drama in the Garden, which centres on Jesus's wakefulness and watchfulness, as one of the primal scenes of the philosophical or spiritual tradition he spent his life reconstructing. It represented, for him, a paradigm for accepting suffering, and affirming spiritual vigilance, in the face of humanity's night of Gethsemane.

Shestov visited the Garden of Gethsemane – the Hebrew name of which, *gat shemanin*, literally means 'oil press' – during the trip to Jerusalem in 1936. '*Aujourd'hui j'étais au jardin de Gethsemani*', he observed to his friend and disciple, the brilliantly talented Jewish Romanian poet Benjamin Fondane, who also lived in exile in Paris. In the next letter Shestov wrote to him, sent from Tel Aviv, he thanked Fondane for sending him an article he had written, tellingly entitled 'Chestov à la recherche du judaisme perdu' (1936) – 'Shestov in Search of Lost Judaism'. There is no detailed record of Shestov's experiences at Gethsemane (in the letter, frustratingly, he told Fondane he promised he would tell him everything once he was back in the French capital: '*Je vous raconterai tout quand je serais à Paris*').[31] But one can imagine him examining the primal, almost monstrous forms of the Garden's olive trees, with their gnarled and barnacled trunks, for these are manifestly Trees of Life. In his poem 'Gethsemane' (2001), Rowan Williams has powerfully evoked these 'trees' clefts', the fissures into which sacred words, 'thick as thumbs', have since biblical times been folded and pressed 'inside the ancient bark'.[32] Certainly, it is plausible to assume that Shestov's visit to Gethsemane was of immense symbolic importance to him and that he too sought these ancient, living words secreted in the deep creases of the olive trees' calloused hides.

One of Shestov's most powerful essays, *La Nuit de Gethsémani: Essai sur la philosophie de Pascal* (1923), is an extremely moving meditation on the night of Gethsemane, in the shape of a sustained interpretation of the great French thinker's minatory reference to the Agony in the Garden in his intriguing fragment known as *Le mystère de Jésus*. It is this essay, *Gethsemane Night: Pascal's Philosophy*, that will ultimately form the focus of this book. For here, Shestov embroiders the theology of insomnia – knotted in what George Steiner has in another context referred to as 'the motif of creative sleeplessness' – that is threaded throughout his religious philosophical writings.[33] The

IN THE GARDEN OF GETHSEMANE.

Figure 1.1 *In the Garden of Gethsemane (engraving), English School (nineteenth century) / Private Collection / © Look and Learn / Bridgeman Images.*

essay's epigraph, the sentence around which Shestov scatters his scintillating reflections, is this remarkable statement of Pascal's, at once apocalyptic and achingly personal:

> *Jésus sera en agonie jusqu'à la fin du monde: il ne faut pas pas dormir pendant ce temps-là.*[34]

'Jesus will be in agony until the end of the world: there must be no sleeping during that time'. No sleep, then, for a thousand and one nights, a million and one nights. No sleep 'til the end of the world.

III

Shortly before his death in 1938, in a letter to his old friend Sergei Bulgakov, the Russian Orthodox priest and theologian, Shestov insisted that, to him, 'the contradictions between the Old and the New Testament seemed always something imaginary' and that the emphasis in both of them on the Tree of Life, as against the Tree of Knowledge, was the only thing 'capable of helping us withstand the horrors we face in life'. 'In my view', Shestov concluded, 'we must make huge spiritual efforts to get rid of the atheistic nightmare and the lack of faith which dominates humanity'.[35] Shestov identified these horrors, throughout his career, with the night; but he remained convinced that darkness had descended on European history not in spite of the Enlightenment but because of it. If Enlightenment, as Adorno and Horkheimer formulated their case in the mid-1940s, was 'the philosophy which equates truth with scientific systematization', and which thereby enforces the identity of reason and domination, then Shestov was a counter-Enlightenment thinker.[36] He testified to the Enlightenment's mechanistic, scientistic cruelties. The 'atheistic nightmare' that Shestov feared – the logical outcome of the entire rationalist project – was a society both faithless and, to put it once more in terms used by the Frankfurt School, totally administered.

Two decades before the letter to Bulgakov, in 'A Thousand and One Nights', at the end of the First World War rather than the beginning of the Second, Shestov referred in angry tones to 'the horrors of these last years'. He nonetheless expressed the hope that, if there was any chance that they might 'bring about the fall of our presumptuous self-assurance', 'then the misfortunes and sufferings that have broken over our heads will perhaps have served some purpose'. But he did not labour under any illusions about this, in part no doubt because his son Sergei Listopadov, a friend of Boris Pasternak, had been killed in action against the Germans in 1915; he therefore added, in bitter tones, 'But it is hardly likely that this will happen'. Shestov regarded the attempt to find redemption in the historical process alone, and in the Enlightenment philosophy of history that rationalized it during the nineteenth and early twentieth centuries, ridiculous. For history, as far as he was concerned, simply repeats its catastrophes, repeats 'the misfortunes of which we have been the witnesses'. And Hegel's description of history, delivered 'with such enviable assurance and such weighty carelessness', does not either resemble its relentless cycles of destruction or offer adequate consolation for them. 'Mankind does not live in the light but in the bosom of darkness', Shestov thundered; 'it is plunged into a perpetual night!'[37] He believed in maintaining a kind of insomniac consciousness – while other people slept their deep spiritual sleep – in the depths of the Enlightenment night.

'I think the world's asleep ...' Shestov selects this line, spoken in exasperation by King Lear in Shakespeare's tragedy of that name (1, 4, 44), to serve as the epigraph to 'Revolt and Submission' (1922–3), which subsequently became the second section of *In Job's Balances* (1929).[38] At midnight in the century – to cite the title of the Russian revolutionary Victor Serge's novel of 1939 – reason has, according to Shestov, plunged humanity into a deep, somnambulistic sleep. 'That "enchantment and supernatural slumber" [*enchantement et assoupissement surnaturel*] of which Pascal spoke has taken possession of us', he wrote in *Athens and Jerusalem*; 'And the more we try to subordinate our life to our thought the heavier our slumber becomes'.[39] On the eve of the Second World War, rejecting Kant's claim that his critiques had enabled him to escape from a 'dogmatic slumber', Shestov energetically argued, to the contrary, that 'the "dogma" of the sovereignty of reason, a dogma devoid of all foundation', is in fact 'an indication not of slumber but of profound sleep, or even – perhaps – the death of the human spirit'.[40] In this context, under what he elsewhere calls 'the autocracy of reason', the Enlightenment is, to use an archaic but evocative term, a state of benightment.[41] According to Shestov, in the face of the profound sleep induced by reason, which is far graver than the slumber invoked by Kant, only a heroic vigilance, in the form of a sort of spiritual sleeplessness that interrupts the individual subject's complacently accepting relationship both to everyday life and the prevailing ideological conceptions that underpin it, can offer potential salvation.

Shestov therefore sought allies among those philosophers and thinkers who, over centuries if not millennia of intellectual history, had proved recalcitrant to the rationalist tradition. He constructed a counter-Enlightenment canon. His philosophical heroes, in this respect, were to be found not only in the Old and New Testament, in the form of the prophets and St. Paul, but in the writings of those he regarded as his great precursors, above all Pascal, Nietzsche and, though he read him only in the 1930s, at the insistence of his unlikely friend Husserl, Kierkegaard.[42] All those, in short, who possessed what Shestov characterized, in an incandescent formulation, as a 'flaming imagination'.[43] To this list, he added the 'underground men' of the nineteenth century, the so-called irrationalists, aggressively militant in their rebellion against the dictates of rational necessity, among whom Dostoevsky was the most significant. Shestov identified Dostoevsky as Nietzsche's spiritual brother, even 'twin'.[44] But he also regarded the Russian novelist as a descendant of Pascal, as a late lecture, 'On the "Regeneration of Convictions in Dostoevsky"' (1937), indicates:

> Dostoevsky almost never speaks of Pascal and apparently knew him little, but Pascal is very closely related to him spiritually. Pascal wrote, 'Jésus sera en agonie jusqu'a [sic] la fin du monde: il ne faut pas dormir pendant ce temps là.' Is not the account of the picture that Ippolit saw at Rogozhin's really a development of this thought of Pascal's?

This rhetorical question is a reference to the atheist Ippolit's description, in Dostoevsky's *The Idiot* (1868), of a copy of Hans Holbein the Younger's painting of the 'The Body of the Dead Christ in the Tomb' (1522). Prince Myshkin had earlier seen it at Rogozhin's house, where he declares, 'That painting! Some people might lose their faith by looking at that painting!'[45] Dostoevsky had himself encountered it, to dramatic effect, in the Basel Museum in 1867, where it directly challenged his faith in Christ's divinity. Anna Dostoevsky, who recorded in her diary its terrible impact on her husband, described its 'fearfully agonised' face, 'the eyes half open still, but with no expression in them, and giving no idea of *seeing*'.[46] This picture, almost intolerable in its unflinching intensity, is the portrait of a broken, rotten human being whose unclosed eyes, as he lies on a mortuary slab as inhospitable as a rack, stare into eternity. Sleepless 'til the end of the world. Shestov sees Holbein's Christ, who has the sad, stupefied gaze of a man who has been drugged and tortured, as an image of Pascal's sleepless Christ, undergoing the agonies of abandonment in Gethsemane, whose kneeling body has been unbent, and left stretched out and stiffened forever. For Dostoevsky, evidently, the painting was a kind of icon for the underground man; in pointing to the 'spiritual affinity' between Pascal and the Russian novelist, Shestov notes that the former's 'desperate struggle against reason', and his 'attacks against our pitiful morality', reminds him profoundly of the introductory chapters of the latter's *Notes from the Underground* (1864).[47]

Nietzsche himself once declared that Pascal's blood flowed in his veins;[48] Pascal's, Kierkegaard's, Nietzsche's and Dostoevsky's blood all finds a kind of confluence in Shestov's veins. And it is as if they transmitted their condition of neurotic, prophetic attentiveness to him too. Restlessness, and the sleeplessness that ensues from it, is a classic characteristic of the underground men with whom Shestov identified. Reading Nietzsche for the first time had itself proved almost traumatic in its impact. He confessed to Fondane in 1938 that, on the occasion when as a young man he first encountered *The Genealogy of Morals* (1887), consuming it continuously from 8.00 pm to 2.00 am, it impressed and upset him so much that it rendered him incapable of sleep: '*Cela m'a remué, bouleversé, je ne pouvais dormir*'.[49] 'It disturbed me, overwhelmed me, I couldn't sleep'. This, from Shestov, is an expression of the utmost admiration. For Shestov believed that philosophers should not only suffer from an inability to sleep but should

Figure 1.2 *The Dead Christ, 1521 (tempera on panel), Holbein the Younger, Hans (1497/8–1543) (after) / Kunstmuseum, Basel, Switzerland / Bridgeman Images.*

also strive to induce insomnia in their readers. The Professor in Chekhov's 'A Tedious Story' (1889), terminally sleepless as he confronts the prospect of his decline and death, is thus perversely an example to be assiduously emulated. Forced 'to remain inactive, to suffer, to remain awake of nights, to swallow with effort food that has become loathsome to him', as Shestov almost enviously observes of him, 'the conception of the world is shattered into fragments!'[50]

'Will men awake', Shestov asked in 'Memento Mori', 'or are they destined to a heavy slumber to the end of time?'[51] Almost from the start, he dedicated his philosophical enterprise, in prophetic spirit, to interrupting this slumber and to provoking in his readers a state of apocalyptic wakefulness. This was the burden of a messianism that, at once political and spiritual, collapsed the distinction that Scholem underlined between the Judaic and Christian eschatological traditions.[52] In the final pages of *Athens and Jerusalem*, in the course of his celebration of the illogical as opposed to the logical, Shestov discriminated between *homo dormiens* ('sleeping man') and *homo vigilans* ('waking man' or 'wakeful man'). The rationalists, implicitly, are incarnated in *homo dormiens*; the anti-rationalists, like him, are incarnated in *homo vigilans*. Shestov then hailed what he called 'the moment of awakening'. When this moment arrives, he intimated, 'the rumbling of the thunder is heard: revelation'.[53] Revelation, to invent a false etymology, is for Shestov a form of reveille. It is a prophetic alarm. A fire alarm. As the French Ukrainian philosopher Rachel Bespaloff formulated it, Shestov's basic premises – for example, '*la limite posée par l'évidence ne corresponde pas à une limite du réel*', that the limits set by empirical evidence do not correspond to the limits of the real – are in themselves enough to awaken philosophy: '*fait le réveil de la philosophie*'.[54]

Shestov himself remained comparatively modest about his capacity to wake people from their spiritual slumbers: 'I certainly do not hope to succeed in waking sleepers', he wrote in the final section of *Athens and Jerusalem*, 'but – no matter – the hour will come and someone else will wake them, not by discourses, but otherwise, quite otherwise'. 'And then', he concluded in a characteristically vatic voice, as if positioning himself as John the Baptist, 'he who is called to awaken will awaken'.[55] This is the spirit of Isaiah: 'Awake, awake, stand up, O Jerusalem, which hast drunk at the hand of the LORD the cup of his fury; thou hast drunken the dregs of the cup of trembling, *and* wrung *them* out' (Isa. 51:

17). And it is the spirit of Matthew's account of the Passion, specifically the scene in Gethsemane, when Jesus three times asks his Father to take the cup of suffering from him, and three times is met both by silence and, when he seeks support from the disciples, their insensible, sleeping forms (26: 39-46). Shestov, like Pascal, identified in the isolated, sleepless Christ an example that might serve in the face not simply of perpetual suffering but the temptation to escape from this perpetual suffering into an eternal spiritual sleep.

Like his precursors Pascal, Kierkegaard and Nietzsche, Shestov might be recruited to the ranks of those whom Karl Jaspers, the subject of a lengthy essay by the Russian in 1937, called the 'Great Awakeners'.[56] It is no doubt not an accident, though Jaspers does not mention the fact, that each of these pre-twentieth-century thinkers suffered from insomnia. Sleeplessness is an indelible symptom of this genetic inheritance. 'It is certain that Pascal never passed a day without suffering', Shestov wrote in *Gethsemane Night*, 'and hardly knew what sleep was (Nietzsche's case was the same)'.[57] Kierkegaard's problems with sleeping and his efforts 'to conquer the insomnia from which he suffered', which included driving his carriage throughout the night, were well documented even in his lifetime.[58] Nietzsche, for his part, not only experienced terrible sleeplessness, as Shestov states, especially in his later years, but was fascinated by the *nocte intempesta*, the 'untimely night', the time of the night when time doesn't seem to exist; and also by the hallucinatory experiences of what he called 'overawake souls'.[59] Camus, discussing Heidegger, Jaspers and Shestov in *The Myth of Sisyphus*, and clearly echoing *Gethsemane Night*, implicitly enlists Heidegger to this line of philosophers: 'For him, too, one must not sleep but must keep alert until the consummation'.[60]

Indebted to this tradition, in which sleeplessness is a philosophical as well as physiological or psychological problem, Shestov elevated the insomniac to the status of a heroic archetype: *homo vigilans*. It is no doubt not irrelevant, too, that Shestov was himself an insomniac – at least towards the end of his life. He refers to this condition more than once in his correspondence with Fondane, who records in a diary entry dated 10 July 1938: 'Chestov est très fatigué. La dernière nuit, il n'a dormi qu'une heure et la nuit devant, pas même une heure. Il n'a rien pris contre l'insomnie'.[61] 'Shestov is very tired. Last night, he only slept for an hour, and the night before even less than an hour. He didn't take any medicine for his insomnia'. In the shape of *homo vigilans*, Shestov heralded the redemptive imperative of a humanity condemned to be sleepless not for one night or even many nights, but 'til the end of time. As he repeatedly makes apparent, Pascal was a hero of his because, in contrast to Aristotle and his descendants, who 'hymn the "golden mean"' rather than affirming that which exceeds reason, he 'does not and will not sleep' – for 'the sufferings of Christ will not allow him to sleep until the end of the world'.[62] Waking, watching and bearing witness, as everyone else struggles to awake from the nightmare of history. In spite of the agonies they endure, the eyes of *homo vigilans* stare at history, and its train of tragedies, with unfailing steadfastness.

Gascoyne – a close friend of Fondane in Paris in the late 1930s and, thanks to him, a passionate admirer of Shestov – restaged this heroic example to portentous effect in his fine poem 'Ecce Homo'. Published in 1940, the year the Germans occupied France, it portrays Christ, and specifically the 'Christ of Revolution and Poetry', gazing out from his 'horrifying face' with 'hollow red-filmed eyes' as he suffers the tortures of crucifixion. Beneath him, 'the centurions wear riding-boots, / Black shirts and badges and peaked caps', and 'Greet one another with raised-arm salutes'. On the crosses to either side of him, 'hang dead / A labourer and a factory hand, / Or one is maybe a lynched Jew / And one a Negro or a Red'. Christ does not speak, but – as in Holbein's portrait of him – his 'putrid flesh, discoloured, flayed, / Fed on by flies, scorched by the sun', tells a 'bitter truth'.[63]

What is this 'subversive truth'? Gascoyne captures its significance in an echo of Pascal, as mediated through Shestov's *Gethsemane Night*: 'He is in agony till the world's end, // And we must never sleep during that time!' Gascoyne means that, if we refuse the spectacle staged by the centurions and the 'black priest', and instead bear witness, perpetually, to the suffering of the oppressed, then 'the rejected and condemned', the agricultural and industrial labourers, the Jews, the Negros and the Reds, might ultimately become 'Agents of the divine'. The agents of revolution. 'The turning point of history', Gascoyne solemnly insists, 'must come'. At this moment, he underlines in reference to the crucified Christ, 'That man's long journey through the night / May not have been in vain'.[64] The last shall be first. And the past, as Shestov taught, will finally be redeemed in the name of the future.

2

Philosophy and anti-philosophy
Shestov's interventions

I

From the end of the nineteenth century, in Russia and in France, and in the course of nomadic excursions to a series of other countries, including Italy, Germany and Switzerland, Lev Shestov evolved an influential variant of religious existentialism, formed in the intellectual ferment of the so-called Silver Age of Russian philosophy and poetry, which celebrated the possibility of fostering human freedom in a realm beyond the dictates of reason.[1] These countries were the stations of a flight first from the moral constraints imposed by his father and then from the intellectual restrictions enforced by the incipient Soviet state as it established its authority in the universities. Teaching philosophy at the University of Kiev in 1919, when he was in his early fifties, Shestov found himself caught between the Bolshevik authorities, who mistrusted him intellectually, on the one side, and the encircling imperialist armies, who briefly reconquered the city, on the other. He fled first to Constantinople and then to Geneva, before finally moving on to Paris, where his article 'Qu'est-ce que le bolchevisme?', which served as a kind of calling card, appeared in the *Mercure de France* in 1920. Shestov's life was a restless one, then, especially before he settled among other Russian and Eastern

European émigrés in Paris and its environs in 1921, the year in which the New Economic Policy was introduced in the Soviet Union. And this restlessness constitutively shaped his philosophy.

Shestov once defined his mature philosophy as 'an art which aims at breaking the logical continuity of argument and bringing man out on the shoreless sea of imagination, the fantastic tides where everything is equally possible and impossible'. Here, he uses characteristically poetic language in order consciously to resist the hegemonic regime of rationalism, whether this is institutionalized in the Enlightenment tradition descending from Hegel or in the increasingly authoritarian Soviet government, both of which effectively identified reason with the state. The search for truth, Shestov underlined both before and after his expatriation from Russia, 'must be undertaken by homeless adventurers, born nomads, to whom *ubi bene ibi patria*'.[2] A prophet out for a stroll, or even on the run, is a better model than a philosopher in his chair, as Shestov might have said if he had lived long enough to read his admirer Gilles Deleuze; 'A breath of fresh air', as Deleuze and Guattari write, 'a relationship with the outside world'.[3] In the opening paragraph of *All Things Are Possible* (1920), an English translation of Shestov's writings based mainly on *The Apotheosis of Groundlessness* (1905), he evokes 'the obscure streets of life', where there is 'no electric light, no gas, not even a kerosene lamp-bracket', where there is only darkness; and depicts a 'wretched pedestrian' who, unlike those who travel 'through brilliant streets', is forced 'to grope his way among the outskirts of life'.[4] This scene, in which a vagabond figure struggles to negotiate the streets of the city's insalubrious suburbs at night, is his allegory for counter-Enlightenment philosophy.

This is the philosopher not as a scholar stooped over a pile of books upon a desk, but as a homeless, empty-handed nightwalker meandering through the streets.[5] Citing St. Paul in an essay on the Russian religious philosopher Vladimir Solovyov, his slightly older contemporary, Shestov insists that philosophizing, like living, is a question of 'going out without knowing where, obeying a call and not giving the slightest thought either about the "sense" or "purposefulness" of the universe'.[6] As Zygmunt Bauman formulates it, in language that deliberately tries to do justice to Shestov's own, the Russian philosopher argued that 'truth found inside a tightly sealed home is hardly of any use outside': 'A non-counterfeit universality may be born only of homelessness.'[7] Shestov's thought, then, was founded on an exilic, fugitive life as opposed to a settled, logically structured metaphysics: in Nietzschean terms, a wanderer's life. Shestov mocks the 'comfortable, settled man' and relishes the fact that, when 'misfortune turns him out of house and home', as it is bound to do in the end, he will be forced to 'live like a tramp', and will moreover find himself unable to rest and 'full of terrors'.[8] Shestov's philosophy is uncompromising in its affirmation of homelessness, restlessness, and even fearfulness. 'It expresses', Ksenia Vorozhikhina observes, 'the mentality of people who do not feel constrained by state borders, who do not adhere to a particular religious tradition, and who do not feel any national roots'.[9]

But it does more than merely reflect this rootlessness, which cannot of course be dissociated from his Jewish identity, as well as from his biographical experiences both as a migrant and an immigrant; it seeks, in an intellectual and spiritual sense, positively to induce rootlessness, to provoke crisis. 'Special spiritual experiences', he wrote in 1938, meaning traumatic shocks to the fragile equilibrium of everyday life, 'are necessary for our soul that has fallen asleep in supernatural torpor to feel in itself the power for the last and great battle against the enchantment'.[10] Shestov places suffering at the centre of thinking; and attempts, through a sort of philosophical drama, and in rhetoric that is often apocalyptic, to disrupt existence and transform the subject, to awaken once and for all. Thinking is thus a heroic attempt to remain awake, like Christ in Gethsemane, and so to bear witness to the horrors of history, in spite of the narcotic temptations to which, in their desire to escape these horrors, humans are, like Christ's disciples, endlessly susceptible. 'In the marketplace, among the crowd, do not men sleep their deadest sleep?', Shestov asks in *All Things Are Possible*; 'And is not the keenest spiritual activity taking place in seclusion?'[11] The loneliness of the nomad and the prisoner, of the outcast Christ, is the paradigmatic social and spiritual condition to which, perversely, Shestov aspires.

The Russian literary theorist Mikhail Bakhtin once insisted on classifying Shestov not as a philosopher, but, like the latter's old friend and *frère ennemi* the Christian Nikolai Berdyaev, a 'thinker'; and this distinction is probably a useful one.[12] Shestov was a stubbornly idiosyncratic thinker who deliberately did not present his philosophical positions in the form of a stable, unified metaphysical system. Instead, he acted them out in the form of a series of interventions with the single, more or less polemical, purpose of critiquing rationalism and its Platonic metaphysics. The Hegelian philosopher Alexandre Kojève, like Shestov a migrant from Russia to France, if a generation or so later, remarked of Solovyov's religious philosophy, in his PhD on the topic, which he conducted under Karl Jaspers, that this influential theologian had developed it 'continuously' – 'the divisions of his books into chapters or lectures bear no systematic significance'.[13] Something of the same might be said of Shestov's philosophical project over the course of his long intellectual career. In revolt from metaphysics, or from his distinctly combative conception of metaphysics, Shestov tended to produce books and articles that, whether aphoristic or essayistic, are unclassifiable meditations on novelists and playwrights as much as philosophers. They amount to an anti-metaphysics that, in its continuousness, is at the same time fitful and relentlessly consistent.

Shestov's writings comprise an ongoing, open-ended attempt to create the intellectual conditions in which truths that are transmitted through being and suffering rather than through abstract thinking might appear. 'Metaphysics', he remarked in 'The Theory of Knowledge' (1916), 'was not only unable to find a form of expression for her truths which would free her from the obligation of proof; she did not even want to'. Shestov condemned metaphysics, which he considered merely the obverse of positivistic thought, for its scientific pretensions and its refusal to confront the horror of being. 'Metaphysics is the great art of swerving round dangerous experience', he exclaims, 'so metaphysicians should be called the positivists *par excellence*. They do not despise all experience, as they assert, but only *the dangerous experiences*.' Dangerous experiences are for Shestov the very precondition of authentic thought. 'A thinking man is one who has lost his balance, in the vulgar, not in the tragic sense', he writes, as if an unsmiling Buster Keaton is his preferred archetype for the public intellectual: 'Hands raking the air, feet flying, face scared and bewildered, he is a caricature of helplessness and pitiable perplexity.'[14] Chaplin or Keaton tumbling into a hole in the road left uncovered by absent-minded labourers is Shestov's model for a philosophy that is adequate to the abyss that lies beneath life. Laughter, as Benjamin Fondane insisted, 'is the sign and the key to a new universe which overflows on all sides the mechanical universe of necessity. It is the sign of a deeper inner life, of a strange *lack of strenuousness* in relation to the real, of a *social maladjustment*.'[15] Keaton, in sum, versus Kant.

Shestov thus privileged not metaphysical truths, but physical, physiological, psychological and spiritual truths. He referred to these as 'ultimate truths' and discriminated them from 'middle truths', 'the logical construction of which we have so diligently studied for the last two thousand years'. Ultimate truths, he insisted, are 'absolutely unintelligible'; unintelligible 'but not inaccessible'. These truths, not elevated but nonetheless pregnant with significance, are momentarily visible in the seizures and spasms of the suffering body. In this context, Shestov cites Dostoevsky, who lived in a kind of hell but, because of his epileptic condition, or perhaps because of his insanity, occasionally 'entered paradise for an instant':

> The hell was obvious, demonstrable; it could be fixed, exhibited, *ad oculos*. But how could paradise be proven? How could one fix, how express, those half-seconds of paradisic beatitude, which were from the outside manifested in ugly and horrible epileptic fits with convulsions, paroxysms, a foaming mouth, and sometimes an ill-omened sudden fall, with the spilling of blood?[16]

Conventional, metaphysical philosophy, in aspiring to scientific status, refuses to take account of the elusive, revelatory truths lived by an individual like Dostoevsky; lived by everyone, potentially, at moments of particular crisis. And it consequently abdicates its claim to universal knowledge.

Shestov himself resisted the notion that he was a professional philosopher, in spite of serving from 1922 as a professor of Russian in the Institute of Slavonic Studies at the Sorbonne. Indeed, on several occasions he declared himself grateful for the fact that he had never had a formal academic training in the discipline: 'It is only because I did not study philosophy that I preserved a freedom of spirit.'[17] Deleuze, who read Shestov attentively as a young man, argued in a seminar of 1956–7 that, like Kierkegaard, Shestov identified with the 'private thinker' as opposed to the 'public professor' – with Job rather than Socrates.[18] In 'On Philosophical Honesty' (1937), his article on Karl Jaspers, Shestov had underlined Kierkegaard's point that, in the Bible, Job 'is not only a much-plagued old man but a *thinker*[;] to be sure, not one celebrated in the history of philosophy, not a *professor publicus ordinarius*, but a private thinker.'[19] Deleuze, who consistently promoted the archetype of the private thinker, or 'idiot', credited Shestov some two decades later with finding 'in Dostoevski the power of a new opposition between private thinker and public teacher'.[20] Public, professional philosophy, as Shestov perceived it, was little more than a game, the aim of which was the accumulation of symbolic capital, wherein ideas functioned as mere strategic counters. 'The whole history of philosophy', he wrote, 'is to no small degree the incessant search for prerogative and privilege, patents and charters'.[21] He effectively sought, instead, to desublimate philosophy; to render it a matter not of 'conceptions of the world', which he considered 'idealistic cemeteries', but of 'nerves', of feelings that must be made to live.[22] 'Shestov's philosophy', Berdyaev concluded shortly after his friend's death, in an article commemorating his 'fundamental ideas', 'belongs to the type of existential philosophy' – 'i.e. it avoids objectifying the process of knowledge and does not tear it away from the subject of knowledge but connects it with the wholeness of man's fate'.[23]

Shestov's is a concrete, embodied philosophy, then, which refuses the abstract categories or entities of the Enlightenment tradition and instead affirms the suffering of individual, implicitly bodily beings as the formative site of humanity's dramatic, and in some fundamental sense tragic, struggle to find intellectual and spiritual meaning in the face of meaninglessness. In *Gethsemane Night* (1923), he presents an existential choice between two almost irreconcilable alternatives. He summarizes the first of these, the one with which he identifies, in terms of 'Pascal's methodological rule'. He summarizes the second, in a cruder synopsis, in terms of Spinoza's. For Spinoza, as a scion of the Socratic and Stoic traditions, 'intelligence' is the 'ideal'; from this perspective, what Shestov calls the 'ego', which stands in for the embodied subjectivity of the individual self, 'is the most refractory, and therefore the most incomprehensible and irrational thing in the world.' In the history of philosophy, according to Shestov, the hegemonic, totalizing authority of the rationalist ideal of 'understanding' is predicated on the elimination of the threat that the ego represents. '"Understanding" only becomes possible when the human "ego" has been deprived of all its individual rights and prerogatives, when it has become a "thing" or a "phenomenon" among other things and phenomena of nature.' Rationalism, Shestov claims, reifies the self and transforms the subject into an object. It thereby 'annihilate[s] it in order to make possible the realization of the objective world-order'.[24]

In these circumstances, Shestov contends, it is necessary to choose between two 'regimes of truth' (as Foucault might have called them).[25] He sets the relevant alternatives out with some urgency in *Gethsemane Night*:

> The choice must be made: either the ideal and intangible order with its eternal and immaterial truths, that order which Pascal had rejected and whose adoption reduces the mediaeval idea of the salvation of the soul to an utter absurdity; or else the capricious, discontented, restless, yearning 'ego' which always refuses to recognize the supremacy of 'truths', either material or ideal.[26]

Shestov's 'ego', with its capricious, disruptive energies and in its innate commitment to undermining the rational order, has a good deal in common, ironically, with Freud's id (although it is noticeably non-libidinal).[27] But Shestov ascribes it a positively messianic spiritual role that is alien both to psychoanalysts and to contemporaneous French and German existentialists. 'In the "ego", and only in the "ego" and its irrationality', he argues, 'lies the hope that it may be possible to dissipate the hypnosis of mathematical truth which the philosophers, misled by its immateriality and eternity, have put in the place of God'.[28] In his perceptive reappraisal of the Russian, Boris Groys usefully refers to 'the Shestovian philosophical eros'. In contrast to Heidegger, Sartre and other existentialists, he argues, Shestov 'insisted rigorously on the literal, exact, this-sided, non-symbolic realization of individual, bodily human wishes'.[29]

Reviewing Shestov's *Apotheosis of Groundlessness* in 1911, Alexandr Zakarzschevsky captured something of the embodied drama of the individual subject in Shestov's philosophy in this notably baroque description:

> One encounters in this book an ailing and extremely beautiful person who is crucified on a dark imageless cross, his whole face is in spasms of an epileptic violent expression of emotion, and drops of bloody sweat fall in the depth of inspiration and terrifying sounds spring up, evil and poisonous flowers of the mysterious and beckoning night.[30]

This hallucinogenic passage, which recalls the Symbolist movement with which Shestov was associated as a young man in Kiev, Moscow and St. Petersburg when he was part of a circle that included Dmitry Merezhkovsky and Aleksey Remizov, identifies his philosophical angst with Christ's agonies both on the cross and in the Garden of Gethsemane.[31] The philosophical vocation with which Shestov identified was centred on finding meaning in the face of godlessness and meaninglessness, in the depths of the night of history, through an irrational or, more precisely, supra-rational affirmation of faith. Christ's cry from the cross, he claimed, contained more truth than all the reasoning of the Greek philosophers. 'How could they admit', he asked, 'that when an ignorant Jew cried from the depths of the abyss (*clamabat de profundis*), God answered him, while when a cultivated Greek reasoned, his reflections led to nothing?'[32]

Shestov sought to make this cry from the depths of the abyss, which was audible at Golgotha and in Gethsemane, resonate again. Throughout his writings, with their uncompromising emphasis on resisting the sleep induced by reason, he insists that sleeplessness, in the form of an eternal attentiveness, represents the individual's only hope of overcoming the physical and spiritual suffering by which she has been torn apart. The individual must be subjected to a violent reawakening; and, if at all possible, must thereafter remain insomniac.

II

Born in 1866, the son of an affluent Jewish textile merchant, Shestov was raised and educated in Kiev. No less than two traumatic events seem to have determinately shaped Shestov's formative years. If it is not excessively reductive to seek specific biographical sources for Shestov's 'philosophy of tragedy', over and above his relatively itinerant, restless life, then these two events are surely among them. Shestov's writings themselves to some extent licence this biographical approach, for they repeatedly emphasize that only through acute individual suffering does life reveal its secrets; only in new Golgothas are new truths born. Thinking of one of his foremost philosophical masters, Nietzsche, he quoted from *Thus Spake Zarathustra* (1883–91) to this effect: 'Before my highest mountain do I stand, and before my longest wandering: therefore I must first go down deeper than I ever climbed – deeper down into pain than I ever ascended, even into its darkest flood.'[33]

In the first of these incidents, which according to legend occurred in 1878, a group of anarchists apparently kidnapped the twelve-year-old boy, and only returned him to his parents after some six months, once it had become clear that no ransom money was forthcoming (Geneviève Piron has recently speculated that this incident in fact took place in 1881).[34] Shestov's abduction was, naturally, a shocking irruption into the security and stability supposedly safeguarded by the family. As his great-nephew, Igor Balachovskii, observed of this incident, 'How after that can one stop looking for a threatening sign of something invincibly horrible, hiding in the corners and ready to jump out at any time from things that are most common and routine?'[35] The impact of this permanent state of uncertainty on his thinking can be summarized by Sineokaya and Khokhlov's more general claim, in a recent article, that 'intuition of existential anxiety is the starting point of Lev Shestov's philosophy of freedom'.[36]

The second and in some respects more significant traumatic event, though less spectacular, remains even more enigmatic. This existential and psychological crisis took place in 1895, when Shestov was almost thirty, and it seems to have been caused in part by the fact that he had fallen in love, successively, with two sisters, both of whom were unacceptable to his father because they were gentiles.[37] Clearly, there must have been other, complicating factors in motion here. These surely included Shestov's resentment of his father's business activities, which were proving an embarrassment to his militant political sympathies. After all, as a young man pursuing his legal studies in Kiev, Shestov wrote a controversial socialist thesis about state legislation against the Russian working class, one that was subsequently rejected by the Committee of Censors in Moscow because of its 'revolutionary' sentiments. But however overdetermined its causes, Shestov evidently suffered a 'serious nervous illness' because of this incident, as one of the two sisters with whom he had been entangled expressed it in a recollection written in 1934.[38]

Shestov commemorated the second of these major emotional crises in a diary entry dating from 1920 where he echoed Shakespeare's *Hamlet*: 'Twenty-five years have already passed since "the time fell out of joint"? 'I mark this down', he added, 'in order not to forget it since often the most important events in one's life, events about which nobody but oneself knows might in fact be easily forgotten'.[39] Hamlet's declaration that 'the time is out of joint' (1, 5, 189) was one of Shestov's favourite quotations. Personal as well as historical in its implications, as his retrospective reference to the cryptic psychological crisis of 1895 indicates, this sense of both the individual and the collective as fundamentally self-divided is something like the fulcrum of his philosophical enterprise. Shestov had loved Shakespeare since his youth, and his first book, published in Russian in 1898, was a monograph entitled *Shakespeare and his Critic Brandes*. It was in part a critique of the Danish scholar Georg Brandes that focused its attack on fashionable positivist interpretations of literature. Shakespeare *'me bouleversait au point de ne pas me laisser dormir'*, Shestov told Fondane in recollecting his obsessive reading habits as a PhD student in 1935. 'He moved me so much I could hardly sleep nights.' Shestov asseverated on this occasion that Brandes, who merely repeated liberal platitudes about Shakespeare, remained in contrast serenely undisturbed by his plays: *'En un mot, Shakespeare le laissait dormir, lui'.*[40] 'In a word, Shakespeare left *him* to sleep.' An inability to sleep, it is already apparent, is always symptomatic of something intellectually or spiritually important in Shestov's biography, as in the biographies of those philosophers he most admired.

A couple of years later, in an article written a few weeks before his death, Shestov reiterated Shakespeare's significance to him: 'My first teacher of philosophy was Shakespeare, with his enigmatic, incomprehensible, threatening, and melancholy words: "the time is out of joint." 'What can one do, how can one act,' Shestov meditated, 'when the time is out of joint, when being reveals its horrors?'[41] Several decades later, the disjunctive temporality dramatized by Shakespeare came to interest Jacques Derrida, who allegedly conducted a seminar on Shestov in 1991.[42] In *Specters of Marx* (1993), his negotiation with the Marxist tradition, Derrida included an extended discussion of *Hamlet*, and of the phrase 'the time is out of joint' in particular. As Derrida formulated it, in terms that might have seemed familiar to Shestov, this temporality wherein 'time is *disarticulated*, dislocated, dislodged', wherein 'time is run down, on the run and run down, *deranged*, both out of order and mad', poses a fundamental challenge to the subject.[43] It renders the subject mad. It deranges its reason. And the insanity it induces, if it entails a rejection of the entire logic of order, the reasonable and so on, represents in Shestov's thinking an opportunity to redeem or save the subject through an encounter with the horrors of being. The non-contemporaneous present that is the historical precondition for the subject's crucial failure to coincide with itself is, to put it in the Benjaminian terms within which Derrida operates in his discussion of *Hamlet*, the 'strait gate through which the Messiah might enter'.[44]

Berdyaev confirmed that, in contrast to the kind of philosopher who performed the intellectual rituals associated with the academic profession, Shestov 'was a philosopher who philosophised with his whole being, for whom philosophy was not an academic specialty but a matter of life and death'.[45] It is because of his emphasis on the embodied individual subject, which involves a refusal of the abstract endeavour to construct truths *sub specie aeternitatis*, that Shestov consistently gravitated to imaginative literature, with its attention to the concrete struggle to create meaning in specific historical and cultural contexts. Above all, in addition to Shakespeare, he valued Dostoevsky, Tolstoy, Chekhov and other representatives of nineteenth-century Russian literature. He might have concurred with the Trinidadian Marxist C. L. R. James's claim, from 1948, that the nineteenth-century Russian novelists constituted 'as distinct a stage of the European *consciousness* as was, in its way, the Classical Philosophy, and [that] they deserve a place in a new *Phenomenology of Mind*';

indeed, he might have gone further and insisted that they constituted a more distinct stage.[46]

Shestov praised the Russian novelists he favoured, fairly pointedly, for their 'restlessness'. 'Never were there so many disturbing, throbbing writers,' he writes in one thrilling sentence, for instance, 'as during the epoch of telephones and telegraphs'.[47] Shestov effectively treated the philosophy he favoured, too, as a form of fiction. As John Bayley put it in a sprightly essay on him, 'Shestov has much of the superb stylistic vitality of his heroes, Nietzsche and Kierkegaard, whom he sees more as novelists and dramatists of the inner life than as philosophers'.[48] In thus treating novelists as philosophers and philosophers as novelists, he reflected the unique intellectual conditions he had inherited in Russia before the revolution, when educated readers tended to be resistant to philosophy, in part because of its European associations, preferring journalistic and literary genres instead.[49]

The nineteenth-century novel, then, in its emphasis on individuality and interiority, and its investment in linking this dimension to the fate of the collective, was in a sense Shestov's model for philosophizing. For Shestov, so his admirer E. M. Cioran claimed, 'literature was a method of undermining philosophy': Tolstoy against Hegel; even Ivan Karamazov against Kant and Hegel.[50] Shestov's is an anti-logocentric mode of philosophizing, which predicates its critique of reason, and of metalanguage more generally, on a radically decentred, disjunctive concept of the subject (though any attempt to domesticate him by comparing his thought to post-structuralism or other philosophies supposedly characteristic of postmodernism can only be misleading, not least because his critique of reason is prophetic rather than deconstructive in its method). It is premised on the conviction that life is only spiritually meaningful if it refuses reason's supremacy and, as in Chekhov's writings, constantly confronts both the fact of death and its physical encroachments.[51] Chekhov's narratives, Shestov notes approvingly in 'Creation from the Void' (1905), his extraordinary essay on the playwright, in which he discusses 'A Tedious Story' (1889) at length, 'have to do with the decomposition of a living organism'. A 'sorcerer' or 'necromancer' like Chekhov, according to Shestov – someone with 'a singular infatuation for death, decay and hopelessness' – persistently and productively pitches reason into crisis.[52] This is the presupposition underlying Shestov's philosophy of tragedy, which mediates what he calls, in the title of one of his books, *Les Révélations de la mort* (1923): The Revelations of Death.

Philosophy, according to Shestov, should function as 'a preparation for death and a gradual dying'.[53] Here, in *Potestas Clavium*, he is thinking with approval of Plato's example, in spite of the suspicion that he reserved in other contexts for the Greek philosophers who had pioneered the rationalist tradition. At approximately the same time, in the early 1920s, he admiringly observed in 'Revolt and Submission' that 'the ancients, to awake from life, turned to death'; 'the moderns', in contrast, 'flee from death in order not to awake, and take pains not even to think of it'. In vehemently sarcastic tones that are typical of Shestov's polemics, he continues:

> Which are the more 'practical'? Those who compare earthly life to sleep and wait for the miracle of the awakening, or those who see in death a sleep without dream-faces, the perfect sleep, and while away their time with 'reasonable' and 'natural' explanations? That is the basic question of philosophy, and he who evades it evades philosophy itself.[54]

The rationalists, presuming that death is a dreamless, perfect sleep, are incapable of grasping that, in life, 'we are all sleep-walkers, moving automatically in space, spell-bound by the non-being which lies still a little way behind us'.[55] The thinkers with whom Shestov himself identifies, who are routinely dismissed as 'irrationalists', believe in contrast that to live is in effect to sleep, and that it is in consequence their responsibility to point to and prepare the miraculous conditions in which this insensible, somnambulistic state, which appears perpetual, might be dramatically and decisively interrupted.

'Sleep, you say, is the image of death,' as Pascal once protested in a statement that remained unpublished until the 1960s; 'for my part I say that it is rather the image of life'.[56] For Shestov, too, sleep is the metaphor that most fully explains people's semi-unconscious experience of life. To believe that one's earthly life entirely encompasses reality, as those whom Shestov condemns as somnolent do, is to insulate oneself from the shocks of the flesh, as Hamlet phrases it in his meditation on dreaming and dying and sleeping, 'the whips and scorns of time' (3, 1, 71). It is to shuffle off a sense of one's mortality and therefore to fail to live. It is to sleep like a beast even when one is ostensibly sensible. The ironic epigraph to Shestov's essay on Chekhov, which he quotes again in the final sentence, is a quotation from Baudelaire's 'Le Goût du néant' (1861): '*Résigne-toi, mon Coeur, dors ton sommeil de brute*.'[57] 'Be resigned, my heart, sleep your brutish sleep.' Perhaps this is in part what Prospero means when, in *The Tempest*, he comments that 'our little life is rounded with a sleep' (4, 1, 147–8). It is not so much that something resembling sleep defines the periods before birth and after death, as that something resembling sleep encompasses life itself, and defines the actual process of living. The temptation to escape life by living it in the form of a dream must be resolutely resisted and refused. Above all, as far as Shestov is concerned, it is the threat of death that prevents us from sleeping through life; it is what keeps us wakeful and watchful. The presence of death prevents us from submitting to what William Desmond, in his insightful commentary on Shestov, calls 'the sleep which is the false double of peace.'[58]

In our inverted, illusive lives, as Shestov perceives them, 'we create something like the veil of Maia: we are awake in sleep, and sleep in wakefulness, exactly as though some magic power had charmed us.'[59] Shestov's philosophizing promises to rip the veil apart. His prose, though not subtle or sophisticated enough to deploy the sort of dialectical images that Walter Benjamin developed, used its provocative, revelatory rhetoric in order to awaken the collective subject, or at least an individual one in the form of the reader, from the dream state into which their consciousness has elapsed. 'On every possible occasion', he urges, 'the generally accepted truths must be ridiculed to death, and paradoxes uttered in their place.'[60] Shestov's philosophy constitutes not some polite attempt to understand and accommodate the world, as in the Socratic and Stoic paradigms, and in the Enlightenment one incarnated by Kant and Hegel and others, but a frantic agonistic struggle with it. Philosophy, for him, is the creative, self-defining activity of a suffering being. It entails shattering conceptions of the world into fragments. 'Philosophy', he argued, 'is not a curious looking around, not *Besinnung*, but a great struggle.'[61]

Those whom Shestov approvingly calls the 'profane', in contrast to the professional, philosophers do not sacrifice everything for the sake of their ideas, including the truth; 'to them philosophy – more exactly, that which they would call philosophy if they possessed a scientific terminology – is the last refuge when material forces have been wasted, when there are no weapons left to fight for their stolen rights'.[62] Philosophy must be demotic, militant, but at the same time desperate. It is a last resort – an application of the emergency brake.

III

Alain Badiou has helpfully discriminated between those for whom philosophy 'is essentially a reflexive mode of knowledge', the appropriate form of which is the 'school', and those for whom, in contrast, 'philosophy is not really a form of knowledge, whether theoretical or practical'. For the latter, philosophy 'consists in the direct transformation of a subject, being a radical conversion of sorts – a complete upheaval of existence'. Shestov can be counted among those anti-scholastic thinkers whose philosophy is 'an affair of personal commitment', not least because it entails a 'combative affirmation' against the sophists themselves.[63] Shestov is uncompromising in his emphasis on the travails of the concrete individual as the fundamental and irreducible premise of philosophical thinking. Deleuze called him and Kierkegaard 'philosophers of the scandal, of provocation'.[64]

This is, in effect, the tradition of anti-philosophy.[65] And, for Badiou, writing in a different context, one of its paradigmatic representatives is St. Paul: 'Paul is a major figure of antiphilosophy.' For Paul, as for later anti-philosophers such as Luther, Pascal, Kierkegaard and Nietzsche, 'the subjective position figure[s] as a decisive factor in discourse', and 'existential fragments, often anecdotal in appearance, are elevated to the rank of guarantor of truth'.[66] Not coincidentally, Paul is one of the principal protagonists of the intellectual and spiritual drama that Shestov repeatedly stages in his writings. Shestov values Paul because he affirms faith, and the contingency of grace, in opposition to the authority of knowledge; furthermore, Shestov relishes the fact that 'most of the ideas that he develops in his epistles and the quotations from the Old Testament with which his reflections are interspersed can awaken in educated people only feelings of irritation and revulsion'.[67] Paul is a perpetual affront to philosophical reason. Shestov, identifying with this history of intellectual scandal, of provocation, is thus – as Groys recognizes – a scion of the anti-philosophical tradition that descends from the Old Testament prophets, through Paul, to Nietzsche.[68] In his book on Wittgenstein, where he goes so far as to identify Paul as 'the inventor of the antiphilosophical position', Badiou notes that, 'for the anti-philosopher, the pains and ecstasies of personal life bear witness to the fact that the concept haunts the temporal present all the way to include the throes of the body'.[69] Ideas, ineluctably shaped by biographical crises, are embodied; they are lived physically and psychologically.

As a renegade English surrealist living in poverty in Paris in the 1930s, David Gascoyne emphatically identified Shestov with an existentialism that, in contrast to the official, programmatic school sponsored by Sartre and his phenomenologically minded confederates on the Left Bank, aimed 'not at making as complete and rational a discursive exposition as possible of the purely conceptional problems of existence, but at launching individuals into a more fully conscious and authentic real existence of their own'.[70] Gascoyne's friend Fondane, another poet who modelled his own self-consciously anti-philosophical writings on Shestov, encapsulated the Russian's basic philosophical position in terms of this 'daring formulation': 'It is not man who was made for truth but truth which was made for man.' Fondane added, 'The old existential philosophy – of the Prophets, of Jesus, of St. Paul, of Luther – here attains its maximum of *speculative* daring'.[71] He meant, I think, that his mentor appropriated this prophetic, revelatory tradition for philosophical, speculative purposes. Shestov himself forcefully insisted that 'prophetic inspiration is something quite different from philosophical investigation'.[72] Certainly, in underlining the inheritance with which he identified, as a militant opponent of hypostasized reason, he never tired of citing the piece of paper that Pascal secretly sewed into the lining of his jacket after his dramatic encounter with God on the so-called 'night of fire' in 1654: 'the God of Abraham, the God of Isaac, the God of Jacob, and not the God of the philosophers'.[73] He opposed the Hellenized God of Spinoza and the Enlightenment thinkers who came after him, above all Kant and Hegel.

But the apophatic, distinctively Pascalian God whom Shestov reinvented, in the aftermath of the death of God announced by Nietzsche, did not signify some readily identifiable divine being in whom it is possible simply to have faith. For him, God is instead a force, a capricious, disruptive force, which gives its name to all that is aleatory; to the accidents and shocks that undermine and undo the mechanistic coherence of the universe in which rationalists believe. 'Chance or the accidental', Shestov insists, 'irrupts brutally and, as some think, illegitimately into well-regulated and organized unity'.[74] Again, St Paul represents an important precedent, since his paradigmatic 'conversion' on the road to Damascus, like Pascal's spiritual epiphany, constitutes what Badiou calls 'a thunderbolt, a caesura', and, in consequence, 'a conscription instituting a new subject'. 'What this absolutely aleatory intervention on the road to Damascus summons', Badiou continues, 'is the "I am" as such'.[75] The subject is thus brought into being by a crisis that it is impossible to predict. Shestov talks in *Gethsemane Night* of the 'shock[s]' that redefined the lives of St. Paul, Luther, Pascal and Nietzsche, shocks of 'discovery' that philosophy was unable to assimilate because of its constitutive 'fear of the irrational "ego"'. 'At a certain moment', he writes of Pascal, 'a force, an incomprehensible shock drove him in exactly the opposite direction to that favoured by men'. And this shock, 'the saving gift without which he would never have discovered the truth', was a combination of 'his terrible, senseless illness, and his equally terrible and senseless abyss'.[76]

Here is a philosophy, it might be said, of the spiritual encounter. As the Polish poet Czeslaw Milosz put it in a penetrating essay on Shestov, the Russian's God was 'pure anti-Necessity'.[77] More recently, in a brief, refreshing discussion of Shestov at the end of his recent book on the atheist tradition, John Gray has reminded us that, for this philosopher, 'boundless contingency was God incarnate'.[78] Shestov, then, is the prophet of God as the eternal principle of the contingent; a God of the encounter. He wages war against the 'task of philosophy' adduced by the Aristotelian tradition, which 'consists in teaching men to submit joyously to Necessity, which hears nothing and is indifferent to all'.[79] Shestov affirms instead what, in 'The Theory of Knowledge', he calls the 'miracle of sudden metamorphosis'.[80]

As his remarkable studies of Chekhov, Dostoevsky and Tolstoy indicate, Shestov implicitly identified prose fiction as a privileged site for the representation of the transformative effect of contingent experiences on the subject. For example, he praises Chekhov's *The Seagull* (1896) because its action evolves not according to 'the logical development of passions, or the inevitable connection between cause and effect, but naked accident, ostentatiously nude'.[81] Dramatic and novelistic prose is the medium in which the relationship between the incommensurable and the everyday can be limned most fully and richly. The ordinary and the miraculous or mysterious, Necessity and anti-Necessity, are intimately interwoven in the very texture of the novel in particular. And, according to Shestov, it is Dostoevsky's narratives, above all, that stage the latter's disruption of the former; unreason's irruption into reason:

> The author wants, as it were, to force into a story regulated and protected by the laws of contradiction and causality, events of the human soul which can have no place in it, in the secret hope that the laws, unable to resist this strong pressure from within, will suddenly break up and give way, and that he will then find the second dimension of time.[82]

This 'second dimension of time' is the medium of anti-Necessity.

We might look to a contemporaneous Russian novelist like Andrei Bely, who was born fourteen years after Shestov and died four years before him, for an illustration of the role that this philosopher ascribes to anti-Necessity in sabotaging the supremacy of reason. For both men were the products of an epoch that, because of certain distinctive historical and intellectual circumstances, above all the First World War and the period of revolutionary upheaval in Russia, called into question the premises of the Enlightenment. Sidney Monas has justifiably assumed that 'the hoaxing and magicking about with literary convention and religious ritual' that is typical of Bely's novels, and which makes him such an important modernist, was 'foreign to Shestov';[83] but this overlooks their shared interest in 'naked accident' and its disruption of plots predicated on logical development or the indissoluble connection between cause and effect. Bely was, above all, a disciple of Berdyaev, at least before he became an acolyte of the anthroposophist Rudolf Steiner. But like Shestov, he was one of a small number of early twentieth-century Russian intellectuals who not only championed Nietzsche because of his seminal philosophical importance but also argued that his thinking was absolutely central to understanding Christian thinking.

According to both Bely and Shestov, Nietzsche's thought played a compulsory part in the persistence and even the survival of Christianity. 'For a whole group of Russian Symbolists Nietzsche was, in his time, a transition to Christianity', Bely wrote in retrospect, after he had himself come to decide that Nietzsche and Christianity were ultimately incompatible: 'Without Nietzsche, the prophecy of neo-Christianity would not have arisen among us'.[84] It is Shestov and Bely's shared commitment to claiming Nietzsche for religious philosophy that, for comparative purposes, makes invoking the latter's pioneering modernist fiction *Petersburg* (1913–14), perhaps the greatest Russian novel of the twentieth century, seem productive. For if it is full of Dostoevskyan echoes, *Petersburg* is Nietzschean through and through, as commentators have long recognized. Carol Anschuetz, for example, has claimed that it 'simultaneously interprets Nietzsche's philosophy in terms of Russian literature and represents Russian literature in terms of Nietzsche's philosophy'.[85] This formula, if ultimately reductive, applies with equal force to Shestov's philosophical *oeuvre*. Both writers, for example, seem to have been profoundly interested in what Shestov calls 'the "exceptional" experience of Kierkegaard and Nietzsche', which 'revealed to them that the terrors of life do not, as it were, exist for reason'. 'Here', he adds, 'is to be sought the meaning of the intoxicated, one could almost say inspired, glorification of cruelty that is so stunning and repulsive to "all of us" in Nietzsche and Kierkegaard'.[86] And also, arguably, in Bely.

Petersburg is set during the pre-revolutionary events of 1905. Its protagonist, Nikolai Apollonovich, who has been commissioned by an underground revolutionary organization to assassinate his father, a senior Tsarist official, is not a Nietzschean – at least in the first instance – so much as a committed Kantian. Or to frame it more accurately, he is a committed Kantian until the bomb that he has been reluctantly concealing detonates an existential crisis that, in a kind of trance, he subsequently reconstructs for his comrade, Aleksander Ivanovich. Suddenly, Nikolai Apollonovich announces, 'Kant is out of it completely!' He explains to Aleksander Ivanovich that, recoiling from his responsibility for the explosives, which have been packed into a metal container that he compulsively seems to associate with a revolting, rotten sardine tin, his mind and body appear to explode, thereby fatally collapsing the Cartesian distinction between these two hitherto separable entities. 'My skin was inside my sensations. Was that it?' he asks; 'Or had I been turned inside out, with my skin facing inwards, or had my brain jumped out?' It is as if the existential equivalent of a bomb has been set off inside him: 'the sensations of my organs flowed around me, suddenly expanded, dilated and exploded into space: I exploded, like a bo-'.[87] A few years later, Shestov will affirm this sort of experience both for its transformative effect on the individual and for fatally undermining the notion that truth is eternal and immutable. What is needed, he wrote in 'Revolt and Submission' (1922–3), echoing Psalm 22, is 'to melt inwardly, to shatter the skeleton of one's own soul and to break that which is held to be the basis of our own being'. He concludes: 'We must feel that all in us has become fluid.'[88]

In *Petersburg*, Nikolai Apollonovich has not simply spontaneously combusted, in some psychological or spiritual sense; he has effectively converted, instantaneously, from Kantianism to Nietzscheanism. 'Of course', Aleksander Ivanovich tells him, 'a modernist would call this sensation the sensation of the abyss'. Because of this crisis, the abyss is not merely some empty, fashionable term, a mere existential philosopheme; it has 'acquired depth, become a vital truth'. Aleksander Ivanovich is himself susceptible to this sort of experience, for insomnia, combined with an addiction to alcohol and cigarettes, precipitates an episode of 'acute insanity' that he characterizes, superbly, in terms of 'a report by his diseased organs of sense – to his self-conscious "I"'.[89] These are instances of those decisive incidents, to put it in Shestov's language, 'when the natural ground begins to disappear under our feet, [and] reason tries to create through its own powers an artificial ground'.[90] Tries and fails. Bely's philosophical position in this novel, encapsulated in the delightful claim that 'we often drink coffee with cream over the abyss', is comparable to Shestov's philosophy of the void.[91] It is an aesthetics of nothingness to set beside Shestov's ethics of nothingness, which is predicated on the conviction that just as Chekhov and his characters heroically strive to 'create[e] out of a void', so we must 'live on' in spite of 'hopelessness, helplessness, [and] the utter impossibility of any action whatsoever'.[92] Shestov relished Pascal's admonition that 'we run heedlessly into the abyss, after having put something before us to prevent us seeing it'.[93]

Shestov ultimately makes for a limited literary critic, mainly because he evinces so little interest in the formal dimensions of fiction; but his philosophical attention to anti-Necessity offers rich opportunities for apprehending the significance of narrative crises like those to be found in Dostoevsky's novels as well as in later ones like *Petersburg*. For example, he is brilliantly incisive about those moments in Dostoevsky when, as he puts it, 'violently there wells up from the depth of [a character's] soul that more than rational, unknown, that primal chaos, which most of all horrifies our ordinary consciousness'.[94] 'In Dostoevsky', he comments parenthetically, but with stunning insight, in another context, 'everything happens suddenly'.[95] A Shestovian interpretation of the crucial scene from Bely's novel that I have reconstructed might, for example, emphasize the decisive role of entirely unpredictable occurrences in transforming the subject and radically undermining its stability. It might also emphasize that in 1905, the year of the revolution, Shestov published his *Apotheosis of Groundlessness*. And, moreover, that the year 1905, a moment of acute political vertigo, thrilling in its dangers and opportunities, might itself be regarded, in historical terms, as the apotheosis of groundlessness. Louis Althusser, formulating his materialist philosophy of the encounter at the end of his life, and thinking specifically of Nietzsche, refers suggestively to 'the great commencements, turns or suspensions of history, whether of individuals (for example, madness) or of the world, when the dice are, as it were, thrown back on to the table unexpectedly'.[96]

In aleatory occurrences of this kind, the unpredictable irrupts unforgivingly into what Shestov satirically calls 'well-organised unity'. In Part I of *Potestas Clavium*, a collection principally compiled from pieces published in Moscow in 1916 and 1917, at the time that *Petersburg* first appeared in book form, Shestov offers examples of apparently miraculous, though nonetheless ordinary, transformations that rational thought struggles to classify, including the fact that, on occasions, 'someone who had black hair on lying down to sleep finds himself completely white on waking'. 'If this is so', he observes, 'if such transformations are possible on earth, how can we speak of the immutable principles of thought?'[97] In the prefatory chapter to this volume,

'One Thousand and One Nights' (1917), he points furthermore to the apparent arbitrariness of the universe's origins: 'from the point of view of reason the appearance of the world is a matter of pure chance'. The miracle of its existence should be celebrated, he thinks, rather than regarded merely as a source of embarrassment because it remains 'obscure to human calculation'.[98]

G.K. Chesterton, an exactly contemporaneous religious thinker with whom Shestov at times seems to have much in common, called this, in 1923, 'the towering miracle of the mere fact of existence'.[99] If Chesterton's Christian thinking is essentially comic, though, Shestov's is essentially tragic, for it is grounded in the vertiginous idea of groundlessness. It is founded on the lawlessness and illogicality of the universe rather than on its secret order.

IV

Shestov's theory of the encounter is manifestly commensurate with a time shaped by sudden, often unexpected revolutionary, transformations like the ones dramatized in Bely's novel about the events of 1905. This was a time when, in Shestov's at once homely and millenarian terms, 'old men are transformed overnight into young people' – in some historical sense.[100] It is consistent moreover with a time when individual commencements, including madness, coincide with collective ones, such as insurrection, so that in both dimensions, which are inextricably linked to one another, as Althusser notes, 'the "elements" are unloosed in the fit of [a] madness that frees them up for new, surprising ways of taking-hold'.[101] It is the intellectual product, in short, of a time that is out of joint.

Shestov's commitment throughout his career as a thinker is to opening philosophy up to the unexpected and the inexplicable; to that which reason cannot predict or properly explain. Ventriloquizing the voice of Enlightenment reason in order to satirize its constitutive limitations, he writes: 'We must at all costs show ourselves and others that there is not and cannot be anything unexpected in the world; that the unexpected is only a misunderstanding, something chance, something transitory, which can be removed by an effort of reason'.[102] His philosophy, recoiling from these presuppositions, thus prosecutes a militant campaign in what, in the title of one of his essays on Dostoevsky, he called 'The Conquest of the Self-Evident'. Tellingly, Fondane published a substantial article on him in 1938 entitled '*Léon Chestov et la lutte contre les évidences*': 'Lev Shestov and the Struggle against Evidence'.

'One thing only interests him and that is the exception, whether in the domain of the heart or the mind', Albert Camus wrote of Shestov in *The Myth of Sisyphus* (1942), 'he tracks down, illumines and magnifies the human revolt against the irremediable'.[103] In the section of *Potestas Clavium* from which I have quoted, in the course of his discussion of the irruption of apparently miraculous transformations into everyday life, Shestov asks: 'Of what value then are the foundations on which Kant's famous postulates rest?' Echoing Hamlet, he attacks Kant for failing to consult 'men who had lived and experienced much', on the grounds that 'they would have made him see that there are many things on earth and in heaven of which the most learned of the scholars do not even dream'. Kant, he continues, 'would then have felt what appeared to him entirely inconceivable', and would in consequence 'have felt a great disgust for himself'. But this encounter with the inconceivable, and the experience of disgust, revulsion or what Sartre subsequently called 'nausea', is according to Shestov something to be celebrated, because 'it is the condition of important revelations':

> St. Theresa, St. Bernard, Luther, Shakespeare, Dostoevsky, Tolstoi – I could continue the list indefinitely – all felt a disgust for themselves and all repeated with terror the words of the psalmist: *de profundis ad te clamavi, Domine* ['Out of the depths have I cried unto thee, O Lord']. Why then did Kant conclude that everything that leads man to a horror of himself must be rejected?[104]

It is only through the subject's most abject crises, through the unpredictable and often undefinable climacterics that commute a life in an instant, inducing a sense of horror and self-disgust, that truth is encountered. 'Men respond only faintly to the horrors that take place around them', he writes in *All Things Are Possible*, 'except at moments, when the savage, crying incongruity and ghastliness of our condition suddenly reveals itself vivid before our eyes, and we are forced to know what we are'. Nikolai Apollonovich's experiences in Bely's novel are exemplary of these horrifying moments 'when the ground slides away from one's feet'.[105] Only in recoiling from oneself can one fully identify with oneself. 'The true saint', Shestov argued in 'Speculation and Apocalypse', echoing his reading of Dostoevsky, 'is the eternally disturbed underground man'.[106] This conviction is the basis of Shestov's philosophy of tragedy; a philosophy of faith that, paradoxically, is predicated on despair. It is a question, as in Chekhov, of creating out of the void.

It is thus the duty of the philosopher, according to Shestov, not to remain detached from life but to be entirely immersed in it, susceptive and responsive to its ordeals, its trials. It is the duty of the philosopher, that is, not to be a philosopher; not to be merely contemplative or reflective. It is for this reason that Shestov affirmed the prophetic mode over the philosophic one. In contrast to the philosophers, he insisted, the prophets 'never know any rest': 'They are anxiety incarnate'.[107] Shestov eventually counted the third-century Greek philosopher Plotinus, too, whose reputation he did a good deal to revive, among these prophetic archetypes. He praised Plotinus, in an article from 1926 on what he termed his 'Ecstasies', for feeling that 'he must not lull to sleep the unrest and spiritual tension within him, but goad it on to the highest degree, where sleep becomes impossible'.[108] The role of these anti-philosophers – initial patients in an epidemic of insomnia – is both to cultivate a permanent state of agitation in themselves and to transmit it to others. They must impart this restlessness to other people so that they find it impossible to lapse into some complacent, ideological acceptance of the world (a disposition that Shestov characterizes in terms of 'the universally accepted dreams'), so that sleep becomes impossible. 'We must be awakened, if only in part; to this end what is usually done to a person sound asleep must be done to us', Shestov wrote with almost cartoonish vim in 'The Theory of Knowledge': 'He is pulled, pinched, beaten, tickled, and if all these things fail, still stronger and more heroic measures must be applied.' Philosophy, then, or the agonistic and prophetic version of it that Shestov so vehemently sponsors, 'should live by sarcasm, irony, alarm, struggles, despairs'.[109]

The true philosopher does not passively reflect; they actively open themself up to the sort of contingent events that, though they might be ordinary enough, nonetheless dramatically disrupt existence and force them to reconsider it: 'a temperature of 120°, an epileptic fit, or something of this kind, which facilitates the difficult task of seeking'.[110] Shestov even valorizes *senilia* – those 'manifestations of sickness, of infirmity, of old age' that he associates with both Ibsen and Turgenev at the end of their careers – as a condition that produces almost incommunicable insights into fundamental truths.[111] The anti-philosopher's slogan is, in effect, *In febris veritas*. In an article on Martin Buber published in June 1933, some five months after this remarkable Jewish philosopher had resigned his professorship at the University of Frankfurt in protest at Hitler's accession to power in Germany, Shestov cited the postscript to his *Die Chassidischen Bücher* (1928), which quotes the eighteenth-century founder of Hasidic Judaism, Israel ben Eliezer:

> He (man) takes unto himself the quality of fervor. He rouses himself from his sleep with fervor, for holiness is imparted to him and he becomes a different man and is worthy to create and is become like the Holy One Blessed Be He, when He created His world.

Buber then added, as Shestov reports, that it was on reading this that, 'instantaneously overpowered', he 'experienced the Hasidic soul' and the 'primordially Jewish opened to [him]'.[112] Shestov presumably relished this record of what, to cite again a prophetic passage from 'Speculation and Apocalypse' that I repeated at the beginning of this chapter, he calls those 'special spiritual experiences [that] are necessary for our soul that has fallen asleep in supernatural torpor to feel in itself the power for the great and last battle against the enchantment'; for his own philosophy is built on such ecstatic, often painful epiphanies.[113] And it is throughout committed to pitting fervour against torpor, restlessness and sleeplessness against sleep.

3

Angels of history and death
Shestov's constellations

I

By the later 1930s, at least among his scattering of admirers in Paris, Shestov had the reputation for being a sort of Judaeo-Christian prophet – *Vox clamantis in deserto*, to invoke the subtitle of one of his final books, *Kierkegaard and the Existential Philosophy* (1936). At once diffident and strident, he was a prophet who for decades had been making aphoristic, often ironic, pronouncements in which he fulminated, sometimes in slightly relentless, repetitious tones, against the entire philosophical tradition of rationalism, from Plato to the present. Benjamin Fondane, in his attempt to canonize Shestov as a philosopher, complained retrospectively of his mentor's refusal, both in print and implicitly in person, to appeal for professional respectability. 'If it had only depended on me, on me giving his texts a slight nudge in the right direction', Fondane remarked, 'he could have marched confidently into the history books, revered as a philosopher, instead of remaining, as has been the case, an object of suspicion, a voice shouting in the desert [*une voix clamant dans le désert*]'.[1]

Shestov himself, who once remarked with a certain defensive pride that 'prophets are kings without an army', seems to have been less ashamed by his intellectual isolation.[2] David Gascoyne, reflecting on his time as a youthful expatriate in Paris in the 1930s when he first became a passionate admirer of Shestov's thinking, thanks in part to his friendship with Fondane, observed in retrospect that 'at the end of his life, Chestov was resigned to being neglected or mischievously misinterpreted by his contemporaries, who if they ever referred to him, did so to pour scorn on his crazy "anti-rationalism".[3] Gascoyne pointed out that, in this context, the elderly Russian finally died the death that, in a typical provocation, he himself had once described as desirable. This was a self-consciously lonely one. 'The best death', Shestov wrote in *The Apotheosis of Groundlessness* (1905), 'is really the one which is considered the worst: to die alone, in a foreign land, in a poor-house, or, as they say, like a dog under a hedge'. Why? Because 'then at least one may spend one's last moments honestly, without dissembling or ostentation, preparing oneself for the dreadful, or wonderful, event'. By contrast, Socrates spent the last month of his life, according to legend, 'in incessant conversations with his pupils and friends'. This seems to have been Shestov's idea of torture: talk, talk, talk. 'That is what it is to be a beloved master and to have disciples', the Russian added with sly humour; 'You can't even die quietly'.[4]

Alone in a foreign land, living in what Fondane described as 'an absolute and terrifying isolation', Shestov did die quietly.[5] He lived his lonely, nomadic thought to the end, committed to the idea that philosophy is predicated not on rational reflection, but on irrational suffering that violently displaces the subject's relationship both to everyday life and to those common-sense assumptions, underpinned by rationalist principles, that provide its ideological and philosophical framework. It is perhaps because of this social isolation, and because his thought was calculatedly concrete and idiosyncratic, that Shestov effectively precluded the possibility of positioning himself at the centre of an intellectual or philosophical milieu, not excluding that of French existentialism. For with the famous exception of Fondane, who was the Russian's most eloquent and most creative interpreter, there are no Shestovians. '*Qui voudra* suivre *Chestov?*' Fondane had asked, according to Gascoyne.[6] 'Who would want to follow Shestov?' No one, is the tacit response.

II

In his *Second Diasporist Manifesto* (2007), a glorious book of autobiographical interventions, written in a kind of free verse and published the year he died, the Jewish American painter R.B. Kitaj intriguingly included one numbered entry relating to Shestov. In confessional mode, Kitaj has been cataloguing and celebrating his principal intellectual influences (among which Franz Kafka and Walter Benjamin seem to be pre-eminent):

> 206 LEV SHESTOV (1866-1933 [*sic*]). This largely unsung Diasporist Jew in Paris was a progenitor of the absurdist climate of DADA and Surrealism. He has been called 'Russia's greatest thinker of the 20th century' no less. Some of the guys who were drawn to him were Bataille, Gide, Fondane (see 205), Artaud, D.H. Lawrence et al. Now me, better late than ever![7]

The date of Shestov's death may be erroneous, and the claim that he directly fostered the climate of Dadaism and Surrealism misleading, but Kitaj's affirmation of the Russian philosopher's significance, and his sphere of influence, is as suggestive as it is infectiously enthusiastic.

For even if there are no Shestovians, the list of those whom Shestov influenced during his Parisian exile, at a time of philosophical ferment in Europe, is a formidable one. In addition to Fondane, Shestov performed the role of mentor of one kind or another to Georges Bataille, as Kitaj implies, but also to Rachel Bespaloff and, later, Émile Cioran. At one time or another, these were among his closest relationships. Furthermore, as I have already indicated, and in spite of the fundamental opposition between their philosophies, he formed a firm friendship with Edmund Husserl. Shestov, who met him in 1928, regarded the German phenomenologist's work, with a certain amount of conflicted but nonetheless profoundly felt admiration, as the acme of the rationalist tradition he had committed his life to refuting. Husserl, for his part, respected Shestov not in spite of the latter's merciless critique of the former in 'Memento Mori' (1916), but because of it. In his commemoration of their friendship, published in 1938, the year that both of them died, Shestov proudly recalled Husserl introducing him to several American visiting professors in Freiburg with the following words: 'No one has ever attacked me so sharply as he – and that's why we are such close friends.'[8] In a letter sent a decade before, Husserl had placed on record both his intellectual respect for Shestov and their philosophical differences: 'You know how seriously I take your efforts to disclose God's world [*Gotteswelt*] for yourself and for all of us; a world in which one can live and die authentically, even though your ways could never become my ways.'[9]

More diffusely, the list of those on whom Shestov's philosophical project impinged, more or less decisively, constitutes an impressive list of some of the most influential European thinkers of the 1920s and the 1930s. Camus's *The Myth of Sisyphus* (1942), which is manifestly haunted by Shestov's essay on Pascal, *Gethsemane Night* (1923), discusses him directly at several points. Indeed, it might even be said to originate in a statement Shestov makes in 'A Thousand and One Nights' (1917), which first appeared in French as the Preface to *Potestas Clavium* in 1928: 'The proud tower of European culture is now in ruins. We must begin again the painful work of Sisyphus.'[10] Alongside Camus, others influenced by Shestov included Martin Buber, André Gide, Michel Henry, Vladimir Jankélévitch, Leszek Kolakowski, André Malraux, Gabriel Marcel, Miguel de Unamuno and Jean Wahl, as well as Gershom Scholem. Buber, highlighting the 'unfrightened honesty of his questioning that has made Shestov the eminent religious thinker that he is', insisted as late as 1964, the year before his own death, that he 'is one of the representative thinkers of our epoch'.[11] But Shestov's attacks on the rationalist tradition also left notable traces in the writings of Maurice Blanchot, Gilles Deleuze and Emmanuel Levinas. And they shaped the work of a number of dramatists and poets, including Yves Bonnefoy, Paul Celan and Eugène Ionesco (these last two, like Cioran and Fondane, Romanian in origin).[12]

In addition, Shestov's anti-rationalism had a limited but notable impact in Britain during the first half of the twentieth century. A collection entitled *Anton Tchekhov and Other Essays* was published in Dublin in 1916; another one, *All Things Are Possible*, an English translation of *The Apotheosis of Groundlessness* (1905), which had originally appeared in Russian, was published in London in 1920. Several of the writers and intellectuals associated with the Bloomsbury Group encountered these volumes, and in this way, Shestov's writings played a significant role in mediating the English, as well as the French, reception of nineteenth-century Russian literature, especially Dostoevsky and Tolstoy.[13] Katherine Mansfield and John Middleton Murry, both of whom relished Shestov's neo-Romantic sentiments when they read him in the later 1910s and earlier 1920s, were especially enthusiastic. In a letter to Murry in January 1920, at the time *All Things Are Possible* appeared, Mansfield for example offered this expressive, if cryptic, judgement: 'The Shestov!... *did you ever!*'[14] The translator of this volume was the literary impresario S.S. Koteliansky, known as 'Kot', whose relations with Mansfield (whom he adored) and Murry (with whom he later dramatically fell out) were extremely complicated. Koteliansky, like Shestov a Jew of Ukrainian origin, had judiciously managed to involve his friend D.H. Lawrence, then working on *Women in Love* (1920), in this slightly ill-conceived project. Lawrence collaborated closely with Koteliansky on the translation, substantially revising it (just as Murry had done in the case of *Anton Tchekhov*); he also devised the English title, having rejected 'Apotheosis of Groundlessness' because of its off-putting clumsiness.[15] Lawrence finally wrote a short Foreword too, one that Koteliansky thought patronizing. If this is the impression it gives, perhaps it is partly for this reason that, in spite of Lawrence's imprimatur, the volume sold relatively poorly.

Many of Shestov's Russian contemporaries had singled out his literary style for particular praise when he first started publishing his work, in spite of its repetitiousness, but Lawrence was less persuaded of its merits. In fact, if he was amused by Shestov's prose, he was also rather baffled by it, as this delightful description from his Foreword demonstrates:

> Shestov's style is puzzling at first. Having found the 'ands' and 'buts' and 'becauses' and 'therefores' hampered him, he clips them all off deliberately and even spitefully, so that his thought is like a man with no buttons on his clothes, ludicrously hitching along all undone. Where the armholes were a bit tight, Shestov cuts a slit.[16]

In his correspondence, Lawrence expressed his frustration more fully, but also confessed that he liked Shestov's habit of '"flying in the face of Reason", like a cross hen'.[17] Lawrence was evidently somewhat ambivalent about Shestov then, but he was nonetheless a perspicacious reader of his work. He admired the Russian's refusal to affiliate himself with prevailing ideological fashions and valued his heroic, if also rather quixotic, example as an anti-rationalist. In the Foreword, he emphasizes that, as 'he protests time and again', Shestov 'is preaching nothing'. 'He absolutely refutes any imputation of a central idea,' Lawrence goes on: 'He is so afraid lest it should turn out to be another hateful hedge-stake of an ideal.' Shestov's philosophy – which the English novelist insists is 'not nihilism' so much as simply 'a shaking free of the human psyche from old bonds' – militates in its essence against the kind of systemic appropriations that more openly metaphysical thinking solicits.[18] In spite of his scepticism, Lawrence thus clearly recognized in his slightly older Russian contemporary an intellectual comrade.

Rather more surprisingly perhaps, so did the Scottish socialist poet Hugh MacDiarmid. Indeed, in spite of their political differences, Shestov's dogged critique of systematic, metaphysical philosophizing had a decisive but durable impact on him. Not unlike Lawrence, MacDiarmid praised Shestov, above all, for celebrating the particular and the singular in the face of current philosophical and political fashions, and for inveighing 'tirelessly' against 'that dismissal of everything insusceptible of being generalized'. In his autobiography, *Lucky Poet* (1943), in which he looked back over his intellectual formation, MacDiarmid more than once described Shestov as his 'favourite' philosopher, even declaring, grandly enough, 'I have named Leo Chestov as my master'.[19] MacDiarmid first mentioned Shestov in 1922, but it was in the following decade, after the appearance of an English translation of *In Job's Balances* (1929) in 1932, that he became most fully preoccupied with his thought. His collection *Stony Limits and Other Poems* (1934; 1956) is for example full of echoes of Shestov's characteristic rhetoric. As late as the early 1970s, though, MacDiarmid was still insisting on Shestov's importance to his verse. In *Dìreadh* (1974), a poem that contains a reference to Pascal's abyss that is surely mediated through Shestov, he reflects on his relationship to Scotland's landscape and the Scottish people, and includes a brief tribute to his unlikely philosophical teacher:

> People full of remoteness, uncertainty and hope
> People who were still evolving,
> Suddenly (my master Shestov's *suddenly!*)
> See now the reconciliation of all opposites.[20]

If in Dostoevsky, according to Shestov, 'everything happens suddenly', then in Shestov too everything happens suddenly.[21] MacDiarmid's parenthesis is as insightful as it is affectionate. Some three years before he published these lines, MacDiarmid explicitly informed one enquiring correspondent, in slightly defensive tones, that 'poems like "The Impossible Song" and parts of "Ode to All Rebels"', both written at the high tide of the 1930s, 'are pure Shestov'.[22] 'So reason grounds itself on groundlessness', the poet had solemnly intoned in the former.[23]

Shestov might not have initiated a philosophical school, then, but he was a crucial centre of intellectual attraction – in Britain in the 1920s and the 1930s, but especially in France during these decades – not least precisely because he resolutely refused to initiate a philosophical school. In a period of moral and social crisis, Shestov had a determinate impact on a number of intellectuals who, to cite one of Lawrence's recent intellectual biographers, read him 'as a writer among the ruins, pushing aside all existing belief systems to make way for original utterance'.[24] Bataille's relations with him, precipitated by an encounter at the School of Oriental Languages in Paris, where he had enrolled as a student, are revealing in this context precisely because once he had propelled himself into a closer relationship with both Marxism and Surrealism, he effectively disavowed it. The friendship flourished from approximately 1922 until 1925, a brief but important period in which the young Frenchman learned the rudiments of an anti-idealist interpretation of Plato and other representatives of the rationalist tradition. Looking back, Bataille did confess on at least one occasion that Shestov had given him 'the basis of philosophical knowledge which, without possessing the character that is commonly expected from this designation, in the long run was not any less real'. And he admitted that, in spite of Shestov's excessive seriousness, he was 'moved' to recall what he had learned in listening to him, namely, 'that the violence of human thought is nothing if it is not its fulfilment'.[25] But Bataille's references to his former master remained for the most part muted and rather misleading; and he once even dismissed him as 'an old Russian philosopher', disconcerting in his 'humorlessness', whom he merely happened to have visited on various occasions in his youth.[26]

Discussing Bataille's failure to credit Shestov with a significant role in his intellectual development, Stuart Kendall wisely remarks that a perspective like Bataille's, 'predicated on the mutual and violent abandonment of man and god, in which a madman hurls himself on the throat of that which embodies his highest value, cannot confess the patient and nurturing tutelage that engendered it'.[27] Ironically, Shestov and Bataille had fundamentally different understandings of the violence of human thought and the meaning of its self-fulfilment. Bataille nevertheless manifestly inherited a number of the significant features of his mature thought from Shestov, above all his militant anti-idealism and his commitment to a thinking that commenced at the point at which reason effectively fails. He also learned his admiration for both Dostoevsky and Nietzsche – an anti-idealist, anti-nationalist version of Nietzsche – from Shestov. Revealingly, Bataille never completed the book or substantial article on Shestov that, in 1923, he said he was preparing; but he did collaborate with the Russian's daughter, Teresa Beresovski-Shestov, on a French translation of *The Good in the Teaching of Tolstoy and Nietzsche*, which was eventually published in 1925.[28]

At times, Bataille directly echoes Shestov, though he doesn't fully admit to doing so, as when, in the section on 'Torture' in *Inner Experience* (1943), the aphoristic form of which itself owes something to the Russian exile's example, he discusses the problem of reaching 'the extremity of the possible'. At that limit, Bataille prophesies, 'is fulguration, even the "apotheosis" of nonsense'. It is an ambivalent allusion to Shestov's *Apotheosis of Groundlessness*, in English *All Things Are Possible*, one that is symptomatic of Bataille's lasting anxiety of influence. Further proof that he is thinking of Shestov, semi-consciously, comes in the succeeding paragraph, where he characterizes extremity in terms of the perpetual insomnia enjoined by Pascal, as explored in *Gethsemane Night*: 'The extremity implies "one must not fall asleep during that time" (up to the moment of death), but Pascal accepted sleeplessness in view of the beatitude to come (at least he gave himself that reason).'[29] Shestov, writes Bataille's biographer, 'invited him to the abyss of a desperate thought'.[30] But if Shestov remained at its edge, his philosophy creatively poised beside the void, Bataille subsequently plunged into it. He remained a kind of rebellious adolescent in his relations to Shestov, pressing his symbolic father's philosophical premises to the point of destruction.

As a young man, reviewing Shestov's influential, if characteristically unclassifiable, book on Kierkegaard in 1937, Emmanuel Levinas evoked the historical and intellectual conditions in which the Russian's thinking intervened:

> The moral crisis opened by the War of 1914 has given men a pointed feeling of the impotence of reason, of the profound discord between rationalist civilization and the exigencies of the individual soul lost in the anonymity of the general. It has reopened the question, despite the blinding expansion of the sciences and technology, of the value, until now uncontested, of the Greek heritage. From there, under different forms, the reemergence at the same time of irrationalism and doctrines of violence.[31]

Shestov's emphasis on the irrational, and on the abrupt, violent irruption of the miraculous into everyday life, is a homeopathic response to the times through which he lived, which one historian, has characterized in terms of a 'culture of Anti-Necessity'.[32] His was a tragic philosophy for tragic times; a philosophy of the spiritual encounter for an epoch shaped, in spite of the technocratic ambitions of the state, by the irruption of unpredictable but decisive events that undermined the claims of scientistic reason.

Before he became a Marxist, in the years before the First World War, the young Hungarian intellectual György Lukács, like Shestov a great admirer of Dostoevsky at this time, developed a humanist philosophy of tragedy, invested in the redemptive role of violence, which is roughly comparable to the Russian's philosophy with which it was contemporaneous. Lukács too underlined the transformative role of accident, which he too understood in more or less spiritual terms, in defining this anti-rationalist conception of life. In 'The Metaphysics of Tragedy' (1910), for example, he identified 'empirical life' with a condition of 'numbness' comparable to the state of somnambulism that Shestov associated with everyday life in post-Enlightenment society. And he argued, in the spirit of romantic anti-capitalism characteristic of him at this stage of his career, that this 'empirical life' is secretly susceptible to miraculous irruptions that expose the underground presence of what he called instead 'real life'. 'The miracle is what determines and is determined', he writes: 'It bursts incalculably into life, accidentally and out of context, and ruthlessly turns life into a clear, an unambiguous equation – which it then resolves.' 'Only the miracle', Lukács concludes, in language that Shestov would have recognized, 'has reality before the face of God'.[33]

Shestov made a unique contribution to European thought in the period between the two world wars because, without reinforcing the irrationalist ideological tendencies then becoming entrenched throughout the continent in the form of fascism, his anti-rationalism reflected the prevailing, ever-deepening crisis of the Enlightenment and its instrumentalization of reason. His complaint about reason was not that it was not illuminating and revealing – his polemics did not completely blind him to its value – but that it 'unveils every mystery save one – the existence of an abyss beneath out feet'.[34] According to Shestov, however, this is effectively the single most important fact of life. This helps explain his appeal for a generation of European intellectuals between the wars, living through what Camus called their 'nights of Gethsemane'.[35] These were thinkers who, to lean on William Desmond's distinction, were less inclined to see history, from within a Hegelian frame, as 'the dialectical progress of *Geist*', than to see it, in an echo of Pascal, as 'the prolonged Gethsemane night of time'.[36]

III

As the example of Bataille implies, Shestov is probably best understood, at least in the context of French metropolitan culture between the Wars, as a semi-visible philosophical force field, perceptible partly through effects on other, more celebrated intellectuals, effects that were sometimes no more than half admitted or credited. Walter Benjamin, who lived in exile in Paris from 1933, that is, during the last four or five years of the Russian thinker's life, is one writer who occupied the peripheries of this force field. And there are intriguing connections and points of contact between their philosophies, especially insofar as these relate to messianic notions of awakening or wakefulness. Here, indeed, is an 'elective affinity' of the sort that Michael Löwy, in his book on 'Jewish Libertarian Thought in Central Europe', characterizes as 'a very special kind of dialectical relationship that develops between two social and cultural configurations, one that cannot be reduced to direct causality or to "influences" in the traditional sense'.[37]

Benjamin probably never met Shestov, but he shared acquaintances with him, among them Bataille, Scholem and the Swiss Protestant theologian and socialist Fritz Lieb, a former pupil of Karl Barth and a close friend of Berdyaev (Scholem characterized Lieb, whose millenarian influence on Benjamin can be felt most sharply in the sixth of his theses 'On the Concept of History' (1940), as 'the only person to whom Benjamin's theological dimension in his later years was directly comprehensible and unabashedly significant').[38] Moreover, Benjamin comments on Shestov incidentally several times in his correspondence. More precisely, as I will go on to explain, the German captured something of the Russian's incongruous, though beguiling, reputation in the French metropolis in a strange, phantasmagoric image, which appears in a letter to Scholem from 1939 (the year after Shestov's death; the year before Benjamin's).

In short, Benjamin's association, or non-association, with Shestov, is oddly revealing of the latter's reputation among the rootless European intellectuals of this period. It is as if they should have encountered one another; as if Benjamin should have written about Shestov. In fact, there is an interesting slip, symptomatic of just this presumption, in an essay about Benjamin by the German literary critic Hans Mayer, who met his older compatriot at Bataille's Collège de Sociologie in the later 1930s. In 'Walter Benjamin and Franz Kafka: Report on a Constellation' (1980), which he dedicated to Scholem, Mayer in one paragraph contrasts Benjamin's relatively scattered reflections on Kafka to what he calls by comparison his 'well-structured composition[s]'. As examples of the latter, less ephemeral category of writing, he offers 'this prodigious essayist's works on Proust, Shestov, Kraus, or Brecht'.[39] Of course, Benjamin never actually wrote about Shestov, even though he expressed a desire to do so. Instead, Mayer surely means the Russian novelist Nikolai Leskov, the subject of Benjamin's essay entitled 'The Storyteller' (1936). But the mistake is delightfully revealing. For Shestov and Benjamin might also be said to constitute a constellation, albeit not one that is immediately visible.

Paul Celan, the Jewish Romanian poet, who wrote largely in German, offered a fleeting glimpse of this constellation when he read and annotated both Shestov and Benjamin in late 1959. If, according to his biographer, Celan 'refract[ed] Western thought through this Russian Jew who died in

exile in Paris' in 1938 (i.e. Shestov), then he refracted Kafka and a number
of other European writers through this 'German Jew exiled in Paris who
committed suicide in 1940' (i.e. Benjamin). One quotation from Benjamin's
essay on Kafka that Celan underlined when reading it, as might be noted, was
Malebranche's maxim that 'attentiveness is the natural prayer of the soul'.[40]
Benjamin's emphasis on attentiveness is comparable, I think, to Shestov's on
wakefulness and watchfulness, though their frame of reference is of course
different. It is no accident not only that Celan read both authors at the same
time but that he quoted them in conjunction with one another a year later in
'The Meridian', his speech on the occasion of receiving the 1960 Georg Büchner
Prize. In this remarkable meditation on the meaning of the poem, *qua* poem,
he repeated a statement of Pascal's cited in the final sentence of Shestov's 'A
Thousand and One Nights' in order to defend the 'obscurity' of contemporary
poetry: '*Qu'on ne nous reproche donc plus le manque de claret, puisque nous
en faisons profession*': 'Do not reproach us with lack of clarity, for we make it
our profession.' Celan then duly recited the dictum from Malebranche quoted
in Benjamin's essay on Kafka in order to valorize 'the attention which the
poem pays to all that it encounters': '"Attention", if you allow me a quote from
Malebranche via Walter Benjamin's essay on Kafka, "attention is the natural
prayer of the soul"'.[41]

Levinas also noticed this apparently strange conjunction of Benjamin and
Shestov in Celan's 'The Meridian', a lecture he admiringly characterized, in an
essay from 1972, as a 'breathless meditation' that 'obeys no norm'. He praised it
in particular for 'daring to cite Malebranche from a text of Walter Benjamin's
on Kafka and Pascal, according to Léon Chestov'. Although he doesn't
specifically link it to Shestov's notions of sleeplessness and vigilance, Levinas
nonetheless interprets attentiveness, in Celan's appropriation of the concept, as
'a mode of consciousness without distraction' and, more significantly, 'the first
meaning of that insomnia that is conscience'. What Levinas, a couple of pages
later, in a striking ontological image, calls 'insomnia in the bed of being, the
impossibility of curling up and forgetting oneself", seems even more indebted
to Shestov, and in particular to Shestov's reading of Pascal, than it does to
Celan.[42] Certainly, Levinas's first book, *Existence and Existents* (1947), the
importance of which only Bataille appears to have grasped at the time of its

publication, repeatedly explores the relationship of being to beings in terms of sleep and sleeplessness. Levinas never mentions Shestov here; but, in a passage in which, not coincidentally, he cites Pascal's *Penseés*, he outlines what he calls the *il y a*, the 'anonymous rustling of existence', in terms that, evoking 'the vigilance of insomnia which keeps our eyes open', manifestly recall the Russian philosopher: 'It is an indefectibility of being, where the work of being never lets up; it is its insomnia.'[43]

As far back as 1934, to reconstruct the Scholem-Shestov-Benjamin triangle, Scholem had implored Benjamin to meet Shestov and read his work. 'How about doing something really daring in Paris', he mischievously asked, 'and going to see Leo Shestov?' Perhaps Scholem, who iterated a month or so later that he thought 'very highly of the man', characterized the idea as 'daring', in this teasing tone, because Shestov was a religious philosopher. After all, relations between Scholem and Benjamin had become fractious or fraught at this point because the former felt betrayed by the latter's strengthening (and, as he perceived it, increasingly confused and intellectually confusing) commitment to communism. Benjamin – who in response slightly testily asked his friend to 'at least hint at [his] designs' in suggesting that he 'look up' Shestov – purported either ingenuously or disingenuously to be nonplussed. 'What I have read of his, e.g., in *Kreatur*, doesn't give me enough background to make such a step', he commented, referring to the journal co-edited by Buber to which he himself had also contributed; 'I cannot find any concrete facts about him in my memory.'[44]

Subsequently, Scholem renewed his pleas on a number of occasions, and in 1935 Benjamin sought to placate him. He observed that he had skimmed Shestov's *Potestas Clavium*, published in German in 1926 and in French in 1928. And he noted that he had 'determined that its polemic against platonic idealism turns out to be more interesting than in the usual stuff of this genre'.[45] At this time, when Benjamin was working on 'The Work of Art in the Age of its Technological Reproducibility', of which there were various versions between 1935 and 1939, Scholem presumably hoped that Shestov's un-selfconsciously spiritual form of anti-rationalism might moderate his friend's materialist tendencies, and he was evidently frustrated by his apparent reluctance to engage with the Russian's thought more fully. 'In one of my letters I emphatically had drawn his attention to the books of Lev Shestov and advised him to seek his acquaintance,' he wrote in his memoir of their friendship: 'He shirked this assignment for a rather long time.'[46]

In a letter from 1935, directly after a discussion of his article on Leskov, which was then still in manuscript form, Benjamin triumphantly declared to Scholem, 'Tomorrow finally I shall make Shestov's acquaintance.'[47] In the same year, Benjamin told his former friend Werner Kraft, who had sent him a poem and mentioned Shestov in connection with it, both that he expected to meet Shestov 'sometime very soon' and that *In Job's Balances*, the collection in which *Gethsemane Night* was collected in essay form, was sitting 'on the shelf right next to [him]'.[48] Scholem later speculated that, insofar as he actively sought an introduction to Shestov at this time, Benjamin 'brought himself to do it only in connection with his essay on Leskov' (a text that Scholem regarded, along with the essay on Kafka, as evidence of Benjamin's continued investment in mysticism as well as Marxism).[49] It might have been simply that one Russian reminded Benjamin of the other, living near at hand in Paris, as in Mayer's conflation of them more than forty years later. It might have been that Benjamin's comparison of Leskov's at times almost 'antinomian ethics' to those of Dostoevsky reminded him of Shestov, who had first created a stir in the French metropolis when he published a centenary essay on the Russian novelist in *La Nouvelle Revue Francaise* in 1921. Certainly, Shestov himself was a pronounced antinomian. In *Gethsemane Night*, he preached that 'submission to the law is the beginning of all impiety'.[50] And in *Apotheosis of Groundlessness* he insisted, even more militantly, that 'morality, science, logic' are 'police agents'; and that 'laws are a refreshing sleep – lawlessness is creative activity'.[51] In Shestov's idiosyncratic lexicon, 'sleep' is never a positive term. Any activity or experience that provokes sleeplessness is, in contrast, potentially redemptive.

Sadly, though, there is no evidence that Benjamin did make the older man's acquaintance, either in 1935 or later. It was a non-encounter, albeit a suggestive one. Certainly, Benjamin's most substantial reference to Shestov, in a letter to Scholem written some three years later, after Shestov's death, contains no comment that is directly personal. Instead, Benjamin there informs Scholem that the doctor treating Shestov's widow, Anna Eleazarovna, lives in the same building as him, implying that through this neighbour he has made her acquaintance. 'The poor woman sits beneath the volumes of her husband's works, their pages still uncut', Benjamin relates, in a moving evocation of the mortality of a writer's literary remains; 'What will we leave behind someday, other than our own writings with their uncut pages?'[52] This image of the books' uncut pages recalls, a little uncomfortably, a passage from Mallarmé that Benjamin had quoted in one of the sections of *One-Way Street* (1928), where the action of using a knife to slice the paper is compared to the act of penetration whereby a woman loses her virginity.[53] In the letter to Scholem from 1938, where the latent association of these violent sexual politics is of course repressed, it evokes in contrast a sense both of senility and sterility. It is a surgical rather than a sexual image. But there is a more general impression here, in the image of the piles of books, among them ones with uncut pages, of Benjamin's love of the archaic, the discarded and the forgotten; in short, the detritus of capitalist culture from which it might just be possible to sift and uncover a cryptic utopian potential. Shestov's apartment in Paris, that is, implicitly becomes part of the dream logic of Benjamin's *Arcades Project*.

Describing his meetings with the Russian philosopher's widow, Benjamin goes on to explain that, 'to make her interior look a bit more amiable, she hauls away a few of these writings now and then, and in this way I am slowly building up a collection of Shestov's writings'.[54] One might think of Benjamin liberating these books, exhuming them from the mausoleum in which they have been interred, since he believed that, 'to a book collector', as he had observed in 'Unpacking My Library' (1931), 'the true freedom of all books is somewhere on his shelves'.[55] In the letter to Scholem from 1938 about the recently deceased Shestov's books, Benjamin then goes on to pledge that he will read *Athens and Jerusalem* (1938) and to express the hope – it remained unfulfilled when he died, after fleeing Paris, in 1940 – that at some point he will 'have occasion to write a review of the book'.[56]

Finally, in this same letter, Benjamin improvizes a colourful, rather ornate fantasia in relation to Shestov:

If you imagine a good fairy who suddenly gets the urge to transform the filthiest cul-de-sac in the most desolate corner of a large city's outskirts into an inaccessible mountain valley, in which the sides of the mountain flanks plummet as steeply perpendicular as the facades of the block of tenements had before, then you have the image in which Shestov's philosophy appears to me.

Benjamin concludes his brief assessment of Shestov's philosophy by stating: 'It is, I believe, rather admirable but useless.' He adds, though, that he 'can only take off [his] hat to the commentator in him' and, furthermore, that he thinks 'his style is superb'. Cryptically, he even compares Shestov to Kafka, insisting that, apart from the peculiar humour that is essential to the novelist he so admires, the 'route' from the former to the latter 'is not a long one'.[57]

But what did Benjamin mean by depicting Shestov's philosophy, in this dreamlike image, as a sordid proletarian suburb transformed by some genial fairy, on impulse, into an immense, all but impenetrable mountainous terrain? If Adorno notoriously situated Benjamin's thought at the crossroads of magic and positivism, Benjamin appears to situate Shestov, on the outskirts of the French capital, at the crossroads between magic and a sort of Zolaesque naturalism.[58] It seems possible that, if he had not in fact met him, Benjamin had nonetheless seen Shestov, or had at least seen photographs of him, and that the 'fairy' thus deliberately recalls the elderly Russian's elfin features, as well as the frequently playful, puckish quality of his prose, especially in its more aphoristic forms. It also seems possible, given the association between Leskov and Shestov divined by Scholem and then inadvertently intuited by Mayer, that Benjamin was unconsciously recalling his celebration of 'the spirit of the fairy tale' in 'The Storyteller'.[59]

More immediately significant, though, is the series of collisions that Benjamin's dialectical image of a fantastical cityscape implicitly dramatizes in the form of a concatenation of abstract oppositions. These include the ancient and the modern, the natural and the cultural, the country and the city, the East and the West. Also, perhaps, the prophet and the proletariat. These antinomies evoke Adorno's sequence of oppositions in his 'Portrait of Walter Benjamin' (1955), when he summarizes the *Arcades Project*: 'Politics and metaphysics, theology and materialism, myth and modernity, non-intentional matter and extravagant speculation – all the streets of Benjamin's city-tableau converge in the plan of the Paris book as in their Etoile [i.e. the Place de l'Étoile].[60] In other words, the image of Shestov might be seen as a projection, duly distorted, of Benjamin's own contradictions. The letter to Scholem might also be seen as a city-tableau in which various Benjaminian streets, though they contradict or cross one another, converge. He depicts Shestov in terms of a dialectic of theology and materialism, myth and modernity.

In more formal terms, Benjamin implies that Shestov's work, in the context of the contemporary European metropolis, and especially its poorest, least metropolitan quarters, though also no doubt its most cosmopolitan ones, resembles the dreamlike intrusion of a sublime landscape. This glimpse of a forbidding, inaccessible mountainside folded into the city's crowded residential outskirts, its 'flanks plummet[ing] as steeply perpendicular as the facades of [a] block of tenements', recalls a painting or collage by one of Benjamin's surrealist contemporaries. But 'no picture by de Chirico or Max Ernst', as Benjamin puts it in his discussion of the 'surrealistic', and for this reason 'true', 'face' of the city in his essay on 'Surrealism' (1929), 'can match the sharp elevations of the city's inner strongholds, which one must overrun and occupy in order to master their fate and, in their fate, in the fate of their masses, one's own'.[61] Shestov's philosophy, in its bizarre, archaic obtrusions, is for Benjamin, it might be inferred, just such an inner stronghold with sharp elevations. Again, the *Arcades Project*, which Benjamin had originally conceived as a '*dialektische Feen*', a dialectical fairy scene, one specifically concerned with the idea of awakening, provides an overarching logic.

In Benjamin's image of Shestov in the correspondence with Scholem, it is possible to speculate, the sheer facades of suburban tenements and apartment blocks become the perpendicular flanks of mountains in part because the elderly bearded Russian represents an intellectual tradition that transmits the primal force of biblical prophets in the everyday context of industrial metropolitan modernity – the Mount of Olives, as it were, in the 15ème arrondissement. It is not implausible to assume that, in thinking about Shestov, Benjamin recollected that his own heroes as a young man included Tolstoy and Dostoevsky, the authors at the centre of the Russian's published studies from the early 1900s of a prophetic, underground tradition in literature. There is a passage in the prefatory section of *Potestas Clavium*, one of the books that Benjamin professed at least to have inspected, in which Shestov celebrates the 'cry' – 'whether from the depths of an abyss or from the height of a mountain'. 'Educated men of all times', Shestov complains in this context, regard such an utterance, in contrast to logical statements, as 'a completely useless and absurd thing' that has 'no connection with truth'. For Shestov, as I intimated in the previous chapter, cries, groans, roars and other pre-verbal utterances, erupting from the depths of the embodied subject, comprise the most intimate medium of truth. Shestov was fond of quoting Pascal's dictum: '*Je n'aime que ceux qui cherchent en gémissant*'.[62] 'I love only those who seek with groaning.' Or lamentation. These are the utterances of Job and the Old Testament prophets. They constitute the elemental human cry that emanates from the heights of the mountain and from the depths of the abyss that lies in its shadows. It is the cry of Nietzsche's Zarathustra as well as the biblical prophets.

As a student, Benjamin had immersed himself in Nietzsche's 'critique of identity, continuity, causality', as his biographers record, and, as a corollary of this, in Nietzsche's 'radical eventism', which 'furnished the theoretic ground (the groundless ground) for the generation that came of age in the artistically explosive years before the First World War'. 'Benjamin never afterward evaded the challenge of thinking simultaneously within and beyond the antinomies of traditional metaphysics', they add, 'and he never abandoned the interpretation of reality as a spatiotemporal sea of forces, with its depths and its tides of transformation'.[63] Benjamin seems to have perceived Shestov's writings, after his death, in terms of some alien geological phenomenon embedded in the modern metropolitan city like the remains of an ancient meteorite half-buried by time. But he intuitively valued Shestov's Nietzschean protest against identity, continuity and causality, his insistence on a certain 'eventism' as a groundless ground during an epoch of social upheaval. After all, Shestov portrayed his own thinking, to repeat a sentence I cited at the start of the previous chapter, as 'an art which aims at breaking the logical continuity of argument and bringing man out on the shoreless sea of imagination, the fantastic tides where everything is equally possible and impossible'.[64]

IV

Benjamin was evidently suspicious about Scholem's motives for pressing him to meet and read Shestov; and it is no doubt the case, as Michael Weingrad argues, that 'Benjamin rejected Shestov's irrationalism and interior metaphysics from the start as politically retrograde'.[65] But in spite of this, I think it is possible to detect residues of the Russian's messianism, or comparable trace elements of it at least, in Benjamin's writings of the late 1930s (complicated though their admixture is, especially insofar as these writings were shaped by his Judaism as well as his Marxism). Certainly, there are affinities, elective or not, between the two writers, both of whom refused, at the level of form and content, the neo-Kantian philosophical paradigms of their time. Both of them perhaps refused philosophical paradigms per se, for if Benjamin's was a 'philosophy directed against philosophy', as Adorno once said, then so was Shestov's.[66]

These affinities can briefly be enumerated. They include, first, an emphasis in Shestov's thought on the agent of psychological or social transformation as a contingent force, which I explored at length in my discussion of his anti-philosophy. Shestov characterizes it in relation to the individual and in terms of the miraculous; Benjamin characterizes it in relation to the collective and in terms of the messianic.[67] For both of them, to embed it in the Judaic framework adapted by the latter in his theses 'On the Concept of History', 'every second of time [is] the strait gate through which the Messiah might enter'.[68] Second, the two thinkers share a salvific emphasis on hopelessness. Benjamin's famous formulation, 'Only for the sake of the hopeless ones have we been given hope', which concludes his essay on 'Goethe's Elective Affinities' (1924-5), that is, his insistence that hopelessness is the precondition of hope, resonates with Shestov's powerful slogan that 'he who can weep can hope'.[69] The Russian's repeated claim, central to his philosophy of tragedy, is that hopelessness 'is the most solemn and supreme moment in life', and that, as such, it is the precondition of any form of thinking that might ultimately prove redemptive.[70]

For Shestov, in fact, hopelessness is the precondition of thinking *tout court*. His philosophy, then, is a Dostoevskyan and Nietzschean one. It is stripped of all faith in the consolations that a rationalist understanding of the world, with its comforting emphasis on cause and effect, superficially appears to offer. In his early book, *Dostoevsky and Nietzsche: The Philosophy of Tragedy* (1903), Shestov emphasized that it is at the point when 'fearful loneliness' first afflicts the individual, and he or she discovers that the consolations of idealist and rationalist philosophy are useless, that the philosophy of tragedy begins: 'Hope is lost forever, but life remains, and there is much life ahead'.[71] As Edith Clowes comments in relation to Shestov, 'in contrast to systematic philosophy, tragic philosophy is based on an acknowledgement of the basic chaos of life'.[72] Not merely an acknowledgement, but an affirmation; one that is filled with joy as well as horror, hope as well as despair.

Clowes quotes Shestov's *Apotheosis of Groundlessness* to this effect in her authoritative account of Russian literary and philosophical culture:

> Laws – all of them – have a regulatory meaning and are needed by a person in search of rest and support. But the first and vital condition of life is lawlessness. Laws are sleep that fortifies. Lawlessness is creative activity.[73]

As this antinomian, if not anarchic statement implies, the points of contact between Benjamin and Shestov also include, most importantly in the present context, an emphasis on wakefulness. This is the third main affinity between them, the one on which I want to concentrate. Benjamin affirms wakefulness in the face of the dream of capitalism, which he portrays in the *Arcades Project* as 'a natural phenomenon with which a new dream-filled sleep came over Europe, and, through it, a reactivation of mythic forces'.[74] Shestov, in contradistinction, affirms wakefulness in the face of the dream of reason. To be more precise, Benjamin characterizes wakefulness, again in relation to the collective, in terms of awakening; Shestov characterizes it, again in relation to the individual, in terms of remaining awake. Benjamin's famous image, in the essay on 'Surrealism', of 'an alarm clock that in each minute rings for sixty seconds', evokes the eternal, and intolerable, wakefulness entreated by Shestov, especially in his interpretation of Pascal in *Gethsemane Night* – even if its rhetorical register, characteristically, is that of a modernist rather than a latter-day prophet.[75]

In spite of this startling image of an alarm that is constant, that threatens to ring in each hour for sixty minutes, in each day for twenty-four hours, Benjamin's poetics of awakening, and their politics, so to speak, are hypnopompic. That is to say, they centre on those liminal moments, still half-filled with dreams, that precede the complete reconnection of consciousness. In contrast, Shestov's poetics of awakening, which also implicitly comprise a politics, are insomniac. They pivot on a permanent state of attentiveness. For Benjamin, as he speculates in his notes for the *Arcades Project*, awakening 'is the synthesis of dream consciousness (as thesis) and waking consciousness (as antithesis)'. It is a dialectical condition, or what he identifies as a 'supremely dialectical point of rupture', and its exemplary instance is 'Proust's evocation of the space of someone waking up'.[76] For Shestov, wakefulness is not a dynamic, dialectical experience but a static, monolithic one – a kind of spiritual discipline. It is about remaining 'wide awake and strenuously living'. If for Benjamin, then, the space of someone waking up, in a physical sense, is the bedroom, for Shestov, the space of someone being awake is the prison cell. 'The keenest spiritual activity tak[es] place in seclusion,' Shestov argues, emphasizing that he means the seclusion not of the philosopher's study, but of the condemned man's cell.[77] Dostoevsky, not Proust, is the archetype here. But both these paradigmatic modes of being, the condition of awakening and the state of wakefulness, implicitly constitute a refusal of the Enlightenment form of enchantment that reached its acme in the Nazis' populist reclamation of the past.

In the context of these intellectual continuities and discontinuities, Benjamin's most famous and most enigmatic allegorical figure, the Angel of History, which appears in the ninth of his theses 'On the Concept of History', that is, his reading of *Angelus Novus* (1920), the little monoprint by Paul Klee that he owned, might be re-imagined in relation to one of Shestov's allegorical figures, namely, *homo vigilans*. *Homo vigilans*, Shestov's archetype of the wakeful, watchful man, appears in both the books by him that Benjamin encountered: *Potestas Clavium*, where the phrase turns up in an essay added to the French edition of 1928, and *Athens and Jerusalem*.[78] Clearly, it is not a case of Shestov influencing Benjamin; but it is nonetheless possible to glimpse a constellation between their thought in relation to ideas of waking and wakefulness. It is a question of reading them alongside one another, of using them to brush one another against the grain. Both *homo vigilans* and the Angel of History are emblematic of Nietzsche's declaration, in 'On the Uses and Disadvantages of History for Life' (1874), an essay of crucial importance to Benjamin in his youth, that 'a man who wanted to feel historically through and through would be like one forcibly deprived of sleep'. Both feel historically through and through and are therefore forced, in Nietzsche's phrase, to live 'without forgetting'.[79]

Once again, Scholem provides a means of mediating the connections between Shestov and Benjamin. As the epigraph to the ninth of the theses 'On the Concept of History', Benjamin reproduced a verse from 'Greeting from the Angelus', a poem about Klee's painting by Scholem, who had looked after it in the early 1920s. It was Scholem who, at least initially, shaped Benjamin's interpretation of the Angelus Novus. For Benjamin's association of Klee's figure, in his essay on 'Karl Kraus' (1931), with those angels 'who, according to the Talmud, are at each moment created anew in countless throngs, and who, once they have raised their voices before God, cease and pass into nothingness', was the product of discussions about angelology that he had conducted with this brilliant scholar of Judaism.[80] And it was Scholem, incidentally, who eventually inherited the *Angelus Novus* after his friend's suicide, thanks to Bataille and Adorno, who protected it in Paris and New York, respectively, in the years following Benjamin's flight.

Klee's angel, half-human half-divine, has staring eyes with eyelids that appear to have been permanently pinned back against its head. The eyes of Benjamin's Angel of History too, as it stares at the 'rubble-heap' of the past accumulating behind it, 'are opened wide':

A Klee painting named 'Angelus Novus' shows an angel looking as though he is about to move away from something he is fixedly contemplating. His eyes are staring, his mouth is open, his wings are spread. This is how one pictures the angel of history. His face is turned towards the past. Where we perceive a chain of events, he sees one single catastrophe which keeps piling wreckage upon wreckage and hurls it in front of his feet. The angel would like to stay, awaken the dead, and make whole what has been smashed. But a storm is blowing from Paradise; it has got caught in his wings with such violence that the angel can no longer close them. This storm irresistibly propels him into the future to which his back is turned, while the pile of debris before him grows skyward. This storm is what we call progress.[81]

Figure 3.1 *Angelus Novus, 1920 (Indian ink, colour chalk & brown wash on paper), Klee, Paul (1879-1940) / The Israel Museum, Jerusalem, Israel / Carole and Ronald Lauder, New York / Bridgeman Images*

The storm that propels the angel backwards into the future, the storm of 'progress' that is 'blowing from Paradise', 'has got caught in his wings with such violence that the Angel can no longer close them'. Benjamin's freely ekphrastic account of the *Angelus Novus* implies that, according to a logic of contagion, it can no longer close its eyes either – 'like one forcibly deprived of sleep', in Nietzsche's formulation. Eyes, mouth and wings are all opened wide in horror: 'His eyes are staring, his mouth is open, his wings are spread'. In the painting, certainly, the unsleeping angel's eyes appear frozen open for perpetuity. Its vision is different from ours, for where 'we perceive a chain of events', it sees a permanent catastrophe that, accumulating layer upon layer, collapses past, present and future into one another – one damned thing on top of another.

The biblical scholar Robert Alter, who suggestively describes Benjamin's angel as 'a kind of dumbfounded refugee from the world of religious symbolism', observes that in the theses 'On the Concept of History' he presents

Klee's *Angelus Novus* 'as a general allegory of unflinchingly witnessing history'. 'The angel here is not annunciating angelman,' he goes on, thinking in this respect of the distinctive role it performs in Scholem's poem, 'but witnessing man, allegorically endowed with the terrible power of seeing things utterly devoid of illusion'.[82] Seeing things as they are and without being able not to see. Here, in the form of the Angel of History, is Benjamin's *homo vigilans*. In this sense, the theses 'On the Concept of History', like the *Arcades Project*, can be interpreted, in Benjamin's formulation, as 'an experiment in the technique of awakening'.[83] His Angel, to echo Shestov's phrases from *Athens and Jerusalem*, emerges amidst the rumbling of the thunder, under the sign of revelation, bearing witness, in the face of barbarism, to little more than the capacity for bearing witness.[84] As Michael Löwy puts it, the Angel of History 'rivet[s] a gaze imbued with a deep, inconsolable sadness – but also with a profound moral revulsion – on the ruins it produces'.[85]

In 'the night of times', to cite a phrase from one of Benjamin's drafts of the ninth thesis, the Angel of History is condemned to remain awake and watch rather than to sleep.[86] Adorno, in his brief reading of Klee's painting, claimed that it confronted the viewer with a choice: 'The machine angel's enigmatic eyes force the onlooker to try to decide whether he is announcing the culmination of disaster or salvation hidden within it'.[87] Adorno here is uncharacteristically undialectical. For interpreted as an image of *homo vigilans*, the angel proclaims both the culmination of disaster and the salvation hidden within it. It might therefore stand, inadvertently, as an emblematic image of Shestov's philosophy of tragedy. In a letter Shestov wrote to his daughters in 1920, he offered a glimpse of this dialectic of damnation and redemption, despair and hope, when he movingly observed that in Tolstoy, as in Plato and Plotinus, 'the thought of death is accompanied by a particular sentiment, by a kind of consciousness that, even while horror rose before them, wings were growing in their backs'.[88] Benjamin's angel's wings, and perhaps its all-seeing, all-witnessing eyes, offer a glimpse of redemption in the face of piling wreckage. Here is hope for the hopeless.

The angel that presides over the philosophy of tragedy in Shestov's *oeuvre*, however, is not the Angel of History. It is the Angel of Death. Shestov invokes this Angel, which is both destructive and redemptive, in his centenary essay on Dostoevsky, 'The Conquest of the Self-Evident' (1922). There, he takes it from 'a very wise old book', by which he presumably means, not the Book of Revelation in the Christian Bible, but the tractate known as *Avodah Zarah* in the Talmud. This Angel of Death, according to Shestov, is a being who, when it 'descends towards man to separate his soul from his body', is covered with 'innumerable pairs of eyes'. If the Angel appears too soon, and 'the man's term of life is not yet expired', Shestov explains, it leaves him with one of the many pairs of eyes with which it bristles:

And then the man sees strange and new things, more than other men see and more than he himself sees with his natural eyes; and he also sees, not as men see but as the inhabitants of other worlds see: that things do not exist 'necessarily', but 'freely', that they are and at the same time are not, that they appear when they disappear and disappear when they appear. The testimony of the old, natural eyes, 'everybody's' eyes, directly contradicts the testimony of the eyes left by the angel. But since all our other organs of sense, and even our reason, agree with our ordinary sight, and since the whole of human 'experience', individual and collective, supports it, the new vision seems to be outside the law, ridiculous, fantastic, the product of a disordered imagination. It seems only a step short of madness; not poetic madness, that inspiration with which even the handbooks of philosophy and aesthetics deal, and which under the names of Eros, Mania, and Ecstasy, has so often been described and justified where and when necessary, but the madness for which men are pent in cells. And then begins a struggle between two kinds of vision, a struggle of which the issue is as mysterious and uncertain as its origin.

Shestov sees salvation in the visitation of this Angel who grants the individual a vision that is in some transcendent sense alien and insane. As in the case of Dostoevsky, who 'was undoubtedly one of those who possessed this double vision', Shestov believes that it places the individual outside the law, and thus curses them, but also blesses them with preternatural insight.[89] Here is the domain of what Shestov called 'the second dimension of time'. The philosopher anointed by the Angel of Death sees life, in all its horrors, not as self-evident, not as defined by necessity, but as free, contingent; susceptible to sudden transformation. The Angel of Death's vision, and that of the individual touched by it, is different from ours, for where we perceive the realm of Necessity, it sees the realm of anti-Necessity. Where we perceive a chain of events, it sees a perpetual cataclysm. But this cataclysm nonetheless constitutes the strait gate through which the Messiah might enter.

The Angel of Death, as Geneviève Piron is correct to point out, is the result of Shestov's reflections on 'political catastrophes'. 'Like Walter Benjamin in 1940', she writes, the angel appears in Shestov's work, first of all in the notebooks he compiled in Geneva in 1920, after his terminal departure from Russia, 'in response to his sense of an historical cataclysm'.[90] But the Angel of Death is in the end the antitype of the Angel of History. The latter, though it would like to awaken the dead and make whole what has been smashed, in Benjamin's poignant description, is forced to face the past and remains powerless before the inevitability of destructive logic that unfurls through time as it ceaselessly accumulates. The former faces the future, in an apparent paradox, and it closes its wings in spite of the violence of the storm blowing from Paradise, thus refusing to accept the logic of progress, the supremacy of reason. Shestov, who once commented emphatically that 'progress so called – the development of mankind in time – is a fiction', teaches that we must all strive for the unsustainable vision that the Angel of Death bestows as both blessing and curse.[91] And that we must all strive to sustain it in spite of its unsustainability. If Dostoevsky is, for Shestov, the exemplary concrete instance of the individual who, simultaneously damned and redeemed, has been touched by the Angel of Death, then *homo vigilans* is its universal archetype.

Shestov also mentions Nikolai Gogol in the course of his discussion of the Angel of Death in the essay on Dostoevsky. There, he identifies Gogol with the legendary monster Viy in his story of that name, published in 1835. Viy, according to Gogol, is a creature whose impossibly heavy, long eyelids 'h[a]ng right to the ground'.[92] 'Legions of demons and powerful spirits could not raise Vii's eyelids from the earth,' Shestov writes in 'The Conquest of the Self-Evident'; 'Nor could Gogol himself open his eyes, though his whole being concentrated on the effort.' In Shestov's appropriation of this tale, he argues that Gogol perceived that his life was a kind of death, but, in spite of this, he couldn't interrupt it – even though 'he, too, had been visited by the Angel of Death, who gave him the accursed gift of second sight'. Gogol could not make redemptive use of the Angel of Death's eyes; 'he was only capable of torturing himself.'[93]

Shestov's imperative is that we actively refuse Viy and actively affirm the Angel of Death. We must awake. We must strain to lift our heavily lidded eyes. And, once awake, we must remain sleepless, staring open-eyed, 'til the end of the world.

4

Garden and wasteland
The art of Gethsemane

I

For Shestov, Christ's existential drama in Gethsemane, when he is at his most human, represents the paradigmatic instance of a wakefulness and watchfulness that is of potentially apocalyptic importance. It is the primal scene of his Pascalian commitment to a perpetual sleeplessness that is spiritual and, at least implicitly, political in its implications.

Shestov had not read Kierkegaard by the time he wrote *Gethsemane Night* (1923) in the early 1920s, but his interpretation of Christ's agony in terms of the theological significance of sleeplessness nonetheless echoes some of the Danish philosopher's reflections on the events that, according to legend, took place in Gethsemane on the eve of Christ's arrest. It wasn't until 1928, when he met both Heidegger and Husserl at a conference in Freiburg, that the latter urged him to engage with Kierkegaard. Later, in the 1930s, Shestov wrote about him extensively of course, arguing among other things that, 'put into modern language', one of Kierkegaard's fundamental precepts is that 'man must awake from his millennial sleep and decide to think in the categories in which he lives'.[1] As Husserl instinctively recognized, Shestov had from the beginning of his career as a philosopher been an unconscious Kierkegaardian (Gilles Deleuze, for one, was astonished both by the depth and the apparent spontaneity of the similarities between their thought).[2] So perhaps it is not surprising that, as an anti-philosopher committed to reclaiming those episodes in the Gospels in which Christ seemed at his most human, Shestov gravitated to the episode in Gethsemane; and, moreover, to an interpretation of it in terms both of 'millennial sleep' and apocalyptic sleeplessness.

In Kierkegaard's notebooks from 1851, to give one example of his engagement with Gethsemane, the Danish thinker expressed his conviction that, at the foot of the Mount of Olives, 'for one moment, Christ is the suffering human being who for his own sake craves the sympathetic participation of another human being'.[3] Of course, the other human beings present fail him by sleeping (Nietzsche, for his part, bitterly complaining of the deceitfulness of friends, subsequently claimed that, more cruelly and shockingly, the disciples weren't asleep in Gethsemane, 'they were lying on the grass, playing cards and laughing').[4] For Kierkegaard, the ignominious failure of Christ's appeal to the sleeping disciples for emotional support at this critical moment of need is the pretext for making an important spiritual opposition between passive and active spiritual states. If 'human beings are more or less drowsiness', he states, then 'spirit is sheer wakefulness and activity'. 'The more spirit the more sleeplessness', is the slogan Kierkegaard contrives.[5] In effect, this is Shestov's slogan too. He grasped the spiritual and political value of interpreting the night of Gethsemane as an allegorical struggle between drowsiness and wakefulness. If the Agony in the Garden is a public 'contest', as its Greek and Latin origins in the word *agon* suggests, then the struggle is not simply between life and death, to polarize it in predictable terms, or Jesus's human and divine natures, to give another obvious example, but between humanity's physiological, psychological and spiritual proclivities for sleeping on the one hand and waking on the other.

Before exploring Shestov's reading of Pascal's fragmentary account of the night in Gethsemane, which I do in some detail in Chapter 4, probing the scene of Christ's destitution as a setting for the Russian's philosophy of tragedy, I propose in Chapter 3 briefly to reconstruct the biblical episode itself and recapitulate its theological significance. I also propose, for contextual purposes, to sketch a series of episodes in the history of its mediation in literature and painting since the Early Modern period. This history traces a shift during the course of which Christ's experience in Gethsemane becomes increasingly interiorized; and, according to a certain historical irony, comes more and more to represent an individual and collective crisis of faith. The Agony in the Garden evolves, over the nineteenth and twentieth centuries, in the writings of Nerval, Kipling and Eliot, and in the paintings of Gauguin, Van Gogh and Rothko, into an almost atheistic allegory of godlessness. Shestov, for his part, writing in the early 1920s, finds in Gethsemane, and in Pascal's re-inscription of it in particular, a means for redemptively thinking through the political and spiritual climacteric of Europe in the devastating aftermath of the First World War.

Later, shortly before the Second World War, and indeed his own death, Shestov will characterize this situation in terms of an 'atheistic nightmare' and will complain of 'the lack of faith which dominates humanity'.[6] By this point, in European culture, Gethsemane no longer resembles a garden, if indeed it ever was a garden; it resembles, in mythopoetic terms, a wasteland. In this respect, the landscape in the Swiss painter Willy Fries's picture of the Agony in the Garden, painted as part of his Passion series in the late 1930s and the early 1940s, which is at once neoclassical in its simplicity and urgently contemporaneous in its reference to the unfolding atrocities of Europe at this time, is ultimately its most appropriate emblem.[7] There, a hunched, hunted Christ crouches beneath a shroud-like cloak in the background, and the three, indistinguishable disciples huddle together against the cold in the foreground. The eyelids of the sleepers, picked out in their dark faces by luminous light, resemble empty sockets. Their eyes seem terminally unseeing. Fries's static, eerily still scene unfolds in a barren, inhospitable landscape cruelly sculpted from mountains and precipices. Populated by skeletal trees that echo those in Carpaccio's *Agony in the Garden* (1502), this landscape looks as if it has been blasted by bombs.

The tragic drama that unfolds at Gethsemane in the synoptic Gospels, centred on a protagonist who appears to have been abandoned by God, especially in Mark's version, is the scene of Christ's life that is most clearly fit for the sort of godless universe invoked by Fries and others in the first half of the twentieth century. Rowan Williams has emphasized that, in Mark, the narrative of Jesus's Passion, not least in its confusing, nightmarish and nonsensical qualities, 'help[s] us see events strictly from the perspective of the victim'. And he has provocatively compared the universe it portrays, furthermore, to the one 'captured so memorably in the fiction of Franz Kafka as well as the records of those who have been caught up in the arbitrary terror of political oppression'.[8] To frame it in terms that deliberately 'brush history against the grain', as Walter Benjamin might have put it, it is as if the Gethsemane narrative, insofar as it represents the moment of Jesus's destitution prior to his persecution and execution, only came to release its secret spiritual meanings many centuries later, through a kind of historical constellation, in the increasingly secular conditions of industrial modernity.[9] It as if it only really makes sense, paradoxically, in the aftermath of the death of God from the mid-nineteenth century on. In the first half of the twentieth century, above all, when Europe was routinely depicted as a wasteland, the Garden of Gethsemane functioned as a proleptic image of the scene of God's abandonment of humanity.

At this time, the garden realizes its hidden identity – one that can be detected in the Gospels' accounts but that remains concealed in the later iconographic tradition of Gethsemane – and becomes a kind of void. An abyss. The task Shestov set himself in the 1920s, in re-appropriating Pascal's fragmentary interpretation, is to redeem this void, this abyss, by insisting that Christ's sleepless isolation in Gethsemane entails an insomniac attentiveness that bears witness, in the first instance, to suffering; and, finally, to a future in which there will no longer be suffering. Christ in the garden is the ultimate embodiment, at once tragic and heroic, of *homo vigilans*.

II

Three of the Gospels, those by Mark, Matthew and Luke, recount the Agony in the Garden. In all three narratives, it comprises a pericope (meaning, in rhetoric, a coherent and self-contained unit) that is probably as much mythical as it is historical in its origins. It is generally assumed that Mark's version, the first to be written, is the source of Matthew's and Luke's, the other so-called Synoptics. It has further been surmised that Mark combined two prior sources, known as Source A and Source B. The first of these, which is probably especially human in its emphases, portrays nothing less than 'a leader on the verge of a nervous breakdown', as Jerome Murphy-O'Connor puts it; 'an individual going through a private hell'.[10]

Here is the version of Gethsemane in Mark, Chapter 14. This folkloric narrative is shaped not only by Source A, with its political and psychological intensities, but the *Odyssey*, where the Homeric poet frequently portrays sleep as a distraction, seduction or temptation that threatens to capsize its hero and his insufficiently faithful companions:

> And they came to a place which was named Gethsemane: and he saith to his disciples, Sit ye here, while I shall pray.
>
> And he taketh with him Peter and James and John, and began to be sore amazed, and to be very heavy;
>
> And saith unto them, My soul is exceeding sorrowful unto death: tarry ye here, and watch.
>
> And he went forward a little, and fell on the ground, and prayed that, if it were possible, the hour might pass from him.
>
> And he said, Abba, Father, all things are possible unto thee; take away this cup from me: nevertheless not what I will, but what thou wilt.
>
> And he cometh, and findeth them sleeping, and saith unto Peter, Simon, sleepest thou? couldest not thou watch one hour?
>
> Watch ye and pray, lest ye enter into temptation. The spirit truly is ready, but the flesh is weak.
>
> And again he went away, and prayed, and spake the same words.
>
> And when he returned, he found them asleep again, (for their eyes were heavy,) neither wist they what to answer him.
>
> And he cometh the third time, and saith unto them, Sleep on now, and take your rest: it is enough, the hour is come; behold, the Son of man is betrayed into the hands of sinners.
>
> Rise up, let us go; lo, he that betrayeth me is at hand.
>
> (MARK 14: 32–42)

Matthew cleaves closely to this version in his narrative of the scene at Gethsemane. For example, Jesus adheres to many of his predecessor's specific formulations, including the reference to the fact that, when he appeals to the disciples for support a second time, 'their eyes were heavy' (Mark 14: 40; Matt.

26: 43). He also reproduces the familiar narrative pattern wherein, for symbolic reasons, three times Jesus discovers the disciples asleep. Both apostles are conscious not only of echoing the redemptive narrative of Jonah, for instance, who 'was in the belly of the fish three days and three nights' (Jon. 1: 17), but also of anticipating the three days that fall between Christ's crucifixion and resurrection (see Matt. 12: 40). Finally, in both of these versions, there is a strong sense of the classical *agon*; the idea that, like Odysseus, or like Jason, the hero must quit his closest comrades in order to struggle with his antagonist alone. Of course, the scene concludes with Jesus rousing his disciples and rising to meet his destiny in the form of Judas Iscariot and the elders and soldiers to whom he has betrayed his leader: 'Rise, let us be going: behold, he is at hand that doth betray me' (Matt. 26: 46). But Jesus's antagonist is in the end neither a mythical monster, as in the *Odyssey,* nor the treacherous disciple with whom he has recently shared supper, but is the psychological and spiritual crisis he has experienced. In short, it is himself.

For Jesus, in both Mark and Matthew, the repeated realization that his closest friends and comrades are incapable of resisting the temptation to sleep, in spite of his appeal for their support as he pleads with his Father to lift the burden of suffering from him, and in spite of his specific request that they 'watch' for the imminent appearance of his enemies, is cumulatively devastating. Jesus's soul, already 'exceeding sorrowful unto death' (Mark 14: 34), is rendered more sorrowful by the distance or even absence of God. Thereafter, Jesus's increasingly painful consciousness that his three disciples, Peter, James and John, who have proved unable to remain vigilant even though the dangers he confronts are both individually and collectively fatal, brings him closer still to complete despair. In an echo of the Garden of Eden in Genesis, the scene in Gethsemane dramatizes another Fall of Man, and the place or space in which Jesus's faith in others collapses, which neither Mark nor Matthew in fact refer to as a garden, is therefore already a wasteland: a place of betrayal, corruption and disillusionment. Hades more than Eden.

The third time Jesus finds the disciples asleep, he can no longer conceal his anger and exasperation. As Adela Yarbro Collins argues, his imprecation, 'Sleep on now, and take your rest', which is tartly followed, in the succeeding verse, by another, contradictory one, 'Rise up, let us go', appears to be ironic, 'perhaps even sarcastic' (see Mark 14: 41, 42).[11] Jesus is finally forced to admit that, on the night of Gethsemane, he alone has been capable of remaining awake in the face of his persecution. He alone has been able to heed the advice he had dispensed in the parable of the faithful servant: 'Take ye heed, watch and pray: for ye know not when the time is' (Mark 13: 33). In this parable and in the Gethsemane pericope itself, Mark uses the Greek term *gregorein*, which signifies both watchfulness and wakefulness. Raymond Brown observes that, if this state 'does involve staying physically awake', then 'it also has a sense of religious alertness'.[12] In Mark and Matthew, Jesus is not simply awake while his disciples sleep; he prays. His state of being is not equivalent to the insomnia from which Job, for example, suffers in the Old Testament, as in this abject complaint: 'When I lie down, I say, When shall I arise, and the night be gone? and I am full of tossings to and fro unto the dawning of the day' (Job 7: 4). In praying, Jesus transforms his wakefulness and watchfulness from a merely passive form of spiritual isolation into an active, even militant one. Prayer is proof of that spiritual alertness and attentiveness which, to fatal effect, Peter and the sons of Zebedee fail to exhibit. It thus contains a certain messianic or redemptive promise in spite of Jesus's proximity, at this point, to a condition of damnation.

What of the other Gospels? That is, those of Luke and John. Luke, decisively, adds three significant details. First, he introduces an angel, who appears to Jesus 'from heaven, strengthening him' (Luke 22: 43). Second, he adds the striking metaphor of the sweat that falls from Jesus like blood: 'And being in agony he prayed more earnestly: and his sweat was as it were great drops of blood falling down to the ground' (Luke 22: 44). (This 'blood', which is sometimes interpreted literally rather than metaphorically, has itself generated an enormous amount of theological debate.) Third, in Luke's version, Jesus discovers the disciples asleep not three times but only once; and, in a further detail that is different to the other Evangelists' accounts, he specifically identifies them as 'sleeping for sorrow' (Luke 22: 45) – thereby partially excusing them for their irresponsibility.[13] Overall, if Luke renders Jesus's pain more graphic, he ultimately sublimates his suffering, elevating and spiritualizing it because it involves some kind of communion with one of God's representatives. Luke can afford, so to speak, to include the vivid detail of the bloody or blood-like gouts of sweat, which superficially intensifies the sense of Jesus's agony, because he has insisted on the prior appearance of the protective angel. 'By mentioning the angel first', Murphy-O'Connor is correct to note, 'Luke ensured that the "agony" of Jesus would not be taken seriously by his readers'.[14] Luke's is the most mythopoeic inscription of the event. Where Mark and even Matthew underscore Jesus's 'dereliction', as Paul Ricoeur summarizes the distinction between these three main accounts, Luke underscores his 'stoic sovereignty'.[15]

St. John's Gospel, for its part, which merely mentions in passing that Jesus crossed over the brook of Cedron into a garden, and that there Judas and the soldiers apprehended him, elides the scene entirely – presumably because Jesus's very humanity and vulnerability in this scene compromises the Evangelist's attempt to reconstruct him not as a historical actor, a Jewish revolutionary, but as the transcendent Christ (John 18: 1–3). John, even more than Luke, has left behind Source A and its perceptible traces in Mark. In John, who is committed not to reinventing the historical Jesus but to inventing the Christological Jesus, we are furthest from the Messiah as an earthly individual incapable of sleep because of his crippling loneliness and self-doubt. Elevating the Son of Man to the Son of God, John cannot countenance the human intensities of the night in Gethsemane. He is the only one of the Evangelists to refer to a garden, which in anticipation of Christ's resurrection he implicitly identifies as prelapsarian. But this second Eden – according to what might be called a future-perfect logic whereby this is what it is because this is what it will have been – is also secretly imbued with darker, more apocalyptic associations. For the upper course of the Cedron, or Kidron, a river that snakes through a ravine in the Judaean desert down to the Dead Sea, was from the time of the Kings of Judah the site of Jerusalem's principal necropolis. This region, called in the Hebrew Bible Emek Yehoshafat, the Valley of Jehoshaphat, a word meaning 'Yahweh judges', is the place where, according to the prophet Joel, God will destroy the heathen: 'Multitudes, multitudes in the valley of decision: for the day of the LORD is near in the valley of decision' (Joel 3: 14). John's garden, then, in eschatological terms, is also already a kind of wasteland.

The Christological significance, in the Synoptics, of the events in Gethsemane, understood as a pericope, one that is perhaps partly legendary in origin, has of course been immense. Indeed, it is not an exaggeration to claim that, because it appears to foreground the earthly, historical Jesus and to relegate to the background the heavenly, transcendent Christ, the night in Gethsemane has, historically, represented a grave theological problem. Certainly, as Kevin Madigan has argued, 'it was a plague and embarrassment to patristic and medieval interpreters', who in consequence employed a variety of hermeneutic strategies so as either to domesticate its unsettling power or ignore it completely.[16] But even in the mediaeval and Early Modern periods, it produced a rich theological literature; one replete with political as well as spiritual implications. Thomas Aquinas, for instance, influenced by Maximus the Confessor, insisted in the late thirteenth century that, at Gethsemane, Christ 'grieved not only over the loss of His own bodily life' but over 'the sins of all others'; that is, he grieved for all sins forever. According to one recent commentator, this means that in this episode Christ assumed not merely the sins of his time but of our times, including 'the unspeakable evils of the Auschwitz gas chambers'.[17]

Thomas More, in the sixteenth century, was especially alert to the ongoing political resonance of the night of Gethsemane. In *De Tristitia Christi* (1534–5), written in the Tower of London, where he had been committed for failing to sign the Oath of Succession, he seized on the parallels between his own isolation in prison and Christ's in the garden, and between England's irresponsibly supine Protestant bishops and the sleeping apostles. He thus offered an interpretation of the Gethsemane pericope that was as timely as it was sympathetic to its protagonist. 'Why do not bishops contemplate in this scene their own somnolence?' he pointedly asks in the course of his sustained, hyper-attentive commentary on the scene.[18] He repeatedly praises the moral example of Christ's 'all-night vigils':

> Christ tells us to stay awake, but not for cards and dice, not for rowdy parties and drunken brawls, not for wine and women, but for prayer. [...] He ex[h] orts us to devote to intense prayer a large part of that very time which most of us usually devote entirely to sleep.[19]

More imparts almost novelistic details to the Gethsemane scene, noting for instance that the night was cold – 'that the night was cold is clearly shown by the fact that the servants were warming themselves around the charcoal fires in the courtyard of the high priest'. He emphasizes, too, the symbolic geography of Gethsemane itself, observing that Cedron, the name of the stream, means 'sadness' and also 'blackness', and insists, 'We must (I say) cross over the valley and stream of Cedron, a valley of tears and a stream of sadness whose waves can wash away the blackness and filth of our sins'. But this redemption will only be possible, he adds repeatedly, if we imitate Christ's 'all-night vigils' rather than the habits of the 'hypocritical pharisee' who 'snor[es] away in his soft bed'.[20]

Beyond the particular personal and political context of *De Tristitia Christi*, in which More affirmed his own spiritual travails in the form of Christ's, others in the sixteenth and seventeenth centuries turned to Gethsemane as the site of peculiar psychological and spiritual potencies. Albrecht Dürer's sketch of the scene from 1521, when he felt particularly embattled in his personal life, has for example been directly compared to More's treatment of it.[21] The English so-called 'metaphysical poets' were also attracted to the spiritual tortures of Gethsemane, in part probably because they were invested in a broader religious and social shift from seeing night as a site of the supernatural to seeing it as a divine time.[22] In 'The Agonie' (1633), for instance, George Herbert identifies Christ at Gethsemane with the corrosive effects of the sins for which he has assumed moral responsibility, elaborating Luke's signature metaphor as he does so: 'A man so wrung with pains, that all his hair, / His skinne, his garments bloudie be'.[23] Early Modern Catholics and Protestants, according to Sarah Covington, thus began 'to project onto Jesus an interior and affective life'.[24] Over time, the drama of Christ in Gethsemane became a less and less public one, a more and more private one – agonizing, increasingly, rather than agonistic.

No doubt the climactic expression of this logic, in the literary tradition of Christian devotion derived from Herbert, Vaughan and others, comes in the explosive compression of the lines in Emily Dickinson's poem 'One Crucifixion is recorded – only –' (c. 1862): 'Gethsemane', she writes there, 'Is but a Province – in the Being's Centre –'.[25]

III

In spite of the interiorization of Gethsemane that took place over the course of several centuries, or because of it perhaps, the iconographical history of the Agony in the Garden, comparatively speaking, is not an especially rich one. According to Diane Apostolos-Cappadona, the subject 'was rarely depicted in Christian art'.[26] For example, it did not form part of the narrative of the Stations of the Cross. But, in spite of her concession that it 'attained some artistic attention in the nineteenth-century revival of Christian art', Apostolos-Cappadona's claim seems slightly cursory. The theme is rare in pre-thirteenth-century painting, certainly. But there is an important mosaic Agony in the Garden in the south-side aisle of St. Mark's Basilica in Venice, probably dating from between 1215 and 1220, which influenced a number of later depictions (for example, the one in Paolo Veneziano's polyptych from c.1350). And, certainly, from the late fifteenth century on – beginning with Mantegna and Giovanni Bellini, brothers-in-law both indebted to the latter's father, Jacopo Bellini, who had himself made a sketch of the scene – many of the greatest European painters depicted Christ's night in Gethsemane.[27]

At the time of the rise of Renaissance humanism, Gethsemane must have seemed an attractive subject for representation precisely because it is the scene from the Gospels in which Jesus's humanity is most clearly apparent (this is surely one of the implications of More's appropriation of it for his personal, political and theological purposes in the 1530s, as when he conceded that Christ 'had the ordinary feelings of mankind', including 'fear, weariness, and grief').[28] But the painters who depicted it tended nonetheless to be relatively reluctant to portray the agonies of Jesus. Their focus was, if not on the ecstasies, then on the pathos of the scene. It is symptomatic of this emphasis that the artists who portrayed the Agony in the Garden from the fifteenth century seem almost exclusively to have modelled their accounts on Luke's Gospel. For Luke, as we have seen, was the only Evangelist to include an angel. This inclination represents a clear attempt to underline Jesus's divinity rather than his humanity, and to impart a spiritually optimistic rather than pessimistic impetus to the episode. A possible or partial exception to this pattern is Carpaccio's painting of the Agony in the Garden, which I mentioned in relation to Fries's Passion series. It features an angel that can at best be glimpsed only in the form of a halo of light confined to the top left-hand corner of the composition, where it crowns the rocks beside which a rather two-dimensional Christ, who kneels in profile in a striking red robe, gazes upward and prays in an attitude of relatively serene supplication.

The pictures of the Agony in the Garden by Mantegna and Bellini, which have been hung beside one another in London's National Gallery since 1893, are the greatest examples of the privilege accorded to Luke's version of Gethsemane in the fifteenth century. Both of them, according to Caroline Campbell, are likely to have been painted for devotional purposes for private individuals (unlike earlier versions of the Agony, which typically appear on predellas or other parts of an altar-piece);[29] and it therefore seems possible to speculate that this material precondition of their production helped create the conditions for the interiorization of Christ's Agony, or its privatization, in the visual arts. Mantegna painted two versions of the scene: the first, of approximately 1455–6, is the one in the National Gallery; the second, of 1456–9, is in the Musée des Beaux-Arts de Tours. Both are set in morning light that illuminates every aspect of the landscape in almost hallucinatory detail. They are striking, among other things, for their adamantine topography, which is rendered in terms of geometric layers of rock; for the exquisitely painted cityscapes in the background; and for their use of extreme foreshortening in the chiselled figures of the disciples sleeping beneath the stage on which Jesus kneels in the foreground. The angel in the second of Mantegna's paintings is a single figure that, in offering support to the sorrowful, apparently fearful Christ, descends at a precipitous angle through a cloud, as if responding to a spiritual emergency – which indeed it is. In the first of his paintings, in striking contrast, five cherubic angels, static rather than dynamic, stand on a cloud that floats above the natural altar before which Jesus prays. Behind him, and directly opposite this celestial delegation, a black bird, probably a cormorant, perches in a moribund tree, an omen of the tragedy that will unfold when the soldiers marching along the road that curves beneath it finally reach the foreground of the picture.

Like Mantegna's paintings, to which it is directly indebted, Bellini's *Agony* is set not at night, but as day breaks. Here, though, the morning bathes the expansive landscape in soft, diffuse light that is entirely characteristic of the Venetian's aesthetic. In the middle-ground, kneeling on a sloping platform of ochre earth, Jesus leans with his back to the viewer against a natural altar

Figure 4.1 *Agony in the Garden, c.1460 (tempera on panel), Mantegna, Andrea (1431–1506) / National Gallery, London, UK / Bridgeman Images.*

made of rock, like the ones in Mantegna, in order to supplicate to God. A diaphanous angel, which Andrea de Marchi nicely describes as 'a little ghost who materialises at the first light of dawn', descends from the clouds with the cup of suffering.[30] In the foreground, the three disciples sleep in various poses; so exhausted, apparently, that their inattentiveness almost seems excusable. Peter, who snores gently on the right of the cluster, is presented in a particularly foreshortened form that is unthinkable without the prior example of Mantegna's versions of the scene. In the middle distance, Judas and the battalion of soldiers wind their way towards Jesus through the picturesque landscape populated with Italian hill-towns; but they don't at this point intrude on the reverent silence of the scene they are about to interrupt so decisively and fatally. The scene is soaked in sadness, but there is little sense of agony or anguish. Nor of urgency. For in contrast to Mantegna's smaller pictures, where the foreshortening of the figures and the compression of the drama create an inescapable, faintly claustrophobic sense of immediacy, there is a serene

Figure 4.2 *The Agony in the Garden, c.1465 (tempera on panel), Bellini, Giovanni (c.1430–1516) / National Gallery, London, UK / Bridgeman Images.*

inevitability to the scene Bellini depicts, evoked in part by the breathtaking depth of the picture plane.

Only El Greco's version of the Agony in the Garden, painted more than a century later in 1590, through its violent torsion of pictorial space, offers a rendition of Luke that does justice to the horrors of the scene. Not least, this is because, like Jean Gossaert's version of 1509–10, which deploys a particularly spectacular use of chiaroscuro, it is set, dramatically, at night. But even El Greco's picture, in which the Angel consoles Jesus with an almost shocking directness, seems to repress the vision of tragic abandonment that Mark's telling of Gethsemane provided in its brutally stark presentation of what Louis Ruprecht calls 'the first – and really the only – moment when Jesus' faith falters'.[31] El Greco presents a dreamlike nocturnal landscape, one radically distorted by the fatal events that are unfolding at an accelerating pace; but he does not present a portrait of Jesus's mental torture and loneliness. Jesus is instead mournful. If the soldiers in the background threaten to drag him to his earthly humiliation, he is already half-heavenly. El Greco's rocks are like clouds, in this painting, and his clouds are like rocks; Jesus, formally mediating between the terrestrial and the celestial, is at once rock-like and cloud-like.

The sleeping disciples (representative of the earthly), the angel (representative of the heavenly) and Jesus himself (who functions as a middle term) are each isolated in a part of the composition so separate as to appear ontologically distinct. But this seclusion does not communicate his loneliness so much as his fundamentally different state of being.

Over the nineteenth and early twentieth centuries, some representations of Gethsemane in the visual arts assume allegorical functions that speak more directly to contemporaneous political and psychological crises. For Goya, who painted his miniature *Christ in Gethsemane* or *Christ on the Mount of Olives* in 1819, it served as an emblem of the oppressiveness and social upheaval of contemporary Spain in the aftermath of the Peninsular War with Napoleonic France (as the similarity of its central figure to the 'Kneeling Man' in the Frontispiece of *The Disasters of War* (1810–20) makes evident).[32] The composition of Goya's painting directly echoes his compatriot El Greco's: the

Figure 4.3 *Agony in the Garden of Gethsemane, c.1590s (oil on canvas), Greco, El (Domenico Theotocopuli) (1541–1614) / National Gallery, London, UK / Bridgeman Images.*

angel bearing the cup descends from the top left corner of the picture and
Jesus kneels with his arms extended at the centre. But Goya's Jesus, a ghostly,
haunted figure, is not politely supplicating the angel so much as desperately,
perhaps even hopelessly, pleading with it; the angel, for its part, is not directly
communing with Jesus, as El Greco's is, but evasively approaching it in profile,
and from an uncomfortably close angle. Strikingly, the arms of Jesus in Goya's
little painting are outstretched, not proudly but as if they are carrying the
weight of the world. He appears already to be slumped forward in defeat on
the criminal's cross to which he will shortly be nailed. Giving up the ghost.
In Goya's version of Gethsemane, moreover, all movement is suspended in
a moment of eerie silence. And the uncompromising use of chiaroscuro
creates a mood of terrible darkness, one that the rather muddy, sketchy light
associated with the angel, which contrasts with the crystalline light that cuts
into the gloom of El Greco's composition, only exacerbates. Here, to put it in

Figure 4.4 *Christ on the Mount of Olives, 1819 (oil on wood), Goya y Lucientes,
Francisco Jose de (1746–1828) / Colegio Escolapios de San Anton, Madrid, Spain /
Bridgeman Images.*

the terms Goya used in *Los Caprichos* (1799), the sleep of reason, incarnated in the slumbering disciples, who are of course excluded from the frame, brings forth, not monsters, not soldiers even, but the monstrosities that come in the soldiers' train – Christ's arrest, flagellation, execution.

In the mid-nineteenth century, to be sure, Alexandre Cabanel's highly sentimental *Agony in the Garden* (1844), in which an exhausted, if not sleeping Christ is draped over the knees of a girlish angel, is probably fairly typical. Recalling sentimental depictions by painters of the previous centuries such as Veronese and Tiepolo, it transmits nothing of the psychological or spiritual drama of the scene in the Synoptics. But as the example of Goya implies, more sophisticated accounts of Gethsemane became increasingly alive to its tragic as opposed to pathetic dimension. It is, ironically, not in the revival of Christian art in the nineteenth century, as Apostolos-Cappadona asserts, but in art that is the product of an incipiently more secular culture, that it receives the most interesting artistic attention. The post-impressionists are pre-eminent in this respect. In Gaugin's and Van Gogh's tragic aesthetic of Gethsemane, the term 'agony' seems far distant from its ancient roots in the Greek notion of a 'contest' or 'struggle'; instead, it has acquired its more modern meaning, originally dating in English from the fifteenth century, of anguished suffering. In these paintings, which noticeably do not feature an angel, there is far less sense of the spiritual consolation that one finds in Renaissance and post-Renaissance antecedents.

Gauguin's *Agony in the Garden of Olives* (1889) is the most enigmatic and intriguing direct rendition of the scene in the later nineteenth century. Evoking a sense not simply of abandonment by others, but self-abandonment, this is a troubling symbolist self-portrait. Gauguin summarized it in something like these terms in an interview in *L'Écho de Paris* from 1891: 'The crushing of an ideal, and a pain that is both divine and human.'[33] Bifurcated by the thin trunk of a dead tree that stands in for the crucifixion, the composition features a sorrowful red-haired Christ in the foreground, his tired figure leaning like the olive trees that have been pummelled by the wind on the ridge behind him. Christ's stooped, drooping posture, his leaden-lidded, unseeing eyes, and his resigned, slightly effeminate hands – all are expressive of a deep sadness. And of exhaustion. In spite of the virile, strangely volatile colour of his hair, which Gauguin classified as 'dark ochre vermilion', he looks as if has aged a hundred years in the space of the night. In the background, in the nocturnal shadow of those olive trees bent by the wind, two or three men in dark robes loiter in one of the clefts of this rugged, corrugated Breton landscape. It is perhaps no accident that these disciples, often said to represent Van Gogh and other younger artists by whom Gauguin felt deserted, might be mistaken for a couple of the anonymous captors who, we know, will soon appear in order to arrest Christ. They are not asleep, interestingly, just as the heavy-lidded Christ is himself not particularly alert or awake; but their ambiguity as figures underlines their complicity in, and their moral culpability for, his betrayal. In a letter from November 1889, which included a sketch of his *Agony*, Gaugin complained to Van Gogh, 'This canvas is fated to be misunderstood, so I shall keep it for a long time'.[34]

Figure 4.5 *The Agony in the Garden of Olives, 1889 (oil on canvas), Gauguin, Paul (1848–1903) / Norton Museum of Art, West Palm Beach, Florida, USA / Bridgeman Images.*

Gauguin probably feared that the flame-haired Van Gogh, on whom the French artist might indeed have partly modelled his Jesus, would himself misunderstand this bitterly sad portrait of social isolation, since in the previous year, prior to his arrival at the asylum in Saint-Rémy, the Dutch artist had twice attempted to paint a picture of Christ in Gethsemane before scraping the oils from the canvas and destroying it. Van Gogh claimed in his correspondence that he did not feel comfortable tackling this topic without a model on whom he might base a view of 'the women gathering and picking the olives'. He didn't in fact like Gauguin's painting, as he told his brother Theo: 'I am not an admirer of Gauguin's "Christ in the Garden of Olives".[35] Nor did he like the look of what he candidly dismissed as his friend Émile Bernard's 'nightmare of a *Christ in the garden of olives*', also painted in 1889, a photograph of which he received in the same week as Gauguin's sketch.[36] Indeed, according to Joan Greer, he became preoccupied with the works of both these friends and rivals 'almost to the point of obsession'.[37] But stimulated or stung by these competitors, Van Gogh seems immediately to have displaced or redirected his desire to portray the Agony in the Garden into several apparently simple, non-narrative paintings of landscapes with olive trees, including *The Olive Trees* (1889). 'If I stay here, I shall not try to paint "Christ in the Garden of Olives"', he informed Theo in November 1889, refusing the temptations of symbolism, 'but the glowing of the olives as you still see it, giving nevertheless the exact proportions of the human figure in it'.[38] As the verb 'glowing' hints, Van Gogh located the transcendental not in the relevant biblical narrative, but in the everyday.

A more compelling model than Gauguin or Bernard, in this regard, was Jean-Baptiste-Camille Corot's *Christ in the Garden of Olives* (1849), which Van Gogh saw at the commemorative retrospective of Corot's work at the École Nationale des Beaux-Arts in 1875. In his correspondence with Theo, he singled it out for comment: 'I am glad he painted that'.[39] In Corot's sombre picture, Christ is depicted prostrate on a patch of earth behind which a copse of contorted olive trees expresses his despair. The heavenly aureole that crowns the composition appears to offer little human comfort. In his description of Corot's canvas, symptomatically, Van Gogh praised its landscape, which he reconstructed in some detail, but did not mention Christ. His investment was

Figure 4.6 *The Olive Trees, 1889 (oil on canvas), Gogh, Vincent van (1853–90) / museo / Bridgeman Images.*

not in the human forms that, in Gauguin's and Bernard's version, conduct the dynamics of the drama, but in the trees themselves. Van Gogh's *Olive Trees*, to take this example, is a landscape in which, in the absence of any accompanying figures, the trees themselves, 'ganglions of living wood responding to the energy of wind and sun' to appropriate an evocative description of John Berger's, embody his own, and perhaps Christ's, tortured emotions.[40]

It is tempting, then, not only to identify Van Gogh with Christ, as the artist himself did on several occasions, but to see the landscape that appears in his numerous paintings of olive groves at this time as his representation of Gethsemane. It is a non-dramatic, non-narrative Gethsemane. Secretly perhaps, these landscapes might even be interpreted as attempts to represent the view onto which the sleepless Jesus gazed on the morning after the night in which, while he prayed, his disciples repeatedly fell asleep and his God persistently failed to appear. The absence of people in these paintings, from this perspective, is crippling; but the trees themselves, for all their agonized contortions, are at the same time a kind of community from which, it seems just possible, some spiritual consolation might be derived. The cloud that hurtles over these trees and the fantastical rocky landscape that lies behind them, however, is a monstrous, muscular angel who races off as if twisting out of the painter's grasp. It pointedly refuses to remain still long enough to remove the cup of suffering from the Christ that, it can be imagined, stares onto the landscape from the spectator's position.

The painting that, in my view, does the fullest justice to the night in Gethsemane as a tragedy of abandonment and emptiness, one that encodes an emblematic image of sleepless vigilance that is of potentially redemptive importance, is the one that Mark Rothko produced in oil and charcoal at the end of the Second World War. Rothko's *Gethsemane* (1944), along with *The Entombment* (1944) and *Entombment I* (1946), is relatively anomalous among his paintings of this period, since these tend to return to Greek myths, under the influence of Nietzsche, rather than Christian ones. But its interest in isolation and loneliness, and its investment in what Rothko's biographer James Breslin calls 'the myth of the tortured and wounded artist', one that makes him into 'a kind of modern, post-Freudian Van Gogh', is relatively typical.[41] *Gethsemane*, set in one of the primeval landscapes that is characteristic of Rothko's work at this time, is a crucifixion scene before the crucifixion. Its semi-abstract, surrealistic forms, which are related to ones found in de Chirico's and Ernst's paintings, are profoundly disconcerting. Given the moment of its composition, when mass deportations of Jews were taking place in Germany and across Eastern Europe, it seems possible to interpret it, from one angle, as a nightmarish allegory of their oppression and persecution. Rothko's own childhood in Russia had been marred by anti-Semitism.

In the foreground of *Gethsemane*, oddly placed on a pedestal or neoclassical column, is a bird-like creature – a familiar figure in Rothko's paintings, among them *Hierarchical Birds* (1944), from the early 1940s. Obscenely, its body has been butchered, flayed and gutted (if the scene anticipates the crucifixion of Christ, then it also anticipates his flagellation). The creature thus resembles nothing so much as an eviscerated bird that has been nailed to a post in order to deter other predators or scavengers from lighting on this godforsaken spot.

Figure 4.7 *Gethsemane, 1945 (oil on canvas), Rothko, Mark (1903–70) Photo: Christopher Burke: New York © 1998 Kate Rothko Prizel & Christopher Rothko ARS, NY and DACS, London.*

On the ground, its disarticulated body parts, which are indebted to André Masson's book *Anatomy of My Universe* (1943), seem to be reflected in a pale slick of blood that, in its depths, looks as if it might conceal Hell itself.[42] Breslin has commented in relation to *Gethsemane* that Rothko's 'birds in paintings done around this time often evoke, not the heavy, rapacious eagles of a few years before, but spiritual flight and renewal'.[43] But this is to misinterpret the painting's infernal mood of defeat and despair, for the painting violently reproduces a scene not of redemption, but damnation. It captures what Rothko, writing in 1943, had referred to as 'the potentiality for carnage which we know so well today'.[44] At the centre of the composition, in startling blood-red, is a wound the size of a bullet-hole. If it is a bullet-hole, though, it is also a single, agonized eye. It gazes implacably both at the spectator and, as it were, at the horrors of contemporary history that pile up like wreckage behind her. In short, it is the blood-shot eye of an insomniac Christ.

But there is something in this composition that has so far eluded either description or interpretation; a mysterious, slightly repulsive residue or surplus. Above the Christ-creature in Rothko's *Gethsemane* floats an ambiguous figure that echoes some of Hans Arp's characteristically amoebic shapes. Its form recalls moreover that of the hurrying olive trees in Gauguin's picture of the Agony in the Garden; and the clouds in some of Van Gogh's paintings of olive groves. Like Van Gogh's clouds, in fact, though more explicitly, it too evokes the numerous iterations of Luke's angel in the history of European painting since the fifteenth century. Except that, here, it is no more than an implausible and uncomfortable memory of the divine messenger. A bad dream of it. In its monstrosity, it is evidently neither of heavenly nor earthly provenance. Incapable of providing solace, it is a crippled shadow scrambling or swimming desperately across the sky in an attempt to escape its responsibilities for the horrific suffering taking place on the ground below. Slightly foetal in appearance, as if it has emerged from the vaginal opening in the bird-like Christ's body, it is a rough beast, its hour come round at last, that slouches towards Bethlehem to be born.

In Lacanian terms, one might interpret this mysterious, palpitating shape as one of those concrete instances of the Real that is known by the name of 'lamella'. 'Whenever the membranes of the egg in which the foetus emerges on its way to becoming a new-born are broken', Lacan writes, 'imagine for a moment that something flies off, and that one can do it with an egg as easily as with a man, namely the *homelette*, or the lamella'. The lamella 'is something extra-flat, which moves just like an amoeba', he adds. It is irreducibly asexual, and it stands in for 'pure life instinct, that is to say, immortal life, or irrepressible life, life that has need of no organ, simplified, indestructible life'.[45] Rothko's formless, sexless angel, the emissary of some fundamentally non-anthropomorphic, non-zoomorphic realm, almost completely un-representable, is precisely an instance of lamella. Žižek, in his reading of Lacan, identifies lamella as 'unreal, an entity of pure semblance, a multiplicity of appearances which seem to envelop a central void'. That is, he sees it as standing in for 'an uncanny excess of life, for an "undead" urge which persists beyond the (biological) cycle of life and death, of generation and corruption'.[46] Rothko depicts the angel, in the form of 'lamella', as undead. He depicts it as an agent of the void that renders the earthly domain, in which Christ has been spiritually eviscerated by his failure to communicate either with his disciples or his God, meaningless. The shape or stain at the top of the composition marks the presence of the abyss. The garden is a wasteland is a void.

As a fable that describes humanity's abandonment by God, the Gethsemane pericope acquired fresh significance in the later nineteenth and twentieth centuries for a series of generations that became increasingly obsessed with their abandonment by God. This curious phenomenon, whereby messianic traces concealed in the past are activated only subsequently, when circumstances become propitious in the present, is the one Walter Benjamin identified in his *Arcades Project* when he quotes from André Monglond's recent book *Le Préromantisme français* (1930):

> The past has left images of itself in literary texts, images which are comparable to those which are imprinted by light on a photosensitive plate. The future alone possesses developers active enough to scan such surfaces perfectly.

The same might also be said about pictorial images. From this Benjaminian perspective, Rothko's *Gethsemane* is an X-ray of the Agony in the Garden. It renders the inadmissible significations of his predecessors' versions of the scene visible. The 'mysterious meaning' of the night of Gethsemane as the Synoptics present it, its dramatization of the dereliction not only of Jesus but also of faith in God itself, remains inadmissible and 'indecipherable' until some eighteen or nineteen centuries after the legendary event.[47]

IV

In order to be a 'true historian', as Benjamin explained in a fragment finally left out of his theses 'On the Concept of History' (1940), one must be inspired by 'a line in Hofmannsthal': 'Read what was never written'.[48] For, eventually, in certain unpredictable circumstances, that which was never explicitly written nonetheless becomes intuitively readable. Here is the retroactive logic, analogous perhaps to that of recollection in a psychoanalytic context, whereby a secret narrative does not simply become legible, after long seeming illegible, but – in some unprecedented sense – comes into being. According to this photosensitive method of interpretation, the messianic force of the Gethsemane pericope turns out, ironically, to reside in its godlessness.

This is the implication – to turn to what Monglond calls 'literary texts' – of Gérard de Nerval's 'Christ at Gethsemane' (1844). This remarkable poem comprises a sequence of five sonnets that takes as its epigraph the nightmare lines from Jean Paul's *Siebenkäs* (1797–8): 'God is dead! The sky is empty... / Weep! Children, you no longer have a father!'[49] The scene is thus set for a retelling of the events in Gethsemane that situates Christ on the edge of a chasm of meaninglessness. Nerval published his poem in the same year that his slightly older contemporary, the conservative poet Alfred de Vigny published his 'Le Mont des oliviers' (1844). But, if the latter's version of the event, partly influenced by his encounter with Mantegna's painting in 1839, is bleakly evocative in its portrayal of Jesus's insomniac loneliness, dramatized in his restless, ghostly walking in the garden, it nonetheless lacks the shocking intensity of the former's positively atheistic performance.[50] In the opening stanzas of 'Christ at Gethsemane', Nerval's Jesus lifts his 'frail arms to the sky', not unlike Goya's Jesus, and stands 'beneath the sacred trees', conscious that, because of 'his friends' ingratitude', he has been betrayed and hence condemned to remain 'lost in his own mute woe'. His disciples are 'benumbed and lost in bestial slumber', dreaming of themselves becoming 'kings, sages, prophets too'. It is this that forces his confession of faithlessness: '"No!" / He started to cry out, "There isn't any God!"'[51]

'They slept,' the poet states, simply, in relation to the three disciples. So, Christ attempts to rouse his friends, telling them that he has suffered a 'bloody and broken' body for nothing, and that instead of God there is only a void:

'Brothers, I have deceived you: Abyss! abyss! abyss!
No God is on the altar where my body is …
There is no God! No longer!' Through all this they snored!

The sleeping disciples are utterly insensible to the bad news of this anti-Gospel. Searching for the eye of God, in the second stanza, Christ sees only a black, bottomless pit, from which 'eternal night / Streams out over the world and ever deepens'.[52] In this apocalyptic night, in which everybody apart from him is terminally asleep, he realizes that only Judas, with his 'criminal's strength', which is almost admirable because of its vitality, is alert and awake. In 'Christ at Gethsemane', channelling his own insomnia and his sense of psychological and spiritual isolation, Nerval finds in the sleepless, almost faithless Jesus that he depicts what Julia Kristeva describes as 'the ultimate refuge of a psychic identity in catastrophic anguish'.[53] He thus presents a retelling of the Agony in the Garden that speaks eloquently not only to the later nineteenth century but also, in some anticipatory sense, to the horrors of the early twentieth century, the period between the Wars when Shestov returns to Pascal's tragic vision of Gethsemane.

For a preliminary sense of this climate, we might glance at Rudyard Kipling's brutally effective ballad 'Gethsemane', which was first published in *The Years Between* (1919), a volume he originally intended to title *Gethsemane*. Interestingly, T. S. Eliot included this poem in his *Choice of Kipling's Verse* (1941), compiled during the Second World War, though in the introductory essay he disingenuously claimed not to understand it – presumably because of its shockingly bleak, unchristian sentiments.[54] This deceptively simple poem, plainly subtitled '1914–18', relocates the scene of Christ's Agony to Picardy, the site of no less than four major battles along the River Somme during the First World War. A soldier explains that what he calls Gethsemane is the place on the near side of the Front to which gas masks where shipped in case of a chemical attack. There, in the momentarily Edenic conditions of a garden, he distracts himself by talking to a 'pretty lass'. The nouns 'lass' and 'grass' – their innocence poisoned by a bitter irony – are made to rhyme not only with 'gas' but the repeated verb 'pass', in an allusion to the relevant biblical narrative: 'I prayed my cup might pass'. But the cup of suffering doesn't pass, as the repetitions of the third and final stanza, which is deliberately truncated, indicate in a tone of rising panic:

It didn't pass – it didn't pass
It didn't pass from me.
I drank it when we met the gas
Beyond Gethsemane!

Beyond Gethsemane, among the trenches, is a scene of mass crucifixion: Golgotha. In Kipling's disturbing ballad, Christ is an ordinary, proletarian soldier, sacrificed not by God, but by the officers. In the pastoral conditions of Gethsemane, the poet informs us, 'the officer sat on the chair', while 'the men', in anticipation of their slaughter, 'lay on the grass'.[55]

In the half-life that he must henceforth lead, as a victim of chlorine or so-called mustard gas, Kipling's soldier can expect no comfort from God. The spiritual example of Christ in Gethsemane is for the poet not one of redemption but damnation. In spite of the poem's apparently simplicity, which is nonetheless complicated both by its unsettling off-rhymes and by a single metrical anomaly in the thirteenth line, Kipling's identification of Gethsemane with gas has something of the blunt provocativeness of George Grosz's 'Ecce Homo' (1924), a drawing in which Christ, who is nailed to the cross, wears a gasmask, and for which he was charged with blasphemy by the German government. The pungency of Kipling's poem, which Donald Davie rightly described as 'overtly and fiercely blasphemous', is no doubt partly a product of the anger and grief he felt at his eighteen-year-old son John's death at the Battle of Loos in 1915.[56] This substantial defeat for the British forces, which suffered a staggering sixty thousand casualties, was the first occasion in which, pioneered by General Haig, they deployed chemical warfare. But tragically, the poison gas not only proved ineffective, stagnating over no-man's-land, where British soldiers advanced directly into its lingering fog – it proved lethally self-destructive too. 'Gasthemene' is the gruesome pun that, deliberate or not, irresistibly comes to mind on reading Kipling's poem.

It can be speculated that, for allegorical reasons, Christ's agonizing drama in Gethsemane – when, in spite of his almost fatal self-doubt, he insisted on remaining vigilant in the face of spiritual and temporal catastrophe – came to seem particularly relevant in Europe in the aftermath of the First World War. That is, at the time when Shestov was reclaiming Pascal's mysterious annotations of the narrative. This was a period when, as Georg Lukács subsequently put it, the atmosphere that had fostered subjectivism, in philosophical terms, darkened dramatically: 'No longer was the world a great, multi-purpose stage upon which the I, in ever-changing costumes and continually transforming the scenery at will, could play out its own inner tragedies and comedies'.

No, it was now 'a devastated area' across which the 'I', decked no doubt in military uniform, passively enacted a collective or universal tragedy, like an automaton or a puppet, under the direction of vast impersonal forces.[57] The larger, world-historical drama unfolding across Europe consisted in the cataclysmically destructive inter-imperial rivalries of the First World War – what Lenin, writing in 1921, characterized as 'the universal ruin caused by the war' – which threatened to push capitalism to the point of collapse.[58] Against this backdrop as Lukács concluded, 'in its abandoned condition, the solitary Ego stood in fear and anxiety.'[59] The scene was thus set, as his coded allusion to Kierkegaard's *Fear and Trembling* (1843) suggests, for the rise of existential philosophy, which from one angle functioned as a last-ditch attempt to salvage the individual subject even as it catalogued its ruination. In this context, along with the crucifixion, the Agony in the Garden became the paradigmatic scene of the Passion.

The German novelist Hermann Hesse, responding to a time of personal as well as historical crisis, implicitly made precisely this claim in his essay 'Thoughts on Dostoevsky's *The Idiot*', published like Kipling's poem in 1919. There, Hesse admitted that whenever he was casually or spontaneously prompted to think about Christ, what flashed into his consciousness was not Jesus 'on the Cross or in the desert, or as miracleworker or as a raiser of the dead', but Jesus 'in that moment when He drinks the cup of solitude to the dregs in the Garden of Gethsemane, when His soul is torn by the agony of death through which He must pass to His higher birth and how He then in a last moving and childlike longing for comfort, turns to His disciples'. Hesse's Christ, a Christ for the troubled times in which he lived, is the solitary man who seeks the solicitude of his friends and, in a 'cruel moment', in his disappointment at their response, stares into an eternal night. Hesse continues:

> He turns to them for a little human warmth, for a fleeting illusion of affection in the midst of His bitter loneliness. He turns to them – and the disciples are asleep. There lie excellent Peter and beautiful John; they are all asleep together, these worthy men, about whom Christ in His goodness has experienced disappointments over and over again. He has shared His

thoughts with them as though they understood His words, as though it were in actual fact possible to communicate His thoughts to such as these, to arouse in them something like a vibration of kinship, something akin to understanding, to relationship, to unity with Himself. And now in the moment of unbearable torment, He turns to these few comrades He has. He is so utterly human, so utterly alone, so utterly the Man of Suffering, that He would now approach them as never before, to find some poor solace, some poor support in any stupid word they might utter, even in a friendly gesture. But no, they are not even there – they are sleeping – snoring.[60]

Hesse, who republished this essay in *Blick ins Chaos* (1920) alongside another essay, '*The Brothers Karamazov*, or the Downfall of Europe', was committed to a certain apocalypticism at this time. In the image of Christ at Gethsemane, to which he also alludes in his distinctly Dostoveskyan novel *Demian* (1919), he implicitly perceives an emblem, in the first instance, of his own political and psychological isolation at the end of the War. At that time, when his marriage to Maria commenced its terminal collapse, he was the victim of jingoistic attacks in the German press because of his anti-nationalism and pacifism. But Hesse, who was himself an insomniac, and who saw 'sleepless nights' as a concrete instance of the Nietzschean idea of eternal recurrence, also perceives in the unsleeping Christ an emblem of the possibility, or impossibility, of resisting the pyretic spiritual sleep into which, in spite of the impending or ongoing cataclysm, an entire culture appeared to have slipped.[61]

I suspect Eliot was thinking of Hesse's account of the night of Gethsemane in 'Thoughts on Dostoevsky's *The Idiot*' when he wrote 'What the Thunder Said', the final section of *The Waste Land* (1922) – a 'self-consciously apocalyptic poem', as Frank Kermode has called it.[62] Eliot's notorious Notes to the poem, one of whose principal themes is 'the present decay of eastern Europe', explicitly indicate that he had been reading *Blick ins Chaos*. He refers to it in his annotation of lines 366–76, a passage of the poem replete with cataclysmic images of 'hooded hordes swarming / Over endless plains' and of 'falling towers' that presage the dreamlike collapse of civilization's great imperial cities – 'Jerusalem Athens Alexandria / Vienna London'.[63] It is in relation to this febrile vision that, in the Notes, Eliot coolly quotes in German from the final sentences of Hesse's essay on *The Brothers Karamazov*:

> Already half of Europe, already at least half of Eastern Europe, is on the way to Chaos, driving drunkenly in a spiritual frenzy along the abyss, and singing as it goes, singing drunkenly in a hymn-like manner, as Dmitri Karamazov sang. The offended Bourgeoisie laughs at these songs, the Saint and Seer hears them with tears.

Eliot confessed in a letter from September 1960 to having been 'very much impressed by' *Blick ins Chaos* when he read it.[64] Indeed, sending it to his friend Sidney Schiff in January 1922, he persuaded him to translate it into English. Entitled *In Sight of Chaos*, the book duly appeared under the latter's pseudonym, Stephen Hudson, in 1923. Eliot also ensured that Hesse's essays on both *The Brothers Karamazov* and *The Idiot* were printed in the *Dial*, in the issues of June and August 1922 respectively. And he published Hesse's 'Recent German Poetry' in the first issue of the *Criterion* in October 1922. There, its references to 'the experience of the Great War, with the collapse of all the old forms and the breakdown of moral codes and cultures hitherto valid', and its warnings of 'the ruin of the world', appeared alongside the decrepitations of *The Waste Land*.[65] Moreover, when he was in Switzerland in May 1922, Eliot visited Hesse in Montagnola, where he was writing *Siddhartha* (1922), a novel that, like *The Waste Land*, turned to Eastern culture as a potential solution to both the chronic and acute problems of Western culture. In short, in the year that Eliot completed the poem, Hesse's reflections on the crisis of contemporary civilization were, if briefly, an important point of reference for him.

It is for this reason that it seems plausible to claim that Eliot's allusion to Gethsemane in *The Waste Land*, in the opening lines of 'What the Thunder Said', was influenced in part by Hesse's comments on the salience and significance of Jesus's 'unbearable agony' there. The section begins:

> After the torchlight red on sweaty faces
> After the frosty silence in the gardens
> After the agony in stony places
> The shouting and the crying[66]

According to the aesthetic of the poem as a whole, which conjures up a time that is dramatically out of joint, these fractured images reorganize the scene in Gethsemane in the form of a collage. The feverish glimpse of 'torchlight red on sweaty faces' in the first line, which signals the moment of Jesus's arrest, here precedes the more measured evocations of the previous night, 'the frosty silence in the gardens' and, in an image indebted to Mantegna's painting in the National Gallery, 'the agony in stony places' – as if time is running backwards. But time also seems to flow forwards, or ooze forwards, for the ruddy sweat on the torchlit faces of those involved in Jesus's arrest recalls Luke's account of the night in Gethsemane, when in his agony 'he prayed more earnestly: and his sweat was as it were great drops of blood falling down to the ground' (Luke 22: 44).

Here, then, is the Passion as a heap of broken images. But, in addition to the repetition of the preposition 'After', the parallelism that structures the second and third lines I have quoted, where the 'frosty silence' is paired with the 'agony', and the 'gardens' are paired with the 'stony places', nonetheless introduces a consistent logic. The silence seems as it were to conceal the agony, the garden to conceal the rocky, mountainous desert that is described more fully in the next stanza. At the same time, a diachronic rhythm inflects or interrupts the synchronic, isotopic relationship between the two lines; so what is effectively a fairy-tale transformation takes place, as silence collapses in a moment into the agony of shouting and crying and the garden is instantaneously rendered barren and stony: 'Here is no water but only rock'.[67] In the same way, the fields of Europe were suddenly reduced to mud and rubble by the World War. Gethsemane implicitly serves Eliot as one of the primal examples of a wasteland – a 'stony place'. And Christ, in this context, waiting in solitude for his arrest, recalls a figure from the second section of *The Waste Land*, the one who plays chess, 'Pressing lidless eyes and waiting for a knock upon the door'.[68] Both figures wait open-eyed and sleepless for a violent fate, the chess-player stooped over his pieces as they traverse the board, Jesus hunched above the hooded hordes that swarm over the plains.

'Jerusalem Athens'. For Eliot, the relationship between these cities, as the unpunctuated line indicates, is seamless. They are what Jerome McGann, in a slightly different context, has called 'the passing historical agencies of the recurrent reality of a spiritual corruption.'[69] From Eliot's apocalyptic perspective, they are the same. Like the other unreal cities – Alexandria, Vienna, London – they are symbolic of a civilization that, eroding and collapsing like rotten geological strata across millennia, is in a state of terminal ruination. All will fall. From Shestov's apocalyptic perspective, in contrast to Eliot's, with which it is contemporaneous, there is a fundamental difference between Athens and Jerusalem. 'What indeed has Athens to do with Jerusalem?' Shestov repeatedly asks, echoing Tertullian.[70] He identifies the former with damnation and ruination, in so far as it enshrines the entire rationalist tradition; the latter with redemption. Jerusalem is the seat of the prophets and the site of Christ's Passion. It is the setting of the spiritual drama that, a year after the publication of *The Waste Land*, Shestov stages in *Gethsemane Night*, his scintillating essay on Pascal.

5

Sleep and the sleepless
The night of Gethsemane

I

In a delightfully fanciful passage in her *Portrait of Pascal* (1927), the English poet, novelist and biographer Mary Duclaux conjured up the immediate context in which – more and more conscious, supposedly, of the trifling nature of his pioneering scientific achievements – Pascal wrote *Le mystère de Jésus*. 'Let us imagine Pascal one sleepless night, in pain, forlorn (as one never is in daylight), abandoned by God and by his dearest,' she wrote, adding that this was 'a mood familiar, surely, to every mystic, and to most nervous invalids'.[1]

Duclaux, who had written several volumes of verse under her maiden name of Robinson in the late nineteenth century, when she was friends with many of the avant-gardists of the English *fin de siècle*, here unapologetically exercised her poetic licence. But it is certainly not implausible to assume that Pascal's feverish emphasis on the physical, psychological and spiritual travails of sleeplessness in his interpretation of the Passion is the result of his own susceptibility to insomnia, which has been well documented. Insomnia, in effect, as a sickness unto death. Duclaux's sketch was surely indebted to Walter Pater's superb essay on Pascal, his final composition, which remained unfinished when he died in 1894 but was published in the *Contemporary Review* in 1895. Duclaux, who had lived a few doors from Pater on Earls

Terrace in London as a child, published her 'Souvenirs sur Walter Pater' in *La Revue de Paris* in 1925. In her 'portrait' of Pascal she was evidently evoking Pater's 'imaginary portraits' of historical figures, as he entitled them, as well as recalling his essay on the French philosopher in particular. There, Pater characterized the *Pensées* as 'the outcome, the utterance, of a soul diseased, a soul permanently ill at ease' and gently insisted that 'we find in their constant tension something of insomnia, of that sleeplessness which can never be a quite healthful condition of mind in a human body'.[2]

Pascal's 'Mystery of Jesus', a brief, fragmentary text composed at some point in the mid-1650s, not only transmits the constant tension of insomnia but also turns reflexively on the condition of sleeplessness. It is an account of the Passion that focuses its close reading on the Gethsemane scene. Like the *Pensées*, if in considerably smaller compass, these meditations might be said to comprise what Georg Lukács, who came to regard Pascal as 'a forebear of modern irrationalism', called with a certain grudging admiration 'an aphoristic phenomenology of the religious experience of despair'.[3] Pascal's fragment begins by making a significant distinction between Jesus's 'passion' and his 'agony'. The former is caused by others, he argues, the latter is caused by himself: 'Jesus suffers in his passion the torments inflicted upon him by men, but in his agony he suffers the torments which he inflicts on himself'.[4] Pascal then turns immediately to the Agony in the Garden, which he seems to re-examine not in Luke's, but in Mark's and Matthew's versions, for it is noticeable that he makes no reference to the apparition of an angel. Pascal's Jesus, in other words, is the human figure rather than the divine one – Son of Man rather than Son of God. 'No other text', argued the Jewish Romanian Marxist Lucien Goldmann in *The Hidden God* (1955), 'could offer us a better understanding of the tragic soul than *The Mystery of Jesus*'. He added that its singular intensity and profundity is the result of Pascal's identification with Christ's experience at Gethsemane as the 'unique and exceptional moment' in his biography as this is narrated in the Gospels. Pascal understands this moment 'because it is the one which he himself lives and experiences at every moment in his life': 'When He feels himself alone and exposed to God's anger Christ is, in Pascal's view, living out the truth of the human condition at an exemplary level'.[5]

Here is the beginning of Pascal's narrative reconstruction of Gethsemane:

> Jesus seeks some comfort at least from his three dearest friends, and they sleep: he asks them to bear with him a while, and they abandon him with complete indifference, and with so little pity that it did not keep them awake for a single moment. And so Jesus was abandoned to face the wrath of God alone.[6]

There is something profoundly painful about the almost novelistic manner in which Pascal here communicates Jesus's abandonment by those closest to him – his Father and his brothers. His reference to his friends' 'complete indifference', their almost sociopathic lack of conscience, embroiders the biblical account, underlining the human drama. So, too, does his shocking reference to God's 'wrath' (the 'anger' noticed by Goldmann), which is not mentioned in the Gospels. Jesus is here caught between, on the one hand, a vengeful Old Testament God and, on the other, disciples who sleep not because they are physically and spiritually exhausted, as in Luke, but because they are brutally, callously oblivious both to their apostolic responsibilities and, equally important, their ordinary human ones. He is trapped between a cruel God and cruel friends.

Pascal continues:

> Jesus is alone on earth, not merely with no one to feel and share his agony, but with no one even to know of it. Heaven and he are the only ones to know.
>
> Jesus is in a garden, not of delight, like the first Adam, who there fell and took with him all mankind, but of agony, where he has saved himself and all mankind.
>
> He suffers this anguish and abandonment in the horror of the night.[7]

The horror of the night. Pascal's formulation for the destitution of Jesus, which seems to take place in a primal, pre-Adamic environment as well as a redemptive, post-Adamic one, is devastating. It anticipates the glimpse of the abyss opened up by Hegel's description of the limits of reason in his Jena Lectures (1805–6), where he appears to identify Night, not merely as a temporality that is more or less foreign or other, but as the most intimate space at the interior of human nature: 'We see this Night when we look a human being in the eye, looking into a Night which turns terrifying.'[8] Gethsemane, for Pascal, is the place in which this 'extimate' Night, to put it in Lacanian terms, this night that is at once present in the innermost recess of the self and utterly, uncannily alien to it, is cultivated.[9] It is a void as well as a garden.

These are the two spaces onto which what Goldmann calls the 'tragic mind' open up: 'The tragic mind sees only two possibilities before it, nothingness or eternity.' Biographically speaking, of course, these might be seen as the two alternatives with which Pascal himself lived. Before him, eternity; beside him, the abyss. According to a legend purveyed by his contemporary l'Abbé Boileau, Pascal required a chair at all times to be positioned on his left side so as to reassure him that he could not fall into the abyss that he apprehended there. This rather theatrical neurosis is sometimes said to originate in an accident Pascal had in October 1654, when his carriage almost careered over the Pont de Neuilly into the Seine; an experience that allegedly induced 'a kind of false sensation', apparent 'in moments of peculiar weakness, or during a sleepless night, [when] he fancied there was a precipice yawning at the side of his bed into which he was about to fall'.[10] Shestov, whose philosophy of tragedy is premised on a perception of the fundamental presence of the void, obviously loved this story. 'All that Pascal wrote proves to us that instead of the solid earth beneath his feet he always felt and saw the abyss (another strange similarity between Pascal's fate and Nietzsche's),' he noted. 'There is perhaps a single error in the story,' he added, significantly and a little mischievously: 'The abyss was clearly not on Pascal's left side but under his feet.'[11] At Gethsemane, the abyss is beneath Jesus's feet, or beneath his knees as he prays.

The night in Gethsemane, Pascal claims, 'is the only occasion on which Jesus ever complained', and he complained not only because God had apparently forsaken him but also because his carefully selected comrades, on whose solidarity his life depended, failed to perform the most basic act of friendship.[12] They couldn't even keep a lookout for him when he was on the point of being arrested as a common criminal by the Roman soldiers who will execute him. In Matthew's Gospel, from which Pascal repeatedly quotes, Jesus says to Peter, 'What, could ye not watch with me one hour?' (Matt. 26: 40). At this moment, Jesus's surprised disappointment is palpable, at least in the King James translation. Jesus is a figure of extreme pathos in Pascal's account because, in spite of his friends' thoughtless disregard for his needs, he repeatedly demonstrates the most tender solicitude to them. And he repeatedly excuses them: 'The spirit indeed *is* willing, but the flesh *is* weak' (Matt. 26: 41). Although he has been 'totally abandoned, even by the friends he had chosen to watch with him', Pascal suggests, Jesus 'is vexed when he finds them asleep because of the dangers to which they are exposing not him but themselves, and he warns them for their own safety and their own good, with warm affection in the face of their ingratitude'. Jesus does nothing to mitigate his vulnerability – a vulnerability that is both practical and emotional: practical because he sees 'all his friends asleep and all his enemies watchful', and therefore comprehends how close he is to being captured and crucified; emotional because, though 'weary at heart', he only gently, even weakly, insists that his disciples actively support him.[13]

It is tempting to see a self-destructive, if not suicidal, impulse in the strange negligence Jesus displays at Gethsemane. Terry Eagleton has argued recently that the Gethsemane scene was 'interpolated by the Gospel writers to demonstrate among other things that Jesus has no desire to die', and that for this reason, 'he is portrayed as convulsed by panic and terror at the thought of his impending execution'.[14] But Eagleton's statement, which underpins his claim that this evidence that Jesus cherishes his life confirms his status as a martyr, seems to me to overstate the matter. For Jesus isn't convulsed by panic and terror in the Synoptics. His soul, as Mark has it in a line that Pascal repeats, 'is exceeding sorrowful unto death' (Mark 14: 34). It is his loneliness and despair that is striking. 'Jesus weary at heart' is how Pascal puts it. The shocking implication, then, to return to Eagleton's terms, is not that he is a martyr but that, momentarily, he is instead a suicide. If he is for the most part a martyr throughout the Passion narrative, because he seems to have everything to lose; at Gethsemane, shockingly, he is a suicide because he seems to have nothing to lose.

Agony, then, in the Synoptics and in Pascal's re-inscription of their narrative of the night of Gethsemane, is a struggle with friends, with enemies, with God, but above all with self. For Pascal, this struggle is a perpetual one. It does not end with the night of Gethsemane. It is, so to speak, the secret of Christ's life and his afterlife. And for this reason, 'while Jesus remains in agony and cruellest distress', he urges, 'let us pray longer'. Implicitly, it is a question of praying, and hence not sleeping, till the end of the world. This idea of eternal suffering and eternal vigilance is at the core of 'The Mystery of Jesus':

> Jesus seeks companionship and solace from men.
>
> It seems to me that this is unique in his whole life, but he finds none, for his disciples are asleep.
>
> Jesus will be in agony until the end of the world. There must be no sleeping during that time.[15]

'In this eternal and atemporal moment which lasts to the very end of the world', Goldmann responds, 'tragic man remains alone, doomed to be misunderstood by sleeping men and exposed to the anger of a hidden and an absent God'.[16]

But if the insomnia of 'tragic man', in the seventeenth century, is a sign of his damnation, then it also points to redemption. For, as Goldmann explains, 'he finds, in his very loneliness and suffering, the only values which he can still have and which will be enough to make him great: the absolute and rigorous nature of his own awareness and his own ethical demands, his quest for absolute justice and absolute truth, and his refusal to accept any illusions or compromise'. Here is sleeplessness – understood as an extreme, if not apocalyptic, sort of vigilance – in the form of an ethical and even political imperative. In the New Testament, the Book of Revelation reiterates it (echoing 1 Thess. 5: 4–6): 'If therefore thou shalt not watch, I will come on thee as a thief, and thou shalt not know what hour I will come upon thee' (3: 2–3). It is a question, then, of converting wakefulness into watchfulness; a night's wakefulness into an eternity of watchfulness; a passive into an active condition. According to Goldmann's persuasive reading of 'The Mystery of Jesus':

> Tragic greatness transforms the suffering which man is forced to endure because it is imposed upon him by a meaningless world into a freely chosen and creative suffering, a going beyond human wretchedness by a significant action which rejects compromise and relative values in the name of a demand for absolute justice and truth.[17]

Sleeplessness, as spiritual vigilance, bears witness that the empirical world, as Adorno put it in another context, 'should be other than it is'.[18]

II

Jésus sera en agonie jusqu'à la fin du monde: il ne faut pas pas dormir pendant ce temps-là. Shestov placed this sentence as the epigraph to his essay on Pascal's philosophy, which Daniel Halévy, director of the *Cahiers Verts*, commissioned as an article for *Mercure de France* in order to celebrate the 300th anniversary of the French philosopher's birth in 1923. Shestov commenced work on it in December 1922. Arriving in Paris in the autumn of 1921, he published no less than three important pieces in his first eighteen months in exile in France. His essay on Dostoevsky, 'The Conquest of the Self-Evident', or a substantial portion of it, appeared in the *Nouevlle Revue Française*, translated and introduced by Boris de Schloezer, in February 1922. *Les Révalations de la mort*, first published as a series of articles in Russian between 1920 and 1922, appeared as a monograph in May 1923. And 'Descartes and Spinoza' was printed in *Mercure de France* in June 1923. It was in that same month that he published *La Nuit de Gethsémani*, which had become too long to print as an article, as a short book.

In seizing on the sentence from 'The Mystery of Jesus' about Christ's eternal insomnia, Shestov was developing an argument central to the essay on Dostoevsky. This essay affirmed 'the painful convulsions of a doubtful awakening', like the ones depicted in the Russian novelist's portraits of agonized, underground men, and negated the 'yawning torpidity of certain sleep', that is, the somnolent condition of the 'omnitude', the mediocre populace whom he repeatedly condemned in his novels.[19] If, in the summer of 1923, Shestov was still setting out his stall in Paris, philosophically speaking, then *Gethsemane Night* was probably the most confessional, if not autobiographical, of his first few publications in French. It is from the opening paragraphs clear that Shestov identifies closely, personally, with Pascal. 'All the strength of his restless, yet profound and concentrated mind', he argues in the second paragraph, 'was applied to resisting the current of history, preventing himself from being carried forward by it.'[20] The word 'restless' (*inquiète*) carries particular force in this context.

Shestov's essay on Dostoevsky, which opens with a fairly severe discussion of Euripides and Socrates, is relatively formal in its approach to the novelist, for all its idiosyncrasies and eccentricities; the essay on Pascal, however, is from the start infused with a sense of Shestov's emotional as well as intellectual investment in the philosopher. In one of Fondane's essays, 'Un philosophe tragique: Léon Chestov' (1929), in which he positions his friend and mentor as *un Pascal Russe*, the Romanian poet communicates a sense of the dynamism with which, in his tricentennial essay, Shestov apprehended Pascal. '*Comprendre Pascal, c'est aller avec lui, plus loin que lui,*' he writes; '*c'est toucher de près l'inquiétude, l'angoisse, la maladie, l'abîme; c'est haïr la raison; c'est chercher éperdument Dieu*': 'To understand Pascal is to go with him, to go further than him. It is to be intimate with anxiety, anguish, sickness, and the abyss; it is to hate reason; to search madly for God.' The strength of Shestov's piece, according to Fondane, is that he doesn't speak to us of Pascal's style, or his thought, or even, more generally, his 'grandeur', for these are the predictable concerns of those who do not comprehend him. No, '*il nous parle de la singularité de Pascal; de sa déraison; de ses faiblesses*'.[21] 'He speaks to us of the singularity of Pascal; of his unreason; of his weaknesses.' It is these particular characteristics – his madness, his loneliness and his weaknesses – that bring him into a dialectical conjuncture with the present. (As Cioran pointed out when interviewed about Fondane and Shestov, Pascal 'still impresses us today' because 'his anguish is stronger than his positive experience'.)[22] This Pascal, with his 'extraordinary and unexpected fears', is less like a saint than a suicide; or – since, according to Shestov's reading of Dostoevsky, 'the true saint is the eternally disturbed underground man' – an underground man.[23]

'It is certain that Pascal never passed a day without suffering, and hardly knew what sleep was,' Shestov writes, in a sentence I have already cited once. Pascal's faithful sister Gilberte, among others, testified to this insomnia, which was particularly acute during the final year of his life. She wrote of his 'sleepless nights' that were 'so frequent and so exhausting', but that nonetheless continued to stimulate his capacity for seminal thinking.[24] 'It is also certain,' Shestov adds in his brief biographical reference to Pascal's suffering, 'that Pascal, instead of feeling the solid earth beneath his feet as other men do, felt himself hanging unsupported over a precipice, and that had he given way to the "natural" law of gravity he would have fallen into a bottomless abyss'.[25] Refusing the canonical, theological Pascal, Shestov uses the existential Pascal to convulse us, to tear apart our reliance on Reason. Pascal's failure to disguise his insecurities, his refusal to repress his lack of faith in Reason, perhaps even in God, is implicitly what makes him so relevant in the aftermath of the First World War. To put it in Benjamin's terms, Shestov seizes hold of Pascal as he flashes up, three hundred years later, in a moment of danger. The essay on Pascal – like the appropriation of Pascal in Bataille's *Inner Experience* (1943) that Sartre noted in his review of the book in 1947 – is an attempt, as Benjamin once more might have stated the matter, to wrest him away from a conformism that threatens to overpower him.[26]

'Of what interest to us can a man be, who tries to make time run backwards?', Shestov asks in the third paragraph of *Gethsemane Night*. He starts the essay, as I have already intimated, by situating Pascal in terms of his attitude to the past: 'He did not feel himself impelled, with all the rest, forward towards a "better" future, but backwards towards the deeps of the past'. He portrays Pascal as someone who disavowed the Cartesian values of the Enlightenment; as someone who refused 'all that humanity had acquired by its common efforts in the two brilliant centuries to which a grateful posterity gave the name of "Renaissance"'.[27] From the opening page of the essay, then, Shestov implicitly identifies Pascal with a rejection of the ideology of progress that, in the history of philosophy, and the philosophy of history, is subsequently identified with the figure of Hegel. 'Is it so necessary to defend Hegel at all costs?', Shestov asks. He continues:

Hitherto history has always been written on the assumption (unverified, it is true) that men, once dead, absolutely cease to exist, that they are consequently defenceless before the judgment of posterity, and without influence over the living. But the time may come when even the historians will feel that the dead were men like themselves; and then they will become more careful and circumspect in their judgments. It is our belief, indeed our strong conviction to-day, that the dead are silent and will always remain silent, whatever we say of them, however we treat them. But if one day we are robbed of this conviction, if we suddenly feel that the dead can come back to life at any moment, can rise from their graves, invade our lives, and stand before us as equals – how shall we speak then?[28]

The time may come. The time has come. Like all those who speak in the voice of the prophet, Shestov denounces the present in announcing the future.

For Shestov himself was living through a period in which the dead suddenly seemed to have come alive. Philosophically, because the crisis of Reason heralded by the First World War made those who had rejected its protocols several centuries ago, such as Pascal, suddenly seem relevant again, as the writings of Bataille, Camus and Sartre, among others of their generation, testified. Historically, because after the War the teeming men slaughtered on the battlefields lived as ghosts alongside those who had survived it, as the revival of spiritualism among other things testified. 'Ghosts move about me / Patched with histories', Ezra Pound wrote in 'Three Cantos' (1917).[29] And they are no longer silent. Like Benjamin in his theses 'On the Concept of History' (1940), Shestov rejected Marx's injunction that, in the era of proletarian as opposed to bourgeois revolutions, the dead should bury the dead. Shestov believed, to the contrary, that history could only be rescued and made meaningful if those declared dead could be disinterred and resurrected. Here he himself resembles Benjamin's Angel of History, his face turned towards the past as he is driven by the storm of progress into the future; still trying to awaken the dead and piece together what has been smashed.

In the aftermath of the First World War, the ideology of progress seemed less sustainable than ever before. It was not merely Marxists like Rosa Luxemburg who pointed this out. The British liberal sociologist L.T. Hobhouse can stand as representative when, in *Questions of War and Peace* (1916), reflecting on the fact that 'three or four times as many men' were killed 'at Loos as at Waterloo', he declared: 'If this is progress I grant you the world moves onward, but the word ceases to express anything in which a rational man can take interest'.[30] More or less apocalyptic alternatives to the ideology of progress, furthermore, seemed more viable than ever before. The First World War was proof, after all, that humanity was eminently capable of creating its own cataclysms.

Reclaiming Pascal in this climate, Shestov celebrates him as an 'apostate'.[31] He insists that, precisely because he has supposedly been superseded by history, Pascal is of pressing relevance. Shestov concedes that Pascal is still printed, read, even praised; but observes that this sanctification is little more than a form of entombment. 'His august face is like the image of a saint, before which a lamp burns that will burn many a long day', the Russian writes; 'But no one listens to him.'[32] 'To-day we have grown used to Pascal, we all read him from childhood, we learn extracts from his *Pensées* by heart,' he writes a few pages later. But the effect of this is soporific: 'We listen to these as though they were just harmless remarks, acute and entertaining; and after hearing them we could go on living and sleeping as quietly as after any other pleasant words.'[33]

The task that Shestov ascribes himself in this essay, then, is to awaken us, in different historical circumstances, to Pascal's perpetual or persistent wakefulness. It is to excavate the underground man interred in the saint's tomb; to make Pascal our equal, to make him invade our lives. Shestov's assertion is that, in some productive and provocative sense, Pascal is untimely; that his meditations are untimely ones; and that he therefore speaks with peculiar force to a time that is peculiarly out of joint. In historiographical terms, it is thus a question not of 'dissect[ing] corpses', as if history were an 'anatomical theatre', as Shestov imagines it, but of invoking spectres.[34] The model is not science, so to speak, but the séance. Here again is an almost Benjaminian strategy. Shestov, like Benjamin, seems to have believed that 'the past carries with it a temporal index by which it is referred to redemption'; perhaps even that, 'like every generation preceding us, we have been endowed with a *weak* Messianic power, a power to which the past has a claim'. As Benjamin puts it, in apocalyptic terms, 'our coming was expected on earth'.[35] From Shestov's perspective, Pascal is one of those who expected the interwar generation, the generation that lived collectively with the abyss beneath its feet.

At the present time, Shestov states, 'men need something "positive"; they ask for something which will resolve their difficulties and calm their fears'. But Pascal is no bromide. He 'becomes ever stranger and more inhuman to mankind'; more and more alien, as if touched by the Angel of Death that, according to Shestov, visited Dostoevsky. And precisely in this untimeliness, this persistent and perhaps intensifying refusal to conform to the demands of an epoch defined by reason, lies his timeliness. Referring to his contemporaries, Shestov asks:

> What can they hope from Pascal who, in the throes of his sombre exaltation, proclaims, or rather cries aloud: '*Jésus sera en agonie jusqu'à la fin du monde: il ne faut pas pas dormir pendant ce temps-là*'? ('Jesus will be in agony until the end of the world: there must be no sleep while that lasts').[36]

'Nothing' is the implicit response to this rhetorical question, which concludes the first section of the essay. For a demand of this kind can only create incomprehension at a time when, officially at least, the most technocratic forms of Reason remain ideologically dominant in European society.

III

The second section of Shestov's *Gethsemane Night*, which repeats Pascal's statement about sleeplessness like a musical motif to which it compulsively returns, opens by pursuing this point:

> Jesus' agony will last until the end of the world, and therefore there must be no more sleep during all that time. One can say this, for one can say anything, but can a man set himself such a task, and is he able to fulfil it? Like Macbeth, Pascal would fain 'murder sleep'; worse still, he seems to demand that all mankind should associate itself with him in this horrid task.

Clearly, this exorbitant ultimatum, that sleep universally be abolished, is completely inconsistent with the dictates of Reason. It aligns Pascal with the madman Macbeth; indeed, Pascal is more insane than Macbeth, since Macbeth murdered sleep not deliberately and gladly, but inadvertently and guiltily. Like some strictly destructive Angel of Death – Abaddon in the Book of Revelation perhaps – Pascal sets out to massacre sleep. According to all rationalist criteria, this is utterly unconscionable. 'Human reason declares unhesitatingly that Pascal's demands are unreasonable and impossible of execution.' And who, asks Shestov, is strong enough to 'refuse to obey reason?'[37]

Not Peter. For this apostle, pre-ordained as the founder of the Christian Church, 'had not the strength to conquer sleep', even when Jesus 'was seized by the soldiers and dragged before his merciless judges', in spite of the appeal that his leader made to him and the other disciples who attended him at Gethsemane.[38] In fact, Shestov argues, Peter's capacity for sleep is a positive prerequisite for his earthly, worldly role as the head of the Church:

> According to the inscrutable will of the Creator, his vicar on earth can be none other than he who is able to sleep as soundly as Peter, who has relied

so entirely on his reason, that he does not awake even when, in an evil dream, he denies his God.[39]

As Shestov's reference to the soldiers perhaps implies, his contempt for Peter is at the same time contempt for those who, in the context of the First World War and its aftermath, compromise with the forces of oppression, or deny their moral liability and responsibility for the persecution taking place. There is, in other words, a significant political dimension to Shestov's argument even if – because of its religious form – it is also, more obviously, spiritual and existential in its implications.

The exorbitance and extravagance of Pascal's prohibition on sleep, his insistence on what William Desmond calls 'this hyperbolic watchfulness', 'this monstrous sleeplessness', is for Shestov exactly the point.[40] It indicates the violent intrusion of irreducibly alien, heavenly values into the orbit of earthly ones; of anti-Necessity into the realm of Necessity. And it is for this reason, Shestov claims, that Pascal's Jansenist contemporaries, Antoine Arnauld, Pierre Nicole 'and the other recluses of Port Royal', in posthumously publishing his *Pensées*, 'felt obliged to abridge, change, and omit so much'. The idea, Shestov writes, 'that the Last Judgment which awaits us will be in heaven and not on earth, and that therefore man may not sleep, no man may ever sleep' is scandalous to Reason – 'monstrous according to human conceptions'. Indeed, none of the Jansenists 'could have endured this thought'. Even for Pascal, Shestov concedes, the imperative not to sleep, to remain eternally vigilant, constituted 'an intolerable burden', and he himself 'alternately rejected and accepted it, without ever being able to abandon it entirely'. Precisely in its impossibility, it is the appropriate spiritual imperative for an epoch that, like the rationalistic, scientistic one in which Shestov lives, does not dare 'to believe in God directly' – as he remarks of Augustine in *Gethsemane Night*.[41] Shestov effectively insists that we should believe in God directly, even if to do so is intolerable, insufferable. We must attempt to stare at the sun even if we are tempted to shield our sight from it. Even if it will damage us to do so.

Augustine, Shestov goes on, 'was the father of *fides implicita*' (here, he appears to be following the arguments of the German Lutheran theologian Adolf von Harnack); that is, 'of the doctrine by which a man need not himself commune directly with heavenly truth, but has only to observe those principles declared by the Church to be true'.[42] But this doctrine entails an abdication of spiritual, and perhaps political, responsibility:

> If we translate the term '*Fides implicita*' into the language of common sense, it means that man has the right, nay is compelled, to sleep while the Godhead travails in agony. This is the unequivocal command of reason, which none may disobey.

To adopt the position that is for Shestov summarized by the concept of *fides implicita*, which here stands in for all those collective, institutionally authorized codes of belief that can be identified in an alternative, more overtly political vocabulary with the term 'ideology', is to renounce our individuality, or 'individual liberty', which he sarcastically calls 'a dangerous an absolutely unnecessary thing', and to cede it 'to some person, institution, or stable principle'. It is, in short, to alienate it. Augustine is exemplary in this context, according to Shestov's un-selfconsciously partisan account, because he 'remained faithful to the tradition of Greek philosophy'.[43]

During the Middle Ages, Shestov claims, Christianity systematically accommodated itself to 'Greek morality', and the rationalist tradition in consequence became fatally incarnated in the Catholic Church. Luther and Pascal, by contrast, preserving their individuality, circumvented rationalist institutions and short-circuited rationalist ideological certainties. They appealed directly to God. When Luther, like Pascal, 'suddenly saw with his own eyes that the earthly keys of the heavenly kingdom were in the hands of him who had thrice denied God, and when, horrified at his discovery, he turned his eyes from earth and sought for truth in heaven, it ended with his breaking completely with the Church'.[44] This was Luther's awakening, the moment at which he saw with his own eyes. 'Man cannot and dares not look at the world through his own eyes,' Shestov states; 'he needs "collective" eyes, the support, the authority of his neighbour.' Luther, touched perhaps by the Angel of Death, was one of those who had the courage to look at the world through his own eyes. To gaze directly at the sun. And this is what we must all strive to do. To remain awake and to gaze implacably at the world, rejecting what is 'strange and even obnoxious' about it, even if 'all others accept it'.[45] Shestov's conception of ideology is not a particularly sophisticated one, it can be agreed, but the political valence of his argument is indisputable. It is about more than simply bearing witness to suffering; it is about refusing the logic of reason and domination that render it possible.

Pascal also had the courage to look at the world through his own eyes. He too was touched by the Angel of Death. If formally he submitted to Reason, Shestov claims, in fact he prosecuted both Rome and Reason 'before the tribunal of God'. 'In the depths of his soul, Pascal despises and hates this autocrat,' Shestov writes in reference to Reason, 'and is only thinking of how he can shake off the yoke of the detested tyrant, to whom all his contemporaries, even the great Descartes, so willingly bowed the knee'.[46] In a climate in which Reason is hegemonic, like Rome in the time of Luther, Pascal's 'truths', once he had 'learned that man must not sleep until the end of the world', 'are harmful, dangerous, exceptionally terrifying and destructive'.[47] It is in this sense that Pascal was an antinomian and an apostate. He militantly fought against Reason and the intellectual and spiritual complacency it fosters. He battled against the certainty, immutability and stability that Reason, flagrantly contradicting the abysmal and abyssal insecurity of everyday life, induces humanity inordinately to 'esteem'. And he battled against them because they are the conditions of security that enable humanity 'to live quietly and sleep in peace'; that enabled Peter, to give the originary example, to sleep while Jesus 'was preparing to die upon the cross'.

To Shestov, and to the Pascal he appropriates and reinvents, this passive, supine attitude in the face of persistent suffering is morally unacceptable:

> But Christ's agony is not yet finished. It is going on, it will last until the end of the world. 'One must not sleep', Pascal tells us. No one must sleep. No one must seek security and certainty.[48]

As long as one person suffers, Christ continues in agony; and as long as he is in agony, Shestov effectively argues, there will be an ideological incentive to sleep. This is roughly analogous to Benjamin's striking declaration that 'as long as there is still one beggar around, there will still be myth'.[49] The task is to abolish begging and hence the need for myth, to abolish suffering and hence the need to sleep. Reason, in Shestov's critique, is in this sense ultimately the rationalization of suffering. 'People who have been cast out of life have no place in Hegel's "system", he comments in vituperative tones in his article on Kierkegaard from 1938.[50] Hence, what Shestov calls 'speculative philosophy' is a species of myth. Reason does not deconstruct myth; it recreates it under the intellectual conditions of modernity. If Shestov seems close to Benjamin, he also seems close here to Adorno and Horkheimer. For in *Dialectic of Enlightenment* (1944), they established that the relentless rationalist procedures of the Enlightenment, which explain 'every event as repetition', and which are pitted against 'mythic imagination', themselves comprise a form of myth. Enlightenment, they argue, 'with every step becomes more deeply engulfed in mythology'.[51]

Shestov goes on to quote a superb, openly apocalyptic passage from the *Pensées* in which Pascal aggressively dismisses the longing with which human beings burn 'to find some firm stance, some ultimate, unshakable basis, on which we may build the tower that can reach up to infinity'. Every day, Babels are built. 'But all our foundations crack and earth opens to the abyss', is Pascal's mocking response to the expression of this pathetic aspiration: 'THEREFORE LET US NOT SEEK CERTAINTY OR SECURITY.' Instead of certainty or security, anxiety. Shestov's Pascal advocates a permanent state of restlessness; that is, both anxiousness and, more literally, sleeplessness. Sleeplessness, in fact, is simply the apotheosis of anxiousness. And the apocalyptic insomnia on which he insists in 'The Mystery of Jesus' is the apotheosis of sleeplessness. Pascal's attack on certainty and security, his vision of the Tower of Babel cracking at its foundations and tumbling into the abyss, according to Shestov, is 'what a man feels, sees, and hears who has decided, or rather who has been condemned, not to sleep until the sufferings of Christ are ended, which will not be until the end of the world'.[52]

Pascal's own physical and spiritual sufferings were intense and all but unsustainable. As a modern biographer observes, 'there are reliable reports' that from September 1647, when he was only twenty-four, 'Blaise had difficulties speaking and experienced headaches, night-sweats, and insomnia'. His sleeplessness, which probably intensified in his final years, does not appear to have been some devotional discipline, even if he forced it in part to perform a religious function, but 'insomnia as such'.[53] It is this heroic man, constantly tested by his body, constantly testing his mind, to put it in Cartesian terms of which Pascal might not have approved, that Shestov celebrates in *Gethsemane Night*. Shestov's archetype is the individual who suffers 'continual torture'. Like Job. Like Nietzsche, whose chronic illness, the symptoms of which included sleeplessness, is the precondition of his philosophy. Shestov cites Nietzsche's statement that, because 'it teaches boundless suspicion', 'only great pain ultimately sets the spirit free'. And he insists that, even though the French philosopher is a 'believer' and the German an 'unbeliever', 'Pascal could have repeated this saying of Nietzsche's word for word, and with equal right.'[54] In their illness, in their sleeplessness, they are our saviours. A messianic line of descent leads through them all the way from the faithless, sleepless Christ of Gethsemane.

Pascal is an impossibly demanding ethical and spiritual example to which to aspire; but this is precisely the point. He poses a fundamental existential question: To sleep or not to sleep? Not to be or to be?

> Will you still follow Pascal, or is your patience exhausted and do you prefer to pass on to other masters who will be more comprehensible and less exacting? Expect no mercy or indulgence from Pascal. He is infinitely cruel to himself, and infinitely cruel to others. If you want to go searching in his company, he will take you with him, but he tells you beforehand that your search will bring you no joy. '*Je n'approuve que ceux qui cherchent en gémissant.*' ('I approve those only who seek with lamentation.') His truths, or what he calls his truths, are hard, painful, remorseless. He brings with him no relief, no consolation. He kills every kind of consolation. Directly man pauses to rest and collect himself, Pascal is there with his disquiet: you must not pause, you must not rest, you must march on, march without ceasing; you are tired, you are worn out; that is just as it should be; you must be tired; you must be utterly exhausted. '*Il est bon d'être lassé et fatigué par l'inutile recherche du vrai bien, afin de tendre les bras au libérateur.*' ('It is good to be tired and exhausted by the fruitless search for true good, that you may stretch out your arms to the liberator.')[55]

To aspire to Pascal's example, to adhere to his excessive, extortionate demands, is to live in a constant, uncomfortable state of restlessness that makes it all but inconceivable to accept conditions as they are. His ceaseless questioning, predicated on a ceaseless self-questioning, thus constitutes a kind of cynicism, though one that provokes to action rather than inaction, that promises to redeem as well as condemn, and that in this respect is not without important political implications. The condition Shestov's Pascal advocates living is one of profound tiredness that leads not to the extinction of consciousness but its intensification. *In febris veritas*. A constant state of exhausted restiveness is, according to Shestov, the proper disposition: insomnia. An experience of everyday damnation, insomnia nonetheless contains the potential for redemption.

Pascal chooses instability over security; the abyss over the 'solid earth'; 'wars and struggles' over peace.

> Men long for rest – he promises weariness, weariness without end; men pursue clear, distinct truths – and he shuffles all the cards, confuses everything, and changes earthly life into horrible chaos. What does he want? He has already told us. No one must sleep.[56]

It is a choice between the ordinary world, which is sustained by the rationalist philosophy that mediates it, and the world of Pascal and Nietzsche, 'another world of which our philosophy can only dream, a world so unlike our own that all which is the rule to us is to them the exception, and things happen continually there which happen here rarely or not at all'.[57] In Lacanian terms, it is a choice between everyday 'reality', constituted by the Imaginary and the Symbolic, and the Real. The Real is that which escapes and disrupts the Imaginary and Symbolic; the 'terrifying primordial abyss' where all identity, all stable subjectivity, dissolves.[58] Pascal, as we have seen, lived with this abyss on his left side. Or, as Shestov sees it, beneath his feet. Shestov quotes Pascal's startling statement that 'we run heedlessly into the abyss, after having put something before us to prevent us seeing it', which he takes from the *Pensées*, and observes that, as this indicates, it is in the end irrelevant whether l'Abbé Boileau's claim about Pascal's positioning a chair in order to conceal or screen the abyss beside him is true. For if the story is an invention 'it is the invention of a seer, of one who could see into the shadows where for others all things melt in a confused twilight'.[59]

Shestov here implicitly identifies himself with Boileau, I think, as someone who sees into the shadows when he reads Pascal, as someone who, because of his own existential fragility or instability, senses the abyss beside or beneath the French philosopher. Like Pascal, Shestov distances himself from 'men in general', from men who 'always feel the solid earth beneath their feet' and 'only know by hearsay of falls into the abyss, or if they experience these things it is only a short and fugitive experience'.[60] Shestov was, like Andrei Bely, conscious that, though we don't admit it, we are only ever 'drink[ing] coffee with cream over the abyss'.[61] His ethics are predicated on the belief that the best and truest way to live is not like those for whom life is, banally enough, 'alternately difficult and easy', so that 'each effort is usually followed by rest and quiet'. Instead, they are predicated on the conviction that we must strive to live in the alien and insane world inhabited by Pascal, Nietzsche and a number of other underground men. 'There nothing is easy, everything is difficult,' Shestov underlines; 'there is no rest, no quiet, only eternal unrest; no sleep, only an endless vigil'.[62] In contrast to Socrates and his descendants, for whom 'only reason can put an end to unrest, can give us a firm ground', we must cultivate a state of restlessness and live as if we are permanently poised over a precipice.[63]

Shestov's scandalous counter-Enlightenment claim is that we must flee the light and live in darkness. Too much clarity darkens, as Pascal put it.[64] The only way to escape from under the inheritance of Reason, according to Shestov's reading of 'The Mystery of Jesus', is 'to renounce the *veritates aeternae*, the fruits of the tree of knowledge; to "brutalize" oneself, to believe in none of reason's promises; to flee the light, for light illuminates the lie; to love shadows'.[65] It is as if the activities of the mysterious creature in 'The Burrow', which Kafka commenced writing in 1923, the year Shestov published *Gethsemane Night*, represented some kind of paradigm for philosophical enquiry. Better to grope in the abysmal darkness to which we have been sentenced than to aspire to the light. The former is a state of nocturnal wakefulness, the latter a state of diurnal sleepfulness. Reason is a form of enchantment that induces dreams. Revelation, which Shestov pits against Reason, rips into this 'enchanted realm of lies'. 'We are all living as though under a spell and we feel it', he proclaims, 'yet we fear awakening more than anything in the world'. For this reason, 'we look upon those who help us to sleep, who lull us and glorify our sleep, as our natural friends and benefactors; while those who try to awaken us we look upon as our worst enemies, aye, as malefactors'.[66] Shestov was proud to count himself, along with Pascal, among the malefactors.

We must embrace the night, but strain to keep our eyes permanently open in the dark. 'Let us forget light,' Shestov declared in *All Things Are Possible*, 'let us go bravely to meet the coming night'. This is a hymn to the night comparable to those written by Romantic poets such as Novalis. 'Night', Shestov continued, 'the dark, deaf, impenetrable night, peopled with horrors – does she not now loom before us, infinitely beautiful?'[67] Night, the scene of terrifying loneliness, is the site of truth. Shestov is a major philosopher of the counter-Enlightenment.

IV

The prophets, the proponents of Revelation, are those like Pascal who cultivate rather than attempt to eliminate 'the incomprehensible, the enigmatic, the mysterious' – the darkness. For Pascal 'sees in the inexplicable and incomprehensible nature of our surroundings the promise of a better existence'. In the capacity of the unexpected to irrupt into the apparently inalterable landscape we inhabit, utopian possibilities open up, exploding the continuum of history, to put it in Benjaminian terms. Shaken by shock, the world we accept so readily, like sleepers complying with the logic of a dream, 'is plucked apart, torn asunder, loses all meaning and all internal unity'. 'If Cleopatra's nose had been a little shorter the history of the world would have been changed,' Shestov iterates, citing one of the most famous of Pascal's formulations.[68] Against 'Hegel's fat volumes', with their sublime commitment to the unfurling logic of history, he affirms 'Pascal's one brief sentence', which is premised on the conviction 'that the history of the world is governed by tiny chances'.[69] Anti-Necessity.

This too finds an echo in Benjamin's messianic understanding of history. In a short piece entitled 'In the Sun' (1932), during a discussion of the delicately transformative effects of the imagination, Benjamin records that 'the Hasidim have a saying about the world to come': there, 'everything will be the same as here – only a little bit different'. The room we inhabit, the clothes we wear, the place 'where our child lies sleeping', all these things 'will be arranged just as it is with us'; but everything will at the same time be subtly altered.[70] The proof that we live in the afterlife will lie folded into almost imperceptible creases in the things familiar to us from our ordinary life. In his essay on Kafka, composed a couple of years later and published in *Jüdische Rundschau* on the tenth anniversary of the writer's death in 1934, Benjamin repeats the same claim, but renders it a little bit different, a little more political. In this especially knotted, enigmatic paragraph, which addresses 'distortion' in Kafka's fiction, he first cites an entry from the novelist's diary. There, the chronically insomniac Kafka describes a method he has devised in order to fall asleep, which involves lying on his back as if 'loaded down' like a soldier reclining with his pack; and then mentions the appearance of a similar trope in a folksong, 'The Little Hunchback'. 'This little man is at home in a distorted life,' Benjamin notes, adding: 'He will disappear with the coming of the Messiah, of whom a great rabbi once said that he did not wish to change the world by force, but would only make a slight adjustment in it.'[71] Here, the delicate but terminal and total transformation that the Messiah effects is an intervention, a revolutionary intervention, in history. If the logic of Benjamin's precept, then, is synchronic in the first instance, it is diachronic in the second. In 'In the Sun', the two worlds co-exist in a static, ahistorical relationship to one another, like pictures in a spot-the-difference competition; in 'Franz Kafka', the world to come succeeds this world, and the relationship between them is therefore historical.

This second restatement of the rabbinical wisdom – which precedes Benjamin's claim, at the end of the same paragraph, that Kafka 'possessed in the highest degree what Malebranche called "the natural prayer of the soul" – attentiveness' – is the one that brings him close to Shestov's interpretation of Pascal.[72] If the route from Shestov to Kafka, as Benjamin remarked to Scholem in 1939, was 'not a long one', then neither was the route from Kafka to Shestov.[73] The Messiah's 'slight adjustment', in Benjamin's reading of the role of distortion in Kafka, is equivalent to the 'tiny chance', the instance of anti-Necessity, that – so Shestov claims – determines or re-determines the course of history. Shestov's conception of change, here, is ironically more dynamic, and more violent, than Benjamin's. It is also more atheistic. For if Benjamin implicitly predicates his conception of history on the notion of a Messiah who actively intervenes in its narrative, Shestov predicates his on an absent, apophatic God who is passively revealed in the aleatory workings of chance. But both thinkers reject the idea that time is, in Benjamin's parlance, homogeneous and empty. Both assume that 'every second of time [is] the strait gate through which the Messiah might enter'.[74]

Interestingly, it can be added that it was Scholem, the thinker that mediated Shestov to Benjamin, who claimed to be the 'great rabbi' responsible for the statement that the Messiah will change the world not by force but by an insignificant adjustment. In a letter to Benjamin dated 9 July 1934, one that encloses a poem inspired by *The Trial*, he asked his friend about the 'source' of this and other 'stories': 'Does Ernst Bloch have them from you or you from him?' In a footnote to his correspondence, Scholem subsequently stated that, in *Spuren* (1930), Bloch had cited 'the same sentence ascribed by W. B. to a "great rabbi"' and credited it to a 'truly kabbalistic rabbi'. 'The great rabbi with the profound dictum on the messianic kingdom who appears in Bloch is none other than *I* myself,' Scholem concluded his letter to Benjamin; 'what a way to achieve fame!! It was one of my first ideas about the Kabbalah.'[75] It also, incidentally, finds its way into the writings of Adorno, who comments in the 'Finale' of *Minima Moralia* (1951) that the 'consummate negativity' of thought that he advocates, and that he associates with 'redemption', 'presupposes a standpoint removed, even though by a hair's breadth, from the scope of existence'.[76] In these ways, the words of a scholar of kabbalism are modified in the guts of his Marxist contemporaries. It is tempting to wonder too whether Shestov's comments on Pascal wormed their way into Scholem's consciousness and from thence, according to the intestinal logic of an intellectual virus, into Benjamin's, and even Bloch's and Adorno's, too.

At the end of the penultimate paragraph of 'Gethsemane Night', discussing Pascal's refusal to acquit Descartes of using reason, paradoxically, to re-enchant the world, to blind humanity and restore it to a state of 'magic and bewilderment', Shestov asks: 'How can the world be freed from this torpor, how can man be freed from the power of death?' Among other rhetorical questions, he also asks, 'Who will give us the great courage to abandon the gifts of reason and to "brutalize" ourselves? Who will make the sorrows of Job weigh more heavily than the sands of the sea?'[77] The final paragraph is as follows:

Pascal replies: '*Jésus sera en agonie jusqu'à la fin du monde*' ('Jesus will be in travail until the end of the world'). God Himself has added His own infinite sufferings to the sufferings of Job, and at the end of the world the sufferings of God and the sufferings of man will weigh more heavily than the sands of the sea. Pascal's philosophy, so unlike any which is usually called by that name, tells us not to seek strength or assurance in this bewitched world; for we must not rest, we must not sleep. ... This commandment is not for all, but only for certain 'elect' or 'martyrs'. For should they in their turn sleep as the great apostle slept upon that memorable night, the sacrifice of God will have been in vain, and death will triumph definitely and for ever in the world.[78]

The opening sentence of the final paragraph of *Gethsemane Night* is something like the eighth or ninth time that, either verbatim or in the form of a close paraphrase, Shestov has cited the formulation from Pascal about sleeplessness that he takes as the essay's epigraph. It is no longer a theological statement; it has become a religious incantation.

Boris Groys characterizes the citations from Shestov's favourite philosophers that, in his articles and books, he typically liked to repeat again and again, as 'wounds or sores that cut into the body of [his] language, and could never be cured', adding that, like Job himself, he 'constantly scratches or licks these sores, but they never heal'. This is persuasive as well as evocative. There is indeed something 'forced, diseased, even pathological' about these repetitions, and they do resemble the symptoms of 'the fixation of traumatic events that Freud described, bound up with frustration or fulfilment of desire'. Of course, it is pointless speculating about the psycho-biographical origins of these obsessive repetitions. The 'Shestovian philosophical eros', as Groys recognizes, cannot be captured so simplistically.[79] Better, I think, to interpret them as relentless attempts to assimilate the most potent thoughts of those he admires – not, certainly, in order to neutralize them, for even if he suffers from an anxiety of philosophical influence in relation to them, he is committed to preserving their potency, their capacity for disrupting rationalist assumptions; but, instead, so as to internalize their meaning in some fundamental, almost physiological sense. He uses his voice, and the ritual of ventriloquizing certain

significant formulations, as a means of inscribing them on his body. In the
context of *Gethsemane Night*, it is as if the repetition of Pascal's imprecation
to sleeplessness will itself induce a sort of spiritual sleeplessness. It needs to be
added, of course, that obsessive repetition, the apparently eternal recurrence
of one or two particular thoughts, is itself characteristic of the operations of
consciousness in an insomniac state. Shestov's repetitions here mime at the
level of form the philosophical content of the piece.

The slight shock, at the end of Shestov's short book on Pascal, though, is
his reference to the 'elect': 'We must not rest, we must not sleep. ... This
commandment is not for all, but only for certain "elect" or "martyrs"'. It
threatens to expose the political limitations of Shestov's insistence that, in
the face of suffering, we must remain eternally, fanatically vigilant. For there
is an implicitly Nietzschean identification here of the mass of people with
an insensible, somnambulant herd. Wakefulness and watchfulness, Shestov
seems to propose, constitute the responsibility or task of a spiritual elite. Here
Gethsemane Night seems to build on an argument in *Dostoevsky and Nietzsche:
The Philosophy of Tragedy*, published in book form exactly two decades earlier, in
1903. There, Dostoevsky and Nietzsche are effectively identified, to paraphrase
James Joyce, as ideal insomniacs. Above all, Shestov singled out Nietzsche,
suffering from 'dreadful anguish' as a result of the travails to which he had been
subjected by the prevailing 'morality', for the agonistic, if not heroic quality of
his sleeplessness, which signally distinguished him from 'the slumbering people
and their soporific virtues'. 'At a time when, to use Dostoevsky's words, the
laws of nature, i.e. sickness, had deprived Nietzsche of sleep and rest', Shestov
observes, 'the laws of mankind, as if in mockery, were demanding composure
and sleep of him and, as is their custom, threatening anathema in case their
demand was not met'. Insomnia is at the same time both a physical and
psychological affliction for Nietzsche and a sort of ethical duty. It is emblematic
of a profound spiritual restlessness and watchfulness that represents humanity's
only chance of salvation, as Shestov remarks of Dostoevsky and Nietzsche:

> They have understood that man's future, if man really has a future, rests
> not on those who now rejoice in the belief that they already possess both
> goodness and justice, but on those who know neither sleep, rest, nor joy,

and who continue to struggle and search. Abandoning their old ideals, they go to meet a new reality, however terrible and disgusting it may be.[80]

If there is hope for the future, to echo George Orwell's *1984* (1949), it lies with the sleepless.

In a fine discussion of Shestov, Deleuze and Fondane, Bruce Baugh has maintained that, if Deleuze and Shestov's shared emphasis on the 'private thinker' seems elitist, then the 'elite' nonetheless 'consists of those individuals blessed and cursed by the personal necessity of thinking and acting outside the conventions governing society'. 'If it is an aristocracy', Baugh underlines, 'it is an aristocracy of the damned'.[81] Paul, Luther, Pascal, Kierkegaard, Nietzsche; Dostoevsky, Chekhov and their underground characters – all are elective members of this aristocracy of the damned. Uncle Vanya, the eponymous character of what Shestov calls Chekhov's 'last rebellious work', his 'last trial of loud public protest', is a heroic example of this elite. For in his hopelessness and, in the end, his mindlessness, 'he is ready to fire all the cannon on earth, to beat every drum, to ring every bell':

> To him it seems that the whole of mankind, the whole of the universe, is sleeping, that the neighbours must be awakened. He is prepared for any extravagance, having no rational way of escape; for to confess at once that there is no escape is beyond the capacity of any man.[82]

Here, folded into Shestov's philosophy of tragedy, are the politics of awakening inseparable from it. Only when there is no escape is it possible to escape. Only when the situation is hopeless is it possible to hope. At this moment of crisis, as humanity sleeps, the neighbours must be awakened by any means necessary.

Conclusion
Auschwitz and the end of the world

I

In his seminar on 'grounding' from the second half of the 1950s, Gilles
Deleuze sketched what he called 'the equatorial zones of thought, a struggle
against evidence'. It is an echo not only of Shestov's essay on Dostoevsky, 'The
Conquest of the Self-Evident', published in the *Nouvelle Revue Française* in
1923, but – more importantly – of his first essay on Husserl, 'Memento Mori',
which first appeared in French in the *Revue philosophique* in 1926, when it
had a decisive impact on the German philosopher's emergent reputation.
In the latter context, attacking Husserl and other rationalist philosophers
for predicating their thought on average bourgeois experience and failing
to account for the extremities of human life, Shestov states: 'We must have
the courage to say it firmly: the middle zones of human and universal life
do not at all resemble the polar and equatorial zones.'[1] Deleuze's 'equatorial
zones', for their part, are the intemperate, tropical regions in which a kind of
overheated, exhausted reason is forced to remain silent – like some senescent
colonialist suddenly forced to admit he is defeated – because 'it has not
learned anything about the singularity'; that is, about some exceptional,
perhaps contingent phenomenon that remains radically resistant to the
logic of generalization. Significantly, Deleuze opened his discussion with
this sentence: 'Shestov asked: "what accounts for all the victims of the
Inquisition?"'[2]

In fact, Deleuze here misattributes to Shestov a famous passage from a letter written by the influential Russian literary critic Vissarion Belinsky in 1841 (Shestov cited it on at least three occasions, almost appropriating it in the process, so perhaps it is possible to excuse Deleuze for his mistake).[3] In this letter, privately confessing that he did not feel fully committed to the principles of humanitarianism, idealism and universal progress that he professed in public, Belinsky colourfully, but also movingly, rejected Hegel's philosophy because of its failure morally to account for the horrors of history:

> If I should succeed in ascending to the highest rung of the ladder of development, even there I would ask you to render me an account of all the victims of circumstance in life and history, of all the victims of chance, of superstition, of the Inquisition of Philip II, etc., etc.: otherwise I would fling myself headfirst from the highest rung. I do not wish happiness even as a gift, if my mind is not at rest regarding each one of my blood brothers.

Belinsky's devastating point, consistent with the sentiments of Dostoevsky, his fanatical disciple at this time, was that, even if he were to benefit individually from the most sophisticated achievements of advanced civilization, he could not remain comfortable in his own skin if he were at the same time conscious that the philosophy he avowed proved unable to explain the cruel, often contingent circumstances in which people had become the victims of history.[4] A philosophy cannot claim to be a document of culture, to put it in Benjaminian terms, if it cannot account for barbarism; indeed, in this situation, it is itself, in consequence, a document of barbarism. Or as Adorno wrote of negative dialectics, 'If thought is not measured by the extremity that eludes the concept, it is from the outset in the nature of the musical accompaniment with which the SS liked to drown out the screams of its victims.'[5]

Shestov had quoted the passage from Belinsky's letter in *The Good in the Teaching of Tolstoy and Nietzsche* (1900) and, more recently, from both a lecture on 'Kierkegaard and Dostoevsky' from 1935 that subsequently served as the introductory chapter of *Kierkegaard and the Existential Philosophy* (1936) and a lecture on Dostoevsky, delivered on the radio in 1937, entitled 'On the "Regeneration of Convictions"'. He was in general profoundly critical of Belinksy, whose emphasis on morality he took to be fatal to the spirit of philosophy; but he discerned in this letter a refusal of the idealism and rationalism to which Belinsky officially adhered – one conducted, moreover, in the name of the victims of history – that it seemed important, if not compulsory, to proclaim.

In the Preface to the book on Nietzsche and Tolstoy, which he devotes entirely to Belinsky's letter, even though he also discusses it in the seventh section of the book, Shestov explores the literary critic's private apostasy in some detail. He opens by mocking Belinsky's credulous assumption that Enlightenment philosophy, with its commitment to the idea that 'the supreme end lies in some general principle to which individuals must be sacrificed', could ever have been expected to reckon in some meaningful moral sense with the destructiveness of history:

> What compensation should Hegel be able to give Belinsky for every victim of history, for every victim of Philip II? Philip II burned hosts of heretics at the stake; but what kind of absurdity is it to demand accounting for it today? These victims were burned long ago; no restoration is possible; the matter is forever ended. No Hegel can do anything here; to demand accounting for these creatures tortured to death and prematurely perished, to become angry because of them, to appeal to the whole world – is obviously too late.[6]

Of course, atrocities of this sort cannot be consigned as neatly to the past as Shestov insists, as current debates about the politics of reparations for the cruelties of the slave trade are enough to indicate. Furthermore, 'the image of enslaved ancestors', as Benjamin referred to it in his theses 'On the Concept of History' (1940), is often the most productive means of fostering both the *ressentiment* and the 'spirit of sacrifice' that are necessary preconditions for the revolt of an oppressed class.[7] But Shestov's substantive claim, that the sentiments in Belinsky's letter comprise a sort of category mistake because they naively misunderstand the ideological and methodological assumptions on which the idealist thinking of the Enlightenment operates, is persuasive.

If Hegel's thought is founded on the belief that 'all that is real is rational' and that history therefore 'cannot and must not be other than it is', as Shestov put it in his discussion of Belinsky in the book on Kierkegaard, then how can it possibly be expected to accommodate an understanding of the tradition of the oppressed?[8] The 'demands that Belinsky directed to Hegel', Shestov concludes in the 1900 text, are 'strange, unfulfillable'. And, in so far as these demands leave the political presuppositions of Enlightenment philosophy intact because they are fundamentally unrealistic, they reinforce its 'quietism' – 'that terrible condition that up until now has frightened back the boldest people before many similar theories'.[9] In 'On the "Regeneration of Convictions"', returning almost forty years later to the letter, Shestov emphasizes that, for both Belinsky and Dostoevsky, Hegel's blandishments about the real being rational represent not 'a decisive end, a calming answer' but, on the contrary, the beginning of 'eternal, terrible, unescapable anxiety'. 'It is impossible to live, impossible to accept the world', Shestov adds in a devastating sentence, 'so long as we have not obtained an account of all the sacrifices of our brothers in blood'.[10]

In the Preface to the book on Nietzsche and Tolstoy, Shestov's most substantive discussion of Belinsky's confession, he goes on to argue that philosophy must not simply account for individual and collective suffering; implicitly, it must also be active rather than passive in the face of it. He pointedly discriminates between mere 'pathos', of the kind presumably exhibited by Belinsky in his correspondence, and philosophy as it should be – what Shestov affirms as 'the genuine, all-embracing philosophy which clearly and distinctly explains why Philip II and world history have tortured and still torture men'.[11] His emphasis here on barbarism in the present as well as in the past, and on the need for philosophy to assume some form of responsibility in the face of it, is extremely powerful. In the prefatory chapter to *Kierkegaard and the Existential Philosophy*, which is in general far more religious in its emphases than the earlier, more secular treatment of Belinsky, he briefly pursues this attention to contemporary history further. The central term of this later discussion of philosophy's responsibility in relation to human suffering is not so much History as the Fall, which Shestov identifies of course with Man's eating of the fruit of the Tree of Knowledge, that is, with the acquisition of reason. But this narrative, too, is implicitly given a political impetus. 'The Fall of Man has troubled human thought since earliest times,' Shestov writes at the start of the second paragraph; 'Men have always felt that all is not right with the world, and even that much is wrong: "Something is rotten in the state of Denmark," to use Shakespeare's words.'[12]

In this allusion to *Hamlet*, and to the rottenness of the political state, it is impossible not to catch an echo too of the line that, as we have seen, Shestov repeatedly cites in his *oeuvre*, namely, 'The time is out of joint'. Shestov does not believe that it is the task of the philosopher, in Hamlet's exasperated phrase, 'to set it right' (1, 5, 189); he does believe that the philosopher must directly address the rottenness of the dislocated, disarticulated, deranged conditions that prevail:

> The question is put to us, the men of the twentieth century, just as it was put to the ancients: whence comes sin, whence comes the horrors of life which are linked with sin? Is there a defect in being itself, which, since it is created, albeit by God, since it has a beginning, must inescapably, by virtue of that eternal law that is subject to no one and nothing, be burdened down by its imperfections, which doom it ahead of time to destruction? Or do sin and evil arise from 'knowledge', from 'open eyes', from 'intellectual vision', that is, from the fruit of the forbidden tree?[13]

The 'open eyes' of Reason, it will be recalled, denote not attentiveness and brightness of vision, but precisely its opposite: that is, a dream-filled, somnambulistic state. Not hyper-consciousness but unconsciousness. Shestov's response to this situation, his solution to a history full of horrors through which people sleepwalk, is – sleeplessness. Wakefulness. Watchfulness. Eternal, vigilant attentiveness before the tragic hopelessness of the present.

Deleuze, to return to the French philosopher, misattributing Belinsky's statement about Philip II to Shestov, reframes it in terms of a question, namely, 'What accounts for all the victims of the Inquisition?' He then goes on to discuss Kierkegaard's and Nietzsche's attempts to 'reconcile thought with the categories of life'. 'Thought must think the absolutely different', Deleuze argues; 'Thought ultimately goes beyond reason, goes all the way to the end.' The text of Deleuze's seminar, recorded or transcribed at the time but not published until many decades later, is at times slightly obscure, but I take the atrocities of the Inquisition in the second half of the sixteenth century to be an instance of the 'absolutely different', an instance of 'the singularity'. For these atrocities pressed a rationalist enterprise to the point at which reason collapsed. Adorno and Horkheimer called it 'the indefatigable self-destructiveness of enlightenment' (though they nonetheless insisted, more than Shestov or Deleuze did, on remaining inside the ambit of enlightenment in order to redeem it).[14] Confronted with this kind of ongoing catastrophe, thought itself has to go beyond reason in order to think the catastrophe. In the first half of the twentieth century, of course, there were all too many instances of the absolutely alien or 'different'. There were all too many collective historical traumas that, as the extreme outcome of reason, and according to a dialectical logic, pitched reason into crisis. In this context, too, and above all in relation to the event of the Holocaust, only a thought that is capable of going beyond reason can think the singularity. What accounts, we might ask, for all the victims of the Holocaust?

In the aftermath of the First World War, Shestov appropriated Pascal's statement that there should be no sleep until the end of the world in an attempt to impart a force to it that was not simply spiritual but, in effect, political. Almost a century later, we need perhaps to reclaim Shestov's restatement that that there should be no sleep until the end of the world in order to reinforce these political implications. Here, Adorno can be of assistance, for he too was inspired by Pascal's imprecation that sleep is impossible, indeed finally undesirable, in the face of insupportable suffering; he therefore presents an opportunity for re-appropriating and politicizing Shestov's interpretation of Pascal. Although they are profoundly different philosophers, Shestov and Adorno were both invested in the idea that the Enlightenment had enacted a dialectic of destruction, and that 'the fully enlightened earth', in the latter's words, 'radiates disaster triumphant'.[15] Both were profoundly indebted, furthermore, to the traditions of negative theology (in a letter to Benjamin, one in which he discussed both Kierkegaard and Pascal, Adorno once described their shared, ongoing intellectual project in terms of an 'inverse theology').[16] Interestingly, in fact, both Shestov and Adorno published studies of Kierkegaard, one of the great thinkers of the counter-Enlightenment, in the 1930s: the German's, *Kierkegaard: Construction of the Aesthetic*, his first book, based on his Habilitation, appeared in 1933; the Russian's, *Kierkegaard and the Existential Philosophy*, his penultimate book, a study in ethics rather than aesthetics, appeared in French in 1936, the year he visited Palestine in honour of his seventieth birthday. But it is in 'Commitment' (1962), which appeared almost forty years after Shestov's *Gethsemane Night* (1923), that Adorno invoked 'The Mystery of Jesus'. There, reflecting on Europe's descent into barbarism in the mid-twentieth century, and on the Holocaust in particular, he wrote: 'The abundance of real suffering tolerates no forgetting; Pascal's theological saying, *On ne doit pas dormir*, must be secularized.'[17]

In secularizing Pascal's shattering injunction, Adorno left out its apocalyptic reference to the temporality of eternity, even though he insistently retained its emphasis on vigilance. But it needs, I think, to be retained. Shestov, for his part, in contrast to Adorno, demanded that Pascal's dictum should be uncompromisingly submitted to as a spiritual, not merely a political, imperative. If he had lived through the first half of the 1940s, he might have insisted that, just as there can be no poetry after Auschwitz, so there can be no sleep after Auschwitz. No sleep after Auschwitz; no sleep 'til the end of the world. Of course, from one perspective, Auschwitz is itself the end of the world. Philippe Lacoue-Labarthe, for example, refers to 'the Auschwitz apocalypse'.[18] It is the climactic self-destruction of reason. The Holocaust announces the self-immolation of the Enlightenment project. And after this end of the world, as distinct from the end of this world, there can be no sleep. At the same time, there must be no sleep 'til the end of the world. This second, climactic apocalypse, the one that is to come, will mark the time when Auschwitz can be redeemed. It will announce a world in which the Holocaust is impossible. An insomnia between two apocalyptic events. No sleep after Auschwitz. No sleep 'til the end of the world.

Perhaps this is the slogan we need to adopt in the early twenty-first century, as memories of the obscene crimes committed by one imperial state or another in the name of rationalism during the first half of the twentieth-century fade; at a time when the forces of reaction, including various forms of fascism, seem to be in the ascendancy in Europe and the United States. As Camus wrote in *The Myth of Sisyphus* in the early 1940s, 'These are our nights of Gethsemane'.[19]

II

In focusing some of the political implications of Shestov's Pascalian incitement to insomnia, we might turn finally to a poem by his disciple, the film-maker, poet and philosopher Fondane, who was the most formally inventive as well as the most passionate exponent of the Russian's philosophy. Fondane, who from 1932 lived on the rue Rollin in Paris, the very street on which Pascal had lived, was arrested by the Gestapo in 1942, after collaborationists reported him to the authorities because of his Jewish identity. He was eventually deported to Auschwitz-Birkenau, There, in October 1944, a mere two weeks before Soviet soldiers liberated the camp, he was exterminated.

In Fondane's sequence of poems titled *Ulysses* (1933), published in the year the Nazis acceded to power, he dedicated one section, the thirty-seventh, to his friend and mentor Lev Shestov. These are its last four lines in French:

je ne peux pas fermer les yeux,
je dois crier toujours jusqu'à la fin du monde:
'il ne faut pas dormir jusqu'à la fin du monde'
– je ne suis q'un témoin.[20]

I cannot close my eyes; I must shout 'til the end of the world. I must shout, at all times, for all time. Here is an emphatic, indeed militant reaffirmation of Pascal's calamitous sentence from 'The Mystery of Jesus', which Fondane cites in Shestov's version: 'There must be no sleep 'til the end of the world.' In a final statement of defiance, one that is no doubt complicated by a faint, mournful sense of defeat, Fondane then concludes, ' – I am only a witness.'

Fondane was a victim of history's horrors, but – as this poem testifies – he was also a witness to them. And a witness not only in the sense of a passive spectator but as someone who actively and vigilantly attempted to account for history's horrors, and to pre-empt them. He shouted in order to prevent people from sleepwalking into the death camps. 'The Fascist offensive, which is imminent, must be stopped,' he warned with chilling prescience in 1934; 'Tomorrow in the concentration camps it will be too late to repent. The struggle must begin now, while there is still time, before the final destruction.'[21] Fondane stared at the horrors of history not merely with passive vision, like Benjamin's Angel of History, but with active vision. The Angel of Death thus visited him in a double sense: as a victim of the Nazis; and, in Shestov's redemptive re-inscription of this figure, as someone who, like Dostoevsky, 'sees strange and new things, more than other men see and more than he himself sees with his natural eyes.'[22] Among these things, he perceived the victims of history concealed beneath the veneer of civilization's vaunted achievements. As Fondane put it in his book on Rimbaud, *Rimbaud le voyou* (1933), published like *Ulysses* the year Hitler became Chancellor of Germany, every Idea 'has at least a hundred thousand murders on its conscience'.[23]

Bruce Baugh has rightly underlined that 'Fondane's unlimited affirmation of the real', like that of Shestov, 'must not be confused with "resignation" or acceptance of the world as it is.' For, on the contrary, like Deleuze's tragic affirmation, it 'is also a critique of accepted values and "things as they are"'.[24] Implicitly, like Benjamin, Fondane recognized that, in Nazi-occupied Europe, or in capitalist society itself, 'things as they are' precisely constitute a state of emergency. And that philosophy, or in Benjamin's case the 'conception of history', had to fight in order to be consistent 'with this insight'.[25] In 1940, at the start of the German Spring offensive, Fondane wrote to his wife and sister, telling them that it was 'better to perish if the world knows no gods but Hitler', but adding: 'But let us take heart. *This is the moment to live our existential philosophy*.'[26] Living an existential philosophy, in the face of an ongoing emergency, entailed what Fondane called 'irresignation', a dramatic, emblematic political refusal, comparable perhaps to Herbert Marcuse's Great Refusal, if undoubtedly more individualistic. Fondane urged people to testify 'by poetry, by cries, by faith, or by suicide'.[27]

The social and political emergency, and the irresignation it provokes in men and women like Fondane, is generative. It stimulates acts of self-creation, and self-destruction, that pitch the rationalist ideology underpinning the oppressive operations of the state and its agents into crisis. It promotes a fundamental questioning of the Enlightenment and its inheritance, as this Shestovian statement from the Preface to Fondane's *Unhappy Consciousness* (1936) indicates: 'Questions such as "What is knowledge? From where does it derive its right to judge and to decree what is self-evident?" do not get raised in the daylight of wisdom but in a night so black that you end up thinking you have gone blind.' Echoing Rimbaud, Fondane goes on to invoke the night as the site of counter-Enlightenment:

Night? So be it! Marvelous and terrible night! Suffocating night, in which everything collapses, where thought finds nothing to cling to if not itself, 'thought latching on to thought and tugging'. This anguished thought is not yet *free*, but freedom is among its *possibilities*. It divines, it senses, that the *most important thing* is not to build a science according to the measure of man but to raise man up to the level of his existence, to decide the outcome of the most terrible of conflicts.[28]

It is not at dusk but in the horrifying depths of the night that the Owl of Minerva flies. It is at the midnight of the century that Shestov's and Fondane's unreason, confronted with the forces of reaction, which press their rationalist dreams of domination to the point of irrationalism, offers the remote but not impossible prospect of some apocalyptic redemption.

Fondane's heroic paradigm, in his attempt to rehabilitate Shestov's philosophy of tragedy in the face of his generation's European apocalypse, is Shakespearean. But he is not thinking of the Russian's hero Hamlet so much as of Macbeth (about whom Shestov had also written, incidentally, in *Shakespeare and his Critic Brandes* (1898)).[29] It is Macbeth's invocations of the chaos of night, a night that tears apart the subject and induces the collapse both of Reason and the State, that Fondane has in mind when he cries, 'Night? So be it! Marvelous and terrible night!' Recall the speech that Macbeth gives after he has murdered Duncan and before he has murdered Banquo:

> Come, seeling night,
> Scarf up the tender eye of pitiful day
> And with thy bloody and invisible hand
> Cancel and tear to pieces that great bond
> Which keeps me pale. (3, 2, 48-52)

In a rotten state in the aftermath of war, when the time seems terminally out of joint, only destructive gestures that 'cancel and tear to pieces' are sufficiently creative. '*Sound and fury!*' Fondane screams in 'Man before History' (1939), directly quoting Shakespeare's darkest tragic hero; 'An immense howl of terror rises up from our wretched earth, and we ourselves are half crushed.'[30]

Macbeth, implicitly, in spite of his insanity, or because of it, promises an escape from the apparently insuperable choice, at this moment, months before the outbreak of the Second World War, between what Fondane calls 'the National Socialist Caliban', clamouring at the gates, and 'the humanist Prospero', 'who used to believe – and, what is worse, continues to believe – that it is still up to him to introduce *die Vernunft in der Geschichte*, reason into history'.[31] Macbeth is the prototype of desperate, tragic rebellion in the face of this false choice because of his sheer abjection, exemplified by his insomniac state, which he vividly describes in terms of lying 'on the torture of the mind … / In restless ecstasy' (3, 2, 23–4). In plunging into the abyss, in becoming intimate with a state of non-being that is both individual and historical, Macbeth becomes a hero. In becoming hopeless, he creates the condition in which hope – 'a hope beyond hopelessness' as the narrator of Thomas Mann's *Doctor Faustus* (1947) puts it – might be possible.[32] Terry Eagleton calls this hope, which is 'grounded in catastrophe', 'tragic hope'.[33] Fondane's claim is that 'the supreme heroism – I mean the most difficult thing for man – is not sacrificing one's life but *admitting spiritual defeat*'. This is why the Macbeth of Act V, when Shakespeare's anti-hero is at his loneliest and most humiliated, is the one he seeks to emulate: 'It is only when man has been broken, defeated, to the point of daring to cry out that life is a tale told by an idiot, a nightmare, that the soul resorts to extraordinary measures.'[34] In his discussion of Shakespeare, Fondane is surely recalling Shestov's observation in *Gethsemane Night* that, 'like Macbeth, Pascal would fain "murder sleep"', and that, 'worse still, he seems to demand that all mankind should associate itself with him in this horrid task'.[35] Shestov and Fondane themselves demand that humanity become sleepless.

The tragic heroism of Macbeth, Fondane continues in 'Man before History', that of a broken, defeated individual who might nonetheless represent a paradigm for political and spiritual redemption, is comparable to 'that offered to us by Christ: "Eli, Eli, *lama sabachtani*?"'[36] But if Fondane is thinking of Christ on the cross, deserted and forsaken, then he might equally be thinking of Christ in Gethsemane, abandoned by his friends as well as by his God. For as Shestov had demonstrated in *Gethsemane Night*, this Christ is arguably an even more compelling precedent in the tragic struggle to redeem personal suffering at a moment of political danger. Like Shestov, Fondane urged an open-eyed vision, eternally insomniac, that is so total it resembles blindness more than ordinary sight. As a witness, he stared at history as if under compulsion to do so, incapable of closing his eyes. Like Kierkegaard, according to Shestov, he 'stood with open eyes before the horrors of being'. In the face of this, though, he insisted not only on remaining awake but also on shouting until the end of the world. He thereby invoked the voices, the inarticulate cries, of those whom Shestov identifies as the representatives of a messianic tradition. He invoked what Shestov describes as 'the "screams" of Job, the "lamentations" of Jeremiah, the thundering of the prophets and the Apocalypse'.[37] These scarcely articulate cries, which resist reason on the one side and refuse silence on the other, force 'all thoughts', as Adorno once formulated it, to 'converge upon the concept of something that would differ from the unspeakable world that is'.[38]

To be sleepless until the end of the world, and to insist on shouting incessantly during that time, is to mark a messianic limit to the ongoing emergency. The sleeplessness, the shouting, will end; but they will end not because they will one day simply cease, but because the conditions that render both shouting and not sleeping necessary or merely possible will themselves one day pass.

III

There is, in the end, a more drastic, even shocking sense in which Shestov, here probably at his most aggressively counter-intuitive, argues for the end or abolition of a world in which intolerable traumatic events such as Auschwitz occur (and, having occurred, effectively go on occurring; for, as Adorno explains in pointing out that Auschwitz represents a 'relapse into barbarism', the horror is that 'barbarism continues as long as the fundamental conditions that favoured that relapse continue largely unchanged').[39] It is not simply that Shestov envisions a world in which horrifying events of this kind do not happen or will not happen; he envisions a world in which such events have not happened. More precisely, to deploy the future perfect tense for the purposes of clarification, they will not have happened. In effect, Shestov imagines a future in which the past can in some fundamental sense be undone. This is the outcome, logical or illogical, of his claim that 'all things are possible'.

Nikolai Berdyaev was especially attentive to this particular anti-rational strain in Shestov's thinking. In the essay he wrote in the immediate aftermath of his friend's death in November 1938, Berdyaev observed that 'the chief point of the Shestovian theme' was the conviction that 'if there is a God, then all possibilities are open, the truths of reason cease to be inevitable, and the terrors of life are conquerable'. This slightly sentimental statement, which implies that Shestov's philosophy offers Christian consolations, appears in part to be an attempt to domesticate Shestov's intrinsically alien ideas; but the succeeding sentences are nonetheless sensitive to Shestov's commitment to the mysterious notion that past events might in the future be erased or reversed:

> Connected with it is that profound shaking which characterizes all of the philosopher's thought. Can God bring it about that that which has been becomes something which has not been? For reason this is the most incomprehensible of things. Shestov can very easily be misunderstood. The poisoned Socrates, so he says, might have been resurrected – the Christians believed this; Kierkegaard might have had his fiancée returned to him; Nietzsche might have been cured of his horrible sickness. But it is not this at all that Shestov wishes to say. He means rather that God might have ordained it so that Socrates would not have been poisoned, that Kierkegaard would not have lost his fiancée, that Nietzsche would not have been stricken by the horrible sickness. An absolute victory is possible over that necessity which rational knowledge imposes on the past.

Shestov, Berdyaev concludes, 'was tortured by the inevitability of the past; he was tortured by the horror of what once happened'.[40]

The matter is not as simple as Berdyaev implies, however. It is not merely that God might have 'ordained it so that Socrates would not have been poisoned'. Shestov's enigmatic argument is more complex than that; and he certainly doesn't resort to God as if to a magic wand, which is the simplistic impression that Berdyaev's attempt to explicate the point creates. In the relevant short sections of *Athens and Jerusalem* (1938), in fact, Shestov doesn't mention God. In the first of these, 'The Possible', which is the thirty-third section of the book's final part, entitled 'On the Second Dimension of Thought', Shestov's thesis is that if it is 'the unshakeable law of existence' that 'everything that has a beginning has an end, everything that is born must die', then this is also true of ... truths: 'For there are truths which have not always existed, which were born in time.' Truth is historical. It is not eternal. There is a time before something is true, he argues, and there might therefore be a time after which something is no longer true:

> Four hundred years before Christ the truth, 'the Athenians poisoned Socrates', still did not exist; it was born in the year 399 [BCE]. And it still lives, although it took place almost 2,500 years ago. Does this mean it will live eternally? If it must disappear like everything that is born, if the general law that we apply with such assurance to everything that exists does not – as a truth *a priori* – admit of any exception, then there will come a moment when the truth about the poisoning of Socrates will die and cease to exist. And our descendants will then have the possibility of affirming that the Athenians did *not* poison Socrates, but that, quite simply (or, on the contrary, not 'simply' at all) men lived a certain time, a very long time even, in an illusion which they took for an eternal truth because they forgot, through chance or intentionally, the law of birth and death and its ineluctable character.[41]

In a subsequent section of *Athens and Jerusalem*, the fifty-eighth, entitled 'The Possible and the Impossible', Shestov reinforces the point. There, he contends that if the idea of a 'round square or a wooden piece of iron' is a contradiction – 'an absurdity and, consequently, an impossibility' – then so potentially is the idea of 'the poisoned Socrates'. 'Could not one discover a tribunal', he asks, which had the authority to establish 'that the poisoning of Socrates, being contradictory, is an absurdity and that, consequently, Socrates was not poisoned, while a round square is not at all absurd and, consequently, it is quite possible that it may someday be found?'[42]

Shestov's implausible but not entirely illogical proposition, which cannot be dismissed as mystical, is that not only the emergence of truth but also its disappearance is historically contingent. There is nothing sinister going on here. He is not gesturing to the sort of 'tribunal' that, erasing the role of inconvenient individuals and social collectives, re-inscribed and reinvented the past for cynically ideological purposes in Hitler's Germany or Stalin's Russia. The 'tribunal' he has in mind, far from being totalitarian, is one that operates on the divine principle, as he perceived it, of anti-Necessity. It does not implement order but disrupts it. It does not 'excise the incommensurable', as Adorno and Horkheimer remark of the Enlightenment, but deliberately cultivates it.[43] Shestov's commitment to the critique of reason involves imagining a time in which that which has happened has in some sense not happened. This is both because Socrates might not have been poisoned, since it was not inevitable that he should be poisoned; and because if there was a time before which it was not true that someone called Socrates was poisoned, then there will be a time after which it will not be true that this event took place. Socrates will not have been poisoned. There will ultimately be a world, Shestov implies, in which the statement 'Socrates was poisoned' will not make sense. The statement will have become impossible.

Here is what might be identified as the utopian impulse that secretly animates Shestov's philosophy of tragedy. 'Creation from the void', he called it in his account of Chekhov … Here is the 'principle of hope', in Ernst Bloch's phrase, concealed in his account of hopelessness.[44] Here is the 'standpoint of redemption', in Adorno's phrase, from which the condition of damnation to which we are condemned might be seen in a 'messianic light'. As Adorno put it in the 'Finale' to *Minima Moralia* (1944), his 'Reflections on Damaged Life', 'the only philosophy which can be responsibly practiced in face of despair is the attempt to contemplate all things from the standpoint of redemption'. 'Knowledge', he added, in a statement whose counter-Enlightenment sentiment might have appealed to Shestov, 'has no light but that shed on the world by redemption; all else is reconstruction, mere technique'.[45] Shestov radically affirms a future perfect tense in which, because he prophesies a universe in which anti-Necessity finally supervenes, transforming the conditions in which cause and effect unfold from one another in linear narrative sequence, terrible historical events that retrospectively seem to have been inevitable simply will not have taken place. Shestov's thinking thus conforms to the demand that Adorno later made so movingly in his *Negative Dialectics* (1966), with the precedent of Auschwitz tacitly in mind, when he affirmed that 'if thought is not decapitated it will flow into transcendence, down to the idea of a world that would not only abolish extant suffering but revoke the suffering that is irrevocably past'.[46] Shestov's philosophy of tragedy, practiced in the face of despair, is an attempt to contemplate past, present and future from the standpoint of redemption; that is, from an apocalyptic perspective in which even the suffering that is irrevocably past might be revoked.

Shestov's messianic claim is that the world in which history is a procession of horrors, from the barbarities of the Inquisition to those of the Nazis' industrial death machine, will one day end, and that – as when Christ was crucified – the meaning of history itself will be retroactively transformed in the process. At this apocalypse, the Angel of Death, unlike Benjamin's Angel of History, will indeed 'awaken the dead, and make whole what has been smashed'.[47] In the meantime, in our collective struggle both to revoke the suffering that is irrevocably past, in Adorno's formulation, and to bring about a future in which suffering itself is irrevocably past, we must be actively, even preternaturally, wakeful and watchful. In these our nights of Gethsemane, we must embody not the somnambulant *homo dormiens* but – subsisting in a state of permanent eschatological tension – *homo vigilans*. Jesus will be in agony until the end of this world; there must be no sleeping during that time.

'Who', Alain Badiou has asked, 'in the darkness in which we find ourselves, and which is the obsolescence and erasure of politics, watches over the morning, wearing out and destroying the night?'[48] Lev Shestov, philosopher of the sleepless night.

Notes

Introduction

1 Joel Chandler Harris, *Balaam and His Master and Other Sketches and Stories* (New York: Houghton, Mifflin, 1891), 34.

2 William Melvin Kelley, 'If You're Woke You Dig It', *New York Times Magazine* (20 May 1962), 45.

3 Amanda Hess, 'Earning the "Woke" Badge', *New York Times Magazine* (19 April 2016), 13.

4 William Melvin Kelley, *A Different Drummer* (London: riverrun, 2018).

5 Kelley, 'If You're Woke You Dig It', 45.

6 Nicole Holliday, 'How "Woke" Fell Asleep' – http://blog.oxforddictionaries.com/2016/11/woke/

7 Lev Shestov, 'Words that Are Swallowed Up: Plotinus's Ecstasies', in *In Job's Balances: On the Sources of the Eternal Truths*, trans. Camilla Coventry and C. A. Macartney (Athens: Ohio University Press, 1975), 366.

8 Gene Ray, 'History, Sublime, Terror: Notes on the Politics of Fear', in *The Sublime Now*, ed. Luke White and Claire Pajaczkowska (Newcastle: Cambridge Scholars Publishing, 2009), 148.

9 See Lucien Goldmann, *The Hidden God: A Study of the Tragic Vision in the Pensées of Pascal and the Tragedies of Racine*, trans. Philip Thody (London: Verso, 2016), xxvi. Compare Lev Shestov, 'Children and Stepchildren of Time: Spinoza in History', in *In Job's Balances*, 252.

10 On this tradition, see Craig Koslofsky, *Evening's Empire: A History of the Night in Early Modern Europe* (Cambridge: Cambridge University Press, 2011), 46–90. For further reflections on its influence in the twentieth century, see Matthew Beaumont, 'R.S. Thomas's Poetics of Insomnia', *Essays in Criticism* 68, no. 1 (2018): 74–107.

11 Boris Groys, *Introduction to Antiphilosophy*, trans. David Fernbach (London: Verso, 2012), 33.

12 Ramona Fotiade, 'Introduction to the Second Edition: Lev Shestov – The Thought from Outside', in Lev Shestov, *Athens and Jerusalem*, 2nd edn, trans. Bernard Martin (Athens: Ohio University Press, 2016), 2.

13 Blaise Pascal, *The Mystery of Jesus*, in *Pensées*, trans. A. J. Krailsheimer (Harmondsworth: Penguin, 1995), 289.

14 Lev Shestov, 'Gethsemane Night: Pascal's Philosophy', in *In Job's Balances*, 284.

15 Shestov, 'Gethsemane Night', 284.

16 Walter Benjamin, *The Arcades Project*, trans. Howard Eiland and Kevin McLaughlin (Cambridge, MA: Harvard University Press, 1999), 391.

17 Lev Shestov, 'The Conquest of the Self-Evident: Dostoievsky's Philosophy', in *In Job's Balances*, 29.

18 Alain Badiou, *Lacan: Anti-philosophy 3*, trans. Kenneth Reinhard and Susan Spitzer (New York: Columbia University Press, 2018), 69.

19 Lev Shestov, 'Memento Mori', in *Potestas Clavium*, trans. Bernard Martin (Athens: Ohio University Press, 1968), 358.

20 Michel Foucault, 'Standing Vigil for the Day to Come', trans. Elise Woodard and Robert Harvey, *Foucault Studies* 19 (2015): 219.

21 See Hannah Arendt, *Men in Dark Times* (San Diego: Harcourt, Brace, 1968).

22 J. M. Coetzee, 'Philip Roth, *The Plot Against America*', in *Inner Workings: Essays 2000-2005* (London: Vintage, 2007), 232.

23 Philip Roth, *The Plot Against America* (London: Vintage, 2016), 16.

24 Benjamin Fondane, 'Preface for the First Moment', in *Existential Monday: Philosophical Essays*, ed. and trans. Bruce Baugh (New York: New York Review of Books, 2016), 39.

25 Albert Camus, *The Myth of Sisyphus*, trans. Justin O'Brien (Harmondsworth: Penguin, 2000), 21.

Chapter 1

1 V. V. Zenkovsky, *A History of Russian Philosophy*, Vol. 2 (London: Routledge, 2003), 783.

2 'Every pseudonym is subconsciously a rejection of being an heir, being a descendent, being a son,' writes Shestov's friend Marina Tsvetayeva, though she was not thinking of him: 'A rejection of the father....'. Shestov provided Tsvetayeva with emotional and financial support when she was in Paris in the late 1920s – see 'A Captive Spirit', in *A Captive Spirit: Selected Prose*, ed. and trans. J. Marin King (Ann Arbor: Ardis, 1994), 89. On the semantics of Shestov's pseudonym, see Dominic Rubin, *Holy Russia, Sacred*

Israel: Jewish-Christian Encounters in Russian Religious Thought (Boston: Academic Studies Press, 2010), 217.

3   Sidney Monas, 'New Introduction', in Lev Shestov, *Chekhov and Other Essays* (Ann Arbor: University of Michigan Press, 1966), viii.

4   Rubin, *Holy Russia, Sacred Israel*, 218.

5   Bernard Martin, 'The Life and Thought of Lev Shestov', in Lev Shestov, *Athens and Jerusalem*, trans. Robert Martin (Athens: Ohio University Press, 1966), 26.

6   Emmanuel Levinas, 'Review of Lev Shestov's *Kierkegaard and the Existential Philosophy*', trans. James McLachlan, *Levinas Studies* 11 (2016): 241–2.

7   Lev Shestov, 'Gnosis and Existential Philosophy', in *Speculation and Revelation*, trans. Bernard Martin (Athens: Ohio University Press, 1982), 261.

8   Lev Shestov, 'Penultimate Words', in *Chekhov and Other Essays*, 91–2.

9   Lev Shestov, 'The Gift of Prophecy', in *Chekhov and Other Essays*, 79.

10 Shestov, 'A Thousand and One Nights', in *Potestas Clavium*, 22.

11 Michael Finkenthal, *Lev Shestov: Existential Philosopher and Religious Thinker* (New York: Peter Lang, 2010), 164.

12 Adam Sutcliffe, *Judaism and Enlightenment* (Cambridge: Cambridge University Press, 2003), 261.

13 Shestov, *Athens and Jerusalem*, 65–6.

14 Gershom Scholem, ed., *The Correspondence of Gershom Scholem and Walter Benjamin, 1932-1940*, trans. Gary Smith and Andre Lefevere (New York: Schocken, 1989), 246.

15 Brian Horowitz, 'The Demolition of Reason in Lev Shestov's Athens and Jerusalem [*sic*]', *Poetics Today* 19, no. 2 (1998): 224.

16 Shestov, *Athens and Jerusalem*, 287.

17 Lev Shestov, 'Kierkegaard as a Religious Philosopher', in *Speculation and Revelation*, 215.

18 Shestov, 'Children and Stepchildren of Time: Spinoza in History', 248.

19 For Shestov's critique of scientism as opposed to science per se, see Teresa Obolevitch, *Faith and Science in Russian Religious Thought* (Oxford: Oxford University Press, 2019), 126–33.

20 Shestov, 'Memento Mori (On Edmund Husserl's Theory of Knowledge)', 359.

21 Shestov, 'A Thousand and One Nights', 10–11.

22 Shestov, *Athens and Jerusalem*, 262.

23 Camus, *The Myth of Sisyphus*, 29.

24 Shestov, *Athens and Jerusalem*, 376.

25 David Gascoyne, 'Essay on Léon Chestov', in *Existential Writings*, ed. Ramona Fotiade (Oxford: Amaté Press, 2001), 57, 60.

26 See, for example, Shestov, 'Foreword', in *Athens and Jerusalem*, 65–6.

27 Jürgen Moltmann, 'Praying with Open Eyes', in Jürgen Moltmann and Elisabeth Moltmann-Wendel, *Passion for God: Theology in Two Voices*, ed. Douglas Meeks (Louisville: Westminster John Knox Press, 2003), 59.

28 Lev Shestov, 'Dostoevsky and Nietzsche: The Philosophy of Tragedy', in *Dostoevsky, Tolstoy and Nietzsche*, trans. Bernard Martin (Ohio: Ohio University Press, 1969), 219, 293.

29 Emmanuel Falque, *The Guide to Gethsemane: Anxiety, Suffering, Death*, trans. George Hughes (New York: Fordham University Press, 2019), 54.

30 Karl Barth, *Church Dogmatics*, Vol. 4, ed. G. W. Bromiley and T. F. Torrance (London: T&T Clark, 2010), 258. For a fuller context, though not one that includes this extraordinary comparison, see Paul Dafydd Jones, 'Karl Barth on Gethsemane', *International Journal of Systematic Theology* 9, no. 2 (2007): 148–71.

31 Benjamin Fondane, *Rencontres avec Léon Chestov* (Paris: Non Lieu, 2016), 126–7. See also John Kenneth Hyde, *Benjamin Fondane: A Presentation of His Life and Works* (Paris: Droz, 1971), 65.

32 Rowan Williams, 'Gethsemane', in *Poems of Rowan Williams* (Manchester: Carcanet, 2014), 59.

33 George Steiner, *Lessons of the Masters* (Cambridge, MA: Harvard University Press, 2003), 30. 'Great teaching is insomnia', Steiner comments in the course of this discussion of the ethics of instruction; adding, suggestively if enigmatically, 'or might have been in the Garden of Gethsemane'. For a preliminary sense of Shestov's investment in the metaphor of sleep and sleeplessness, in relation to Pascal and Plotinus, as well as *Macbeth*, see William Desmond, 'Murdering Sleep: Shestov and Macbeth', in *The Tragic Discourse: Shestov and Fondane's Existential Thought*, ed. Ramona Fotiade (Oxford: Peter Lang, 2006), 67–78.

34 Léon Chestov, *La Nuit de Gethsémani: Essai sur la philosophie de Pascal* (Paris: Bernard Grasset, 1923), xiii.

35 Quoted in Finkenthal, *Lev Shestov*, 137.

36 Theodor Adorno and Max Horkheimer, *Dialectic of Enlightenment*, trans. John Cumming (London: Verso, 1986), 85.

37 Shestov, 'A Thousand and One Nights', 23.

38 Lev Shestov, 'Revolt and Submission', in *In Job's Balances*, 139.

39 Shestov, *Athens and Jerusalem*, 262.

40 Shestov, *Athens and Jerusalem*, 55.

41 Lev Shestov, 'Speculation and Apocalypse: The Religious Philosophy of Vladimir Solovyov', in *Speculation and Revelation*, 41.

42 On Shestov's Kierkegaard, see George Pattison, 'Lev Shestov: Kierkegaard in the Ox of Phalaris', in *Kierkegaard and Existentialism*, ed. Jon Stewart (Farnham: Ashgate, 2011), 355–74.

43 Shestov, 'Speculation and Apocalypse', 41.

44 Shestov, 'Dostoevsky and Nietzsche', 147.

45 Fyodor Dostoevsky, *The Idiot*, trans. David McDuff (Harmondsworth: Penguin, 2004), 255.

46 Quoted in Joseph Frank, *Dostoevsky: A Writer in his* Time, ed. Mary Petrusewicz (Princeton: Princeton University Press, 2010), 549.

47 Lev Shestov, 'On the "Regeneration of Convictions" in Dostoevsky', in *Speculation and Revelation*, trans. Bernard Martin (Athens: Ohio University Press, 1982), 164–5.

48 Cited in Graham Hunter, *Pascal the Philosopher: An Introduction* (Toronto: University of Toronto Press, 2013), 81.

49 Fondane, *Rencontres avec Léon Chestov*, 156.

50 Lev Shestov, 'Creation from the Void', in *Chekhov and Other Essays*, 25.

51 Shestov, 'Memento Mori', 358.

52 See Gershom Scholem, *The Messianic Idea in Judaism and Essays on Jewish Spirituality* (New York: Schocken, 1971), 1–2.

53 Shestov, *Athens and Jerusalem*, 432–3.

54 Rachel Bespaloff, 'Chestov devant Nietzsche', in *Cheminements et Carrefours*, 2nd edn (Paris: Librairie Philosophique J. Vrin, 2004), 202.

55 Shestov, *Athens and Jerusalem*, 376.

56 Karl Jaspers, *The Great Philosophers: The Disturbers*, ed. and trans. Michael Ermarth and Leonard H. Ehrlich (New York: Harcourt Bruce, 1995), 35. See Lev Shestov, '*Sine Effusione Sanguinis*: On Philosophical Honesty', in *Speculation and Revelation*, 171–202.

57 Shestov, *Gethsemane Night*, 291.

58 These are the words of the pastor Tycho E. Spang, who knew Kierkegaard in the 1840s. See Bruce H. Kirmmse, ed., *Encounters with Kierkegaard: A Life as Seen by Contemporaries*, trans. Bruce H. Kirmmse and Virginia R. Laursen (Princeton: Princeton University Press, 1996), 112.

59 See Robin Small, *Time and Becoming in Nietzsche's Thought* (London: Continuum, 2010), 36.

60   Camus, *The Myth of Sisyphus*, 29.

61   See, for example, Fondane, *Rencontres avec Léon Chestov*, 143; and, for the quotation, 168.

62   Shestov, *Gethsemane Night*, 296.

63   David Gascoyne, 'Ecce Homo', in *New Collected Poems, 1929-1995*, ed. Roger Scott (London: Enitharmon Press, 2014), 127.

64   Gascoyne, 'Ecce Homo', 127–9.

Chapter 2

1   For seminal assessments of the Silver Age and its luminaries, including Rozanov and Solovyov, see the anthology of Shestov's friend Nikolai Berdyaev's writings, *The Brightest Lights of the Silver Age: Essays on Russian Religious Thinkers*, ed. and trans. Boris Jakim (Kettering: Semantron Press, 2015). For the overarching context, see Zenkovsky, *A History of Russian Philosophy*, Vols. 1 and 2. Useful and relevant introductions to this philosophical milieu can be found, among other places, in Ruth Coates, 'Religious Renaissance in the Silver Age', in *A History of Russian Thought*, ed. William Leatherbarrow and Derek Offord (Cambridge: Cambridge University Press, 2010), 169–93; Anna Lisa Crone, *Eros and Creativity in Russian Religious Renewal: The Philosophers and the Freudians* (Leiden: Brill, 2010); Rubin, *Holy Russia, Sacred Israel*; and Olga Tabachnikova, 'Between Literature and Religion: Silver Age Ideas Applied to Modernity – Poetic Outlook as a Type of Religiosity?', *Societal Studies* 10, no. 1 (2018): 32–47.

2   Lev Shestov, *All Things Are Possible*, trans. S. S. Koteliansky (London: Martin Secker, 1920), 38.

3   Gilles Deleuze and Félix Guattari, *Anti-Oedipus: Capitalism and Schizophrenia*, trans. Robert Hurley et al. (London: Continuum, 2004), 2.

4   Shestov, *All Things Are Possible*, 15.

5   On the figure of the nightwalker, see Matthew Beaumont, *Nightwalking: A Nocturnal History of London* (London: Verso, 2015).

6   Shestov, 'Speculation and Apocalypse', 37. See, for some useful context, William Desmond, 'God Beyond the Whole: Between Solovëv and Shestov', in *Is There a Sabbath for Thought?: Between Religion and Philosophy* (New York: Fordham University Press, 2005), 167–99.

7   Zygmunt Bauman, *Modernity and Ambivalence* (Cambridge: Polity Press, 1991), 82.

8   Shestov, *All Things Are Possible*, 17.

9 Ksenia V. Vorozhikhina, 'Lev Shestov's Ideas in the French Philosophical and Cultural Context', *Russian Studies in Philosophy* 55, no. 5 (2017): 374.

10 Shestov, 'Speculation and Apocalypse', 87.

11 Shestov, *All Things Are Possible*, 165.

12 Quoted in Maurice Friedman, 'Martin Buber and Mikhail Bakhtin: The Dialogue of Voices and the Word that is Spoken', *Religion and Literature* 33, no. 3 (Autumn 2001): 25.

13 Alexandre Kojève, *The Religious Metaphysics of Vladimir Solovyov*, trans. Ilya Merlin and Mikhail Pozdniakov (Basingstoke: Palgrave Macmillan, 2018), 20. See

14 Shestov, *All Things Are Possible*, 147, 139.

15 Quoted in Bruce Baugh, 'Private Thinkers, Untimely Thoughts: Deleuze, Shestov and Fondane', *Continental Philosophy Review* 48, no. 2 (2015): 335.

16 Lev Shestov, 'The Theory of Knowledge', in *Chekhov and Other Essays*, 162, 165.

17 Quoted in Edith W. Clowes, *Fiction's Overcoat: Russian Literary Culture and the Question of Philosophy* (Ithaca: Cornell University Press, 2004), 135.

18 Gilles Deleuze, *What Is Grounding?*, trans. Arjen Kleinherenbrink (Grand Rapids: &&& Publishing, 2015), 57. More than two decades later, Deleuze reiterated this distinction, though he also nuanced it, in the course of a discussion of 'noology', the study of 'images of thought'. This discipline, he states in *A Thousand Plateaus* (1980), gives rise to 'counterthoughts, which are violent in their acts and discontinuous in their appearances, and whose existence is mobile in history. These are the acts of a "private thinker," as opposed to the public professor: Kierkegaard, Nietzsche, or even Shestov. Wherever they dwell, it is the steppe or the desert. They destroy images'. These thinkers are anti-philosophers, so to speak, who fight against the reification of concrete ideas as abstract concepts. '"Private thinker," however, is not a satisfactory expression', Deleuze continues, 'because it exaggerates interiority, when it is a question of *outside thought*' – see Gilles Deleuze and Félix Guattari, *A Thousand Plateaus: Capitalism and Schizophrenia*, trans. Brian Massumi (London: Continuum, 2004), 415.

19 Shestov, '*Sine Effusione Sanguinis*', 184.

20 Gilles Deleuze and Félix Guattari, *What Is Philosophy?* trans. Hugh Tomlinson and Graham Burchill (London: Verso, 1994), 62.

21 Shestov, 'The Theory of Knowledge', 208.

22 Leon Shestov, 'Anton Tchekhov (Creation from the Void)', in *Chekhov and Other Essays*, 51.

23 Nikolai Berdyaev, 'The Fundamental Ideas of the Philosophy of Lev Shestov', in *Speculation and Revelation*, 1.

24 Shestov, 'Gethsemane Night', 304.

25 See for instance Michel Foucault, 'The Political Function of the Intellectual', trans.
    Colin Gordon, *Radical Philosophy* 17 (1977): 13: 'Each society has its regime of truth,
    its "general politics" of truth: that is, the types of discourse it harbours and causes
    to function as true; the mechanisms and instances which enable one to distinguish
    true from false statements, the way in which each is sanctioned; the techniques
    and procedures which are valorised for obtaining truth; the status of those who are
    charged with saying what counts as true'.

26 Shestov, 'Gethsemane Night', 304.

27 On the psychoanalyst Max Eitingon's attempts to interest Freud in Shestov, which
    were spectacularly unsuccessful (Freud allegedly referred to Shestov's work as a
    'pitiable waste of intellectual energy'), see Mary-Kay Wilmers, *The Eitingons: A
    Twentieth-Century Family* (London: Faber & Faber, 2017), 186. For a fuller sense of
    the context, see Olga Tabachnikova, 'Cultural Anxieties of Russian-Jewish Émigrés:
    Max Eitingon and Lev Shestov', in *The Russian Jewish Diaspora and European
    Culture, 1917-1937*, ed. Jörg Schulte, Olga Tabachnikova and Peter Wagstaff (Leiden:
    Brill, 2012), 127–45.

28 Shestov, 'Gethsemane Night', 305.

29 Groys, *Introduction to Antiphilosophy*, 37, 41. Groys rather evocatively diagnoses
    Shestov's repetitious citations of his philosophical precursors as 'wounds or sores that
    cut into the body of [his] language, and could never be cured'.

30 Quoted in Louis J. Stein, *The Philosophy of Lev Shestov (1866-1938): A Russian
    Religious Existentialist* (Lewiston: Edwin Mellen Press, 1991), 42.

31 On the relation of Shestov to Symbolism, see Avril Pyman's fine account in *A History
    of Russian Symbolism* (Cambridge: Cambridge University Press, 1994), 139–50.

32 Shestov, *Potestas Clavium*, 12.

33 Quoted in Lev Shestov, 'The Good in the Teaching of Tolstoy and Nietzsche:
    Philosophy and Preaching', trans. Bernard Martin, in *Dostoevsky, Tolstoy and
    Nietzsche* (Athens: Ohio University Press, 1969), 134. See Friedrich Nietzsche, *Thus
    Spake Zarathustra*, ed. R. J. Hollingdale (Harmondsworth: Penguin, 2003), 174–5.

34 Geneviève Piron, *Léon Chestov: Philosophe du déracinement* (Lausanne: Editions
    L'Age d'Homme, 2010), 99–100. The principal source for the relevant aspects of
    Shestov's biography is Nathalie Baranoff-Chestov, *Vie de Léon Chestov*, Vol. 1, trans.
    Blanche Bronstein-Vinaver (Paris: La Différence, 1991). In English, the standard
    starting point is Martin, 'The Life and Thought of Lev Shestov', 11–44.

35 Quoted in Olga Tabachnikova, *Anton Chekhov through the Eyes of Russian Thinkers:
    Vasilii Rozanov, Dimitrii Merezhkovskii and Lev Shestov* (London: Anthem Press,
    2010), 178.

36 Julia V. Sineokaya and Anton M. Khokhlov, 'Lev Shestov's Philosophy of Freedom', *Studies in Eastern European Thought* 68 (2016): 214.

37 On this incident, see Piron, *Léon Chestov*, 187–95.

38 Quoted in Julia V. Sineokaya, 'In the Circle of Non-Vengeance: Lev Shestov and Friedrich Nietzsche', *Russian Studies in Philosophy* 55, no. 5 (2017): 358.

39 For these biographical details, see Finkenthal, *Lev Shestov*, 21–3.

40 Fondane, *Rencontres avec Léon Chestov*, 93. Shestov's book on Shakespeare remains untranslated.

41 Lev Shestov, 'In Memory of a Great Philosopher: Edmund Husserl', trans. George L. Kline, in *Speculation and Revelation*, trans. Bernard Martin (Athens: Ohio University Press, 1982), 271.

42 For the claim that Derrida gave a seminar on Shestov, which admittedly I haven't seen verified elsewhere, see Andrius Valevicius, *Lev Shestov and His Times* (New York: Peter Lang, 1993), 6.

43 I take this sentence from Jacques Derrida, *Specters of Marx: The State of the Deb, the Work of Mourning, and the New International*, trans. Peggy Kamuf (London: Routledge, 1994), 18: Hamlet's line stands as the epigraph to Derrida's book.

44 Walter Benjamin, 'Theses on the Philosophy of History', in *Illuminations*, ed. Hannah Arendt, trans. Harry Zohn (London: Fontana Press, 1992), 255.

45 Berdyaev, 'The Fundamental Ideas of the Philosophy of Lev Shestov', 1.

46 C. L. R. James, *Notes on Dialectics: Hegel, Marx, Lenin* (London: Allison & Busby, 1980), 136.

47 Shestov, *All Things Are Possible*, 176.

48 John Bayley, 'Idealism and its Critic', *New York Review of Books* 14, no. 12 (18 June 1970): 4.

49 See Clowes, *Fiction's Overcoat*, 131.

50 E. M. Cioran, 'Reflections on Philosophy, Poetry, and Benjamin Fondane: An Interview with Leonard Schwartz' (1985), in Benjamin Fondane, *Cinepoems and Others*, ed. Leonard Shwartz (New York: NYRB, 2016), 209.

51 Note nonetheless that, interestingly, Bauman identifies Shestov's project with the work of Freud, Kafka, Simmel and Jabès as a precursor to the post-structuralist hermeneutics of Derrida, which (with its insistence on undecidability) 'stands *on the other side of assimilation*' – see *Modernity and Ambivalence*, 193.

52 Leon Shestov, 'Anton Tchekhov (Creation from the Void)', 21, 23.

53 Shestov, *Potestas Clavium*, 40.

54 Shestov, 'Revolt and Submission', 151.

55 Shestov, 'Revolt and Submission', 149.

56 Blaise Pascal, 'Additional Pensées', in *Pensées*, trans. A. J. Krailsheimer (Harmondsworth: Penguin, 1995), 333.

57 Shestov, 'Anton Tchekhov', 3, 60.

58 Desmond, 'Murdering Sleep: Shestov and Macbeth', 67.

59 Shestov, 'The Theory of Knowledge', 168.

60 Shestov, *All Things Are Possible*, 27.

61 Shestov, *Athens and Jerusalem*, 66.

62 Shestov, 'Penultimate Words', 115–6.

63 Alain Badiou, 'The Enigmatic Relationship between Philosophy and Politics', in *Philosophy for Militants*, trans. Bruno Bosteels (London: Verso, 2012), 10–12.

64 Deleuze, *What Is Grounding?* 46.

65 For an excellent introduction to anti-philosophy, especially in relation to Badiou, see Bruno Bosteels, 'Radical Antiphilosophy', *Filozofski vestnik* 19, no. 2 (2008): 155–87.

66 Alain Badiou, *Saint Paul: The Foundation of Universalism*, trans. Ray Brassier (Stanford: Stanford University Press, 2003), 17. Badiou calls Pascal 'that other great figure of antiphilosophy' (47).

67 Shestov, *Athens and Jerusalem*, 324. See Daniel R. Langton, *The Apostle Paul in the Jewish Imagination: A Study in Modern Jewish-Christian Relations* (Cambridge: Cambridge University Press, 2010), 242–50.

68 See Groys, 'Leo Shestov', 33–49.

69 Alain Badiou, *Wittgenstein's Antiphilosophy*, trans. Bruno Bosteels (London: Verso, 2011), 69.

70 Gascoyne, 'Essay on Léon Chestov', 64.

71 Fondane, 'Existential Monday and the Sunday of History', in *Existential Monday*, 25.

72 Shestov, 'Speculation and Apocalypse', 38.

73 Shestov, *Athens and Jerusalem*, 67, 317–18.

74 Shestov, *Potestas Clavium*, 5.

75 Badiou, *Saint Paul*, 17.

76 Shestov, 'Gethsemane Night', 307–8, 311.

77 Czeslaw Milosz, 'Shestov, or the Purity of Despair', in *Emperor of the Earth: Modes of Eccentric Thinking* (Berkeley: University of California Press, 1977), 119.

78 John Gray, *Seven Types of Atheism* (London: Allen Lane, 2018), 154.

79 Shestov, *Athens and Jerusalem*, p. 80.

80 Shestov, 'The Theory of Knowledge', 174.

81 Shestov, 'Anton Tchekhov', 13.

82 Shestov, 'The Conquest of the Self-Evident', 49.

83 Monas, 'New Introduction', xvii. Note that Roland Clark cites Bely in his essay on Shestov, where he argues, implausibly, that 'Shestov's agenda is synonymous with that of Modernism', but his quotations from *Petersburg*, whose date of publication he erroneously gives as 1912, perform an almost entirely decorative function – see 'Lev Shestov and the Crisis of Modernity', *Archaeus* XI–XII (2007–2008): 240, also 233, 243.

84 Quoted in Maria Carlson, 'Armchair Anarchists and Salon Supermen: Russian Occultists Read Nietzsche', in *Nietzsche and Soviet Culture: Ally and Adversary*, ed. Bernice Glatzer Rosenthal (Cambridge: Cambridge University Press, 1994), 118.

85 Carol Anschuetz, 'Bely's *Petersburg* and the End of the Russian Novel', in *The Russian Novel from Pushkin to Pasternak*, ed. John Garrard (Yale: Yale University Press, 1983), 125.

86 Shestov, '*Sine Effusione Sanguinis*', 189.

87 Andrei Bely, *Petersburg*, trans. David McDuff (Harmondsworth: Penguin, 2011), 354–5.

88 Shestov, 'Revolt and Submission', 229.

89 Bely, *Petersburg*, 360, 417.

90 Shestov, *Potestas Clavium*, 80.

91 Bely, *Petersburg*, 501.

92 Shestov, 'Anton Tchekhov', 28.

93 See Shestov, 'Gethsemane Night', 291.

94 Shestov, 'The Conquest of the Self-Evident', 43.

95 Shestov, 'On the "Regeneration of Convictions"', 161.

96 Louis Althusser, 'The Underground Current of the Materialism of the Encounter', in *Philosophy of the Encounter: Later Writings, 1978-1987*, trans. G. M. Goshgarian (London: Verso, 2006), 196. Althusser was also no doubt thinking, though it isn't a conscious apologetics exactly, of the psychotic episode during which he murdered his own wife in Hélène Rytmann. Note incidentally that Althusser, whose debt to Pascal throughout his intellectual career was extensive, not least in this essay, quoted from 'The Mystery of Jesus' in the diary he wrote in a German prison camp in 1943 – see

Panagiotis Sotiris, 'From the "Hidden God" to the Materialism of the Encounter: Althusser and Pascal', in *Althusser and Theology: Religion, Politics, and Philosophy*, ed. Agon Hamza (Leiden: Brill, 2016), 152.

97 Shestov, *Potestas Clavium*, 77. I have silently corrected a typographical error in this quotation.

98 Shestov, 'A Thousand and One Nights', 5. Compare Shestov, 'Dostoevsky and Nietzsche', 289: 'the development of the world is frightfully unnatural: *it would be natural if there were nothing at all* – neither the world nor its development'.

99 G. K. Chesterton, *St. Francis of Assisi*, in *Collected Works*, Vol. 2 (San Francisco: Ignatius Press, 1987), 132. Note, for instance, the distinctly Chestertonian sentiment, and tone, of this statement of Shestov's, which pursues his point about the miraculousness of mere existence: 'Although the Gospel does not at all agree with our scientific notions of the laws of nature, yet it does not in itself contain anything contrary to reason. We do not disbelieve in miracles because they are impossible. On the contrary, it is as clear as day to the most ordinary common sense that life itself, the foundation of the world, is the miracle of miracles' – see 'Penultimate Words', 130. Note too that, though Shestov might not have been conscious of Chesterton, Fondane was: in his book on Rimbaud, he quotes Chesterton's judgement that Blake was 'an inspired idiot, and idiot because he was inspired' – see Baugh, 'Private Thinkers, Untimely Thoughts', 325.

100 Shestov, *Potestas Clavium*, 77.

101 Althusser, 'The Underground Current of the Materialism of the Encounter', 196.

102 Shestov, 'Revolt and Submission', 150.

103 Camus, *The Myth of Sisyphus*, 29–30.

104 Shestov, *Potestas Clavium*, 77, 78–9. Sartre's *Nausea*, his first novel, was published in 1938, the year of Shestov's death.

105 Shestov, *All Things Are Possible*, 31.

106 Shestov, 'Speculation and Apocalypse', 62.

107 Shestov, 'Speculation and Apocalypse', 40.

108 Shestov, 'Words that Are Swallowed Up: Plotinus's Ecstasies', 366.

109 Shestov, 'The Theory of Knowledge', 170.

110 Shestov, 'The Theory of Knowledge', 171.

111 Shestov, 'Penultimate Words', 108.

112 Lev Shestov, 'Martin Buber', in *Speculation and Revelation*, 107.

113 Shestov, 'Speculation and Apocalypse', 87.

Chapter 3

1   See Arta Lucescu Boutcher, *Rediscovering Benjamin Fondane* (New York: Peter Lang, 2003), 114. I have substituted my own translation for Boutcher's.

2   Shestov, 'The Theory of Knowledge', 167. Gascoyne first encountered Shestov in *All Things Are Possible* (1920) – see Robert Fraser, *Night Thoughts: The Surreal Life of the Poet David Gascoyne* (Oxford: Oxford University Press, 2012), 145.

3   Gascoyne, 'Essay on Léon Chestov', 59.

4   Shestov, *All Things Are Possible*, 19.

5   Fondane, *Rencontres avec Léon Chestov*, 51.

6   See Gascoyne, 'Essay on Léon Chestov', 59, 56.

7   R. B. Kitaj, *Second Diasporist Manifesto (A New Kind of Long Poem in 615 Free Verses)* (New Haven: Yale University Press, 2007), #206.

8   Shestov, 'In Memory of a Great Philosopher: Edmund Husserl', 267.

9   For a translation of this letter, see Valevicius, *Lev Shestov and His Times*, 140.

10 Camus, *The Myth of Sisyphus*, 21.

11 Martin Buber, 'On Leo Chestov', in *A Believing Humanism: Gleanings*, trans. Maurice Friedman (New York: Simon & Schuster, 1967), 60.

12 For more details, see Ramona Fotiade, 'La pensée du dehors: posterité et interlocuteurs privilégiés', in *Léon Chestov, 1866-1938: La pensée du dehors*, ed. Ramona Fotiade (Paris: Société d'Études Léon Chestov, 2016), 111–31.

13 On Shestov's role in making Dostoevsky fashionable in Paris, and on the influential nature of his anti-rationalist reading of *Notes from Underground* in particular, see Alexander McCabe, 'Shifting French Perspectives on Dostoevskian Anti-Rationalism', in *Facets of Russian Irrationalism between Art and Life*, ed. Olga Tabachnikova (Leiden: Brill Rodopi, 2016), 227–31.

14 Cherry A. Hankin, ed., *Letters between Katherine Mansfield and John Middleton Murry* (New York: New Amsterdam, 1991), 249.

15 Galya Diment, *A Russian Jew of Bloomsbury: The Life and Times of Samuel Koteliansky* (Montreal: McGill-Queen's University Press, 2011), 122–5.

16 D. H. Lawrence, 'Foreword', in *All Things Are Possible*, 11.

17 D. H. Lawrence, *The Letters of D.H. Lawrence*, Vol. 3, ed. James T. Boulton and Andrew Robertson (Cambridge: Cambridge University Press, 1984), 387.

18 Lawrence, 'Foreword', 10.

19 Hugh MacDiarmid, *Lucky Poet: A Self-Study in Literature and Political Ideas* (London: Methuen, 1943), 28, 402. See Peter McCarey, *Hugh MacDiarmid and the Russians* (Edinburgh: Scottish Academic Press, 1987), 162–200.

20 Hugh MacDiarmid, *Direadh I*, in *Complete Poems*, Vol. 2, ed. Michael Grieve and W. R. Aitken (Manchester: Carcanet, 1994), 1170. See Nancy K. Gish, *Hugh MacDiarmid: The Man and His Work* (London: Macmillan, 1984), 204–6.

21 See Shestov, 'On the "Regeneration of Convictions"', 161.

22 Hugh MacDiarmid, *The Letters of Hugh MacDiarmid*, ed. Alan Bold (London: Hamish Hamilton, 1984), 876.

23 Hugh MacDiarmid, 'The Impossible Song', in *Complete Poems*, Vol. 1, ed. Michael Grieve and W. R. Aitken (Manchester: Carcanet, 1993), 510.

24 Andrew Harrison, *The Life of D.H. Lawrence: A Critical Biography* (Chichester: Wiley, 2016), 190.

25 Quoted in Michael Weingrad, 'New Encounters with Shestov', *The Journal of Jewish Thought and Philosophy* 11, no. 1 (2002): 54. I discovered the existence of this excellent article, the concerns of which closely overlap with my own account of Shestov's possible relations to Bataille and Benjamin, only after drafting this section. I am grateful to Michael Weingrad for sending it to me.

26 Georges Bataille, *On Nietzsche*, trans. Stuart Kendall (Albany: SUNY Press, 2015), 265.

27 Stuart Kendall, *Georges Bataille* (London: Reaktion, 2007), 42.

28 See Michael Surya, *Georges Bataille: An Intellectual Biography*, trans. Krzystof Fijalkowski and Michael Richardson (London: Verso, 2002), 57–63; also, Vorozhikhina, 'Lev Shestov's Ideas in the French Philosophical and Cultural Context', 368–70.

29 Georges Bataille, *Inner Experience*, trans. Stuart Kendall (Albany: SUNY Press, 2014), 48.

30 Surya, *Georges Bataille*, 62.

31 Levinas, 'Review of Lev Shestov's *Kierkegaard and the Existential Philosophy*', 239.

32 See Robert Wohl, *The Generation of 1914* (Harvard, MA: Harvard University Press, 1979), 212. Wohl cites Eugen Weber as the source of this phrase.

33 György Lukács, 'The Metaphysics of Tragedy: Paul Ernst', in *Soul and Form*, ed. John T. Saunders and Katie Terezakis (New York: Columbia University Press, 2010), 176–7.

34 Shestov, 'Gethsemane Night', 313.

35 Camus, *The Myth of Sisyphus*, 21.

36 William Desmond, 'Between Finitude and Infinity: Hegelian Reason and the Pascalian Heart', in *Hegel on the Modern World*, ed. Ardis B. Collins (New York: State University of New York Press, 1995), 27.

37 Michael Löwy, *Redemption and Utopia: Jewish Libertarian Though in Central Europe*, trans. Hope Heany (London: Verso, 2017), 6.

38 Gershom Scholem, *Walter Benjamin: The Story of a Friendship*, trans. Harry Zohn (New York: NYRB, 2003), 259–60. On Lieb's presence in the sixth thesis, see Michael Löwy, *Fire Alarm: Reading Walter Benjamin's 'On the Concept of History'*, trans. Chris Turner (London: Verso, 2005), 46.

39 Hans Mayer, 'Walter Benjamin and Franz Kafka: Report on a Constellation', trans. Gary Smith and Thomas S. Hansen, in *On Walter Benjamin: Critical Essays and Reflections*, ed. Gary Smith (Cambridge, MA: MIT Press, 1995), 200.

40 John Felstiner, *Paul Celan: Poet, Survivor, Jew* (New Haven: Yale University Press, 1995), 152, 164.

41 Paul Celan, 'The Meridian', in *Collected Prose*, ed. Rosemarie Waldrop (Manchester: Carcanet Press, 1986), 46, 50. For the relevant quotations, see Shestov, 'A Thousand and One Nights', 26; and Benjamin, 'Franz Kafka', in *Illuminations*, trans. Harry Zohn (London: Fontana, 1992), 130.

42 Emmanuel Levinas, 'Paul Celan: From Being to the Other', in *Proper Names*, trans. Michael B. Smith (Stanford: Stanford University Press, 1996), 42, 45.

43 Emmanuel Levinas, *Existence and Existents*, trans. Alphonso Lingis (Pittsburgh: Duquesne University Press, 2001), 63.

44 Scholem, ed., *The Correspondence of Gershom Scholem and Walter Benjamin*, 107, 112, 118.

45 Walter Benjamin, *The Correspondence of Walter Benjamin, 1910-1940*, ed. Gershom Scholem and Theodor W. Adorno (Chicago: University of Chicago Press, 1994), 483.

46 Scholem, *Walter Benjamin*, 254.

47 Scholem, ed., *The Correspondence of Gershom Scholem and Walter Benjamin*, 183.

48 Benjamin, *The Correspondence of Walter Benjamin*, 517. In his autobiography, *Spiegelung der Jugend* (1973), illustrating Benjamin's relationship with Marxism, Kraft described a discussion he had with him about Shestov: 'In a conversation about Leo Schestow [*sic*] he himself was also cuttingly curt. I had said that at the centre of Schestow's philosophy was despair. To which he responded: "That is the very reason why things don't work. At the heart of philosophy is the class struggle." That may not have been correct, but it was monumental.' See Volker Kahmen, 'Walter Benjamin and Werner Kraft', in *For Walter Benjamin: Documentation, Essays and a Sketch*, ed. Ingrid and Konrad Scheurmann, trans. Timothy Nevill (Bonn: AsKI, 1993), 37. It is tempting to see Benjamin's rejection of Shestov's philosophy of despair, and his seemingly crude affirmation of class struggle, in terms of what Freud called a reaction formation.

49 Scholem, *Walter Benjamin*, 254. For these essays as *pieces de résistance* against Marxism, which is Scholem's argument, see Gershom Scholem, 'Walter Benjamin and his Angel', in *On Walter Benjamin*, 53.

50 Shestov, 'Gethsemane Night', 308.

51 See Shestov, *All Things Are Possible*, 26, 127.

52 Scholem, ed., *The Correspondence of Gershom Scholem and Walter Benjamin*, 594.

53 Walter Benjamin, 'One-Way Street', in *One-Way Street and Other Writings*, trans. Edmund Jephcott and Kingsley Shorter (London: Verso, 1997), 67.

54 Scholem, ed., *The Correspondence of Gershom Scholem and Walter Benjamin*, 594.

55 Walter Benjamin, 'Unpacking My Library: A Talk about Book Collecting', in *Illuminations*, ed. Hannah Arendt (London: Fontana Press, 1992), 66.

56 Scholem, ed., *The Correspondence of Gershom Scholem and Walter Benjamin*, 594.

57 Scholem, ed., *The Correspondence of Gershom Scholem and Walter Benjamin*, 594. Some four years later, in 1942, Camus will also link Shestov and Kafka, or Kafka's heroes – see *The Myth of Sisyphus*, 121.

58 Walter Benjamin and Theodor W. Adorno, *The Complete Correspondence 1928-1940*, ed. Henry Lonitz, trans. Nicholas Walker (Cambridge: Polity Press, 1999), 283.

59 Benjamin, 'The Storyteller: Reflections on the Works of Nikolai Leskov', in *Illuminations*, 102.

60 Theodor W. Adorno, 'A Portrait of Walter Benjamin', in *Prisms*, trans. Samuel and Shierry Weber (Cambridge, MA: MIT Press, 1983), 237.

61 Walter Benjamin, 'Surrealism: The Last Snapshot of the European Intelligentsia', trans. Edmund Jephcott, in *Reflections: Essays, Aphorisms, Autobiographical Writings*, ed. Peter Demetz (New York: Schocken, 1986), 182–3.

62 Shestov, *Potestas Clavium*, 25–6.

63 Howard Eiland and Michael W. Jennings, *Walter Benjamin: A Critical Life* (Cambridge, MA: Harvard University Press, 2014), 8. Note incidentally that, on p. 640, Eiland and Jennings misread Benjamin's letter about Shestov's books and erroneously assume that the latter lived in the same building as the former. On Benjamin and Nietzsche, see James McFarland, *Constellations: Friedrich Nietzsche and Walter Benjamin in the Now-Time of History* (New York: Fordham University Press, 2013). 'From his juvenilia through his scholarly work to his avant-garde journalism and radio broadcasts in the 1930s', McFarland writes on p. viii, 'Benjamin consistently oriented his own position with respect to Friedrich Nietzsche's, whether he took him to be the avatar of an ardent "youth" or the diagnostician of mortal tragedy or the exiled wanderer through an anachronistic Europe, witness to the hopeless temporality – new and always the same – of bourgeois imperialism'.

64 Shestov, *All Things Are Possible*, 38.

65 Weingrad, 'New Encounters with Shestov', 61.

66 Adorno, 'A Portrait of Walter Benjamin', 235.

67 Zygmunt Bauman remarked in an interview that Shestov 'defined God not by His power to create the laws of universe, but His ability to break them at will – the capacity for miracles' – see 'Interview with Zygmunt Bauman', *JDC International Centre for Community Development* (February 2009): 4 (available at http://www.jdc-iccd.org/publications/interview-with-zigmunt-bauman-2009/).

68 Benjamin, 'Theses on the Philosophy of History', 255.

69 See Walter Benjamin, 'Goethe's Elective Affinities', in *Selected Writings* Vol. 1 (1913–1926), ed. Marcus Bullock and Michael W. Jennings (Harvard, MA: Harvard University Press, 1996), 356; and Shestov, *All Things Are Possible*, 27.

70 Shestov, *All Things Are Possible*, 82.

71 Shestov, 'Dostoevsky and Nietzsche', 197.

72 Clowes, *Fiction's Overcoat*, 143.

73 Quoted in Clowes, *Fiction's Overcoat*, 143. See Shestov, *All Things Are Possible*, 127.

74 Benjamin, *The Arcades Project*, 391.

75 Benjamin, 'Surrealism', 192.

76 Benjamin, *The Arcades Project*, 463–4. An especially apt dramatization of this hypnopompic logic can be found in the scene at the beginning of Dziga Vertov's *Man with a Movie Camera* (1929) in which an anonymous woman, who functions as a metonym for communist society itself, gradually wakes from a night's sleep in her apartment. Her waking dream, the rhythms of which are increasingly calibrated to the pace of numerous industrial machines as these propel the composite city depicted by Vertov into motion at the start of the day, ultimately merge with the activities of the 'Man with a Movie Camera' himself – here, then, as in Benjamin, the hypnopompic constitutes a politics and an aesthetics.

77 Shestov, *All Things Are Possible*, 165.

78 Shestov, *Potestas Clavium*, 400–1; and Shestov, *Athens and Jerusalem*, 432.

79 Friedrich Nietzsche, 'On the Uses and Disadvantages of History for Life', in *Untimely Meditations*, trans. R. J. Hollingdale, ed. J. P. Stern (Cambridge: Cambridge University Press, 1983), 62.

80 Walter Benjamin, 'Karl Kraus', in *Reflections*, 273. On the angelological discussions, see Scholem, *Walter Benjamin*, 100–1.

81 Benjamin, 'Theses on the Philosophy of History', 249.

82 Robert Alter, *Necessary Angels: Tradition and Modernity in Kafka, Benjamin, and Scholem* (Cambridge, MA: Harvard University Press, 1991), 115–16.

83 Benjamin, *The Arcades Project*, 388.

84 Shestov, *Athens and Jerusalem*, 432–3.

85 Löwy, *Fire Alarm*, 65–6.

86 Quoted in Otto Karl Werckmeister, *Icons of the Left: Benjamin and Einstein, Picasso and Kafka after the Fall of Communism* (Chicago: University of Chicago Press, 1999), 26.

87 Adorno, 'Commitment', trans. Francis McDonagh, in Ernst Bloch et al., *Aesthetics and Politics* (London: Verso, 1980), 194–5.

88 Lev Shestov, 'A Letter from Lev Shestov to his Daughters', in *In Job's Balances*, viii.

89 Shestov, 'The Conquest of the Self-Evident', 5–6.

90 Piron, *Léon Chestov*, 288 (translation mine). Piron cites the relevant passage from the notebooks on p. 287: 'L'Ange – de la mort – couvert d'yeux, a ôté ses yeux à D[ostoevsky] et lui en a donné deux autres. Nostalgie des anciens yeux et horreurs révélées par les nouveaux'.

91 Shestov, 'Penultimate Words', 85.

92 Nikolai Gogol, 'Viy', in *Village Evenings Near Dikanka and Mirgorod*, trans. Christopher English (Oxford: Oxford World's Classics, 1994), 404.

93 Shestov, 'The Conquest of the Self-Evident', 31.

Chapter 4

1 Shestov, *Athens and Jerusalem*, 265.

2 'Shestov did not know Kierkegaard until very late [in his life], and the resemblance between their philosophies, even in their way of expressing themselves, is an amazing case of coincidence', Deleuze remarked, summarizing their divergence in these terms: 'At the end, for Shestov, what remains is the human being and his questions: absurd. For Kierkegaard what remains at the end is faith' – see Deleuze, *What Is Grounding?*, 46.

3 Søren Kierkegaard, *Søren Kierkegaard's Journals and Papers*, Vol. 3, ed. and trans. Howard V. Hong and Edna H. Hong (Bloomington: Indiana University Press, 1975), 493.

4 Friedrich Nietzsche's 'Nachgelassene Fragmente', quoted in Paul Van Tongeren, 'Kant, Nietzsche and the Idealization of Friendship into Nihilism', *Kriterion: Revista de Filosofia* 54, no. 128 (2013): 411.

5 Kierkegaard, *Søren Kierkegaard's Journals and Papers*, Vol. 3, 493. See also David R. Law, *Kierkegaard's Kenotic Christology* (Oxford: Oxford University Press, 2013), 75.

6 Quoted in Finkenthal, *Lev Shestov*, 137.

7 Willy Fries, *Passion* (Zurich: Orell Füssli Verlag, 1976), 27–33.

8   Rowan Williams, *Meeting God in Mark* (London: SPCK, 2014), 57.

9   Walter Benjamin, 'Paralipomena to "On the Concept of History"', in *Selected Writings*, Vol. 4 (1938–40), trans. Edmund Jephcott et al. (Cambridge, MA: Harvard University Press, 2003), 407.

10 Jerome Murphy-O'Connor, 'What Really Happened at Gethsemane?' in *Keys to Jerusalem: Collected Essays* (Oxford: Oxford University Press, 2012), 89–90.

11 Adela Yarbro Collins, *Mark: A Commentary*, ed. Harold W. Attridge (Minneapolis: Fortress Press, 2007), 682.

12 Raymond E. Brown, *The Death of the Messiah: From Gethsemane to the Grave: A Commentary on the Passion Narratives in the Four Gospels* (New York: Doubleday, 1994), 156.

13 On recent theological disagreements over the meaning of this verse, see Claire Clivaz, '"Asleep by Grief" (Lk 22: 45): Reading from the Body at the Crossroads of Narratology and New Historicism', *The Bible and Critical Theory* 2, no. 3 (2006): 29.1–29.15; and Karl Olav Sandnes, *Early Christian Discourses on Jesus' Prayer at Gethsemane: Courageous, Committed, Cowardly?* (Leiden: Brill, 2015), 160–3.

14 Murphy-O'Connor, 'What Really Happened at Gethsemane?', 93.

15 Paul Ricoeur, 'Interpretive Narrative', in *Figuring the Sacred: Religion, Narrative, and Imagination*, trans. David Pellauer (Minneapolis: Fortress Press, 1995), 195.

16 Kevin Madigan, 'Ancient and High-Medieval Interpretations of Jesus in Gethsemane: Some Reflections on Tradition and Continuity in Christian Thought', *Harvard Theological Review* 88, no. 1 (1995): 157.

17 See Paul Gondreau, 'St. Thomas Aquinas, the Communication of Idioms, and the Suffering of Christ in the Garden of Gethsemane', in *Divine Impossibility and the Mystery of Human Suffering*, ed. James F. Keating and Thomas Joseph White (Michigan: Eerdmans, 2009), 245.

18 Thomas More, *De Tristitia Christi/The Sadness of Christ*, in *The Complete Works of St Thomas More*, Vol. 14, Part 1, ed. and trans. Clarence H. Miller (New Haven: Yale University Press, 1976), 259.

19 More, *De Tristitia Christi/The Sadness of Christ*, 171.

20 More, *De Tristitia Christi/The Sadness of Christ*, 9, 19, 35, 37.

21 Donald McColl, 'Agony in the Garden: Dürer's "Crisis of the Image"', in *The Essential Dürer*, ed. Larry Silver and Jeffrey Chipps Smith (Philadelphia: University of Pennsylvania Press, 2010), 167.

22 See Chris Fitter, 'The Poetic Nocturne: From Ancient Motif to Renaissance Genre', *Early Modern Literary Studies* 3, no. 2 (1997): 21–61.

23 George Herbert, 'The Agonie', in *The English Poems of George Herbert*, ed. C. A. Patrides (London: J.M. Dent, 1974), 58.

24 Sarah Covington, 'The Garden of Anguish: Gethsemane in Early Modern England', *Journal of Ecclesiastical History* 65, no. 2 (2014): 284.

25 Emily Dickinson, 'One Crucifixion Is Recorded – Only –', in *The Complete Poems of Emily Dickinson*, ed. Thomas H. Johnson (London: Faber & Faber, 1975), 269. For useful and insightful context, see Linda Freedman, *Emily Dickinson and the Religious Imagination* (Cambridge: Cambridge University Press, 2011), Ch. 4.

26 Diane Apostolos-Cappadona, 'Agony in the Garden', in *Dictionary of Christian Art* (New York: Continuum, 1994), 20–1.

27 See Irene Earle, *Renaissance Art: A Topical Dictionary* (New York: Greenwood Press, 1987), 10–11.

28 More, *De Tristitia Christi/The Sadness of Christ*, 51.

29 Caroline Campbell, 'The Agony in the Garden', in *Mantegna and Bellini*, ed. Caroline Campbell et al. (London: National Gallery, 2018), 137.

30 Andrea de Marchi, 'Mantegna/Bellini: Invention versus Poetry', in *Mantegna and Bellini*, 32.

31 Louis A. Ruprecht, Jr., 'Mark's Tragic Vision: Gethsemane', *Religion and Literature* 24, no. 3 (1992): 18.

32 See F. D. Klingender, 'Notes on Goya's *Agony in the Garden*', *The Burlington Magazine* 77, no. 448 (1940): 4–15.

33 Quoted in Michelle Facos, *Symbolist Art in Context* (Berkeley: California University Press, 2009), 35.

34 Quoted in Facos, *Symbolist Art in Context*, 35.

35 Vincent Van Gogh, *The Complete Letters of Vincent Van Gogh*, Vol. 3 (London: Thames & Hudson, 1978), 229.

36 Van Gogh, *The Complete Letters*, Vol. 3, 522.

37 Joan E. Greer, 'A Modern Gethsemane: Vincent Van Gogh's *Olive Grove*', *Van Gogh Museum Journal* (2001): 108. See also Cliff Edwards, *Van Gogh's Ghost Paintings: Art and Spirit in Gethsemane* (Oregon: Cascade Books, 2015).

38 Van Gogh, *The Complete Letters*, Vol. 3, 229.

39 Vincent Van Gogh, *The Complete Letters of Vincent Van Gogh*, Vol. 1 (London: Thames & Hudson, 1978), 27.

40 John Berger, 'Vincent van Gogh (1853-90)', in *Portraits: John Berger on Artists*, ed. Tom Overton (London: Verso, 2015), 269.

41 James E. B. Breslin, *Mark Rothko: A Biography* (Chicago: University of Chicago Press, 1993), 164–5.

42 On Masson's book as a source for Rothko's paintings of the mid-1940s, see Robert Rosenblum, 'Notes on Rothko's Surrealist Years', in *Mark Rothko* (New York: Pace Gallery, 1981), 8.

43 Breslin, *Mark Rothko*, 244.

44 Quoted in Breslin, *Mark Rothko*, 166.

45 Jacques Lacan, *The Four Fundamental Concepts of Psycho-Analysis*, trans. Alan Sheridan (London: Hogarth Press, 1977), 197–8.

46 Slavoj Žižek, 'Psychoanalysis and the Lacanian Real', in *A Concise Companion to Realism*, ed. Matthew Beaumont (Oxford: Wiley-Blackwell, 2010), 226.

47 Benjamin, *The Arcades Project*, 482. See also Benjamin, 'Paralipomena to "On the Concept of History"', 405.

48 Benjamin, 'Paralipomena to "On the Concept of History"', 405.

49 Gérard de Nerval, 'Christ at Gethsemane', trans. Henry Weinfield, *Literary Imagination* 8, no. 2 (2006): 229. See also Gérard de Nerval, *The Chimeras*, trans. Henry Weinfield (Cincinnati: Dos Madres Press, 2019).

50 Alfred de Vigny, 'Le Mont des Oliviers', in *Poèmes*, ed. Louis Roinet (Paris: Librairie A. Hatier, 1961), 45–50.

51 Nerval, 'Christ at Gethsemane', 229.

52 Nerval, 'Christ at Gethsemane', 229–30.

53 Julia Kristeva, *Black Sun: Depression and Melancholia*, trans. Leon S. Roudiez (New York: Columbia University Press, 1989), 164.

54 T. S. Eliot, 'Rudyard Kipling', in *A Choice of Kipling's Verse*, ed. T. S. Eliot (London: Faber & Faber, 1941) 16.

55 Rudyard Kipling, 'Gethsemane', in *The Years Between* (London: Methuen, 1919), 85.

56 Donald Davie, 'A Puritan's Empire: The Case of Kipling', *The Sewanee Review* 87, no. 1 (1979): 45.

57 Georg Lukács, *The Destruction of Reason*, trans. Peter Palmer (London: Merlin Press, 1980), 490.

58 V. I. Lenin, 'Preface to the French and German Editions', in *Imperialism: The Highest Stage of Capitalism* (Harmondsworth: Penguin, 2010), 6.

59 Lukács, *The Destruction of Reason*, 490.

60 Hermann Hesse, 'Thoughts on Dostoevsky's "Idiot"', in *In Sight of Chaos*, trans. Stephen Hudson (Zurich: Verlag Seldwyla, 1923), 50–2.

61 See Gunnar Decker, *Hesse: The Wanderer and his Shadow*, trans. Peter Lewis (Cambridge, MA: Harvard University Press, 2018), 201–3.

62 Frank Kermode, 'Waiting for the End', in *Apocalypse Theory and the Ends of the World*, ed. Malcom Bull (Oxford: Blackwell, 1995), 260.

63 T. S. Eliot, *The Waste Land*, in *The Poems of T.S. Eliot*, Vol. 1, ed. Christopher Ricks and Jim McCue (London: Faber & Faber, 2015), 69.

64 Quoted in George Wallis Field, *Herman Hesse* (New York: Twayne, 1970), 74.

65 Herman Hesse, 'Recent German Poetry', *The Criterion* 1, no. 1 (October 1922): 90.

66 Eliot, *The Waste Land*, 68.

67 Eliot, *The Waste Land*, 68.

68 Eliot, *The Waste Land*, 60.

69 Jerome J. McGann, *The Beauty of Inflections: Literary Investigations in Historical Method and Theory* (Oxford: Clarendon Press, 1985), 222.

70 Shestov, *Athens and Jerusalem*, 287.

Chapter 5

1 Mary Duclaux, *Portrait of Pascal* (London: T. Fisher Unwin, 1927), 171.

2 Walter Pater, 'Pascal', in *Miscellaneous Studies: A Series of Essays*, ed. Charles L. Shadwell (London: Macmillan, 1896), 66.

3 Lukács, *The Destruction of Reason*, 116.

4 Pascal, *The Mystery of Jesus*, 288–9.

5 Goldmann, *The Hidden God*, 79–80.

6 Pascal, *The Mystery of Jesus*, 289.

7 Pascal, *The Mystery of Jesus*, 289.

8 See Leo Rauch, ed., *Hegel and the Human Spirit: A Translation of the Jena Lectures on the Philosophy of Spirit (1805-6), with Commentary* (Detroit: Wayne State University Press, 1983), 87.

9 On 'extimacy', see Jacques Lacan, *The Ethics of Psychoanalysis, 1959-1960: The Seminar of Jacques Lacan, Book VII*, ed. Jacques-Alain Miller, trans. Dennis Porter (New York: Routledge, 2008), 171.

10 See Anonymous, 'Biographical Sketch', in *Thoughts of Blaise Pascal, Translated from the French, Preceded by a Sketch of His Life*, trans. Edward Craig (Andover: Allen, Morrill & Wardwell, 1846 [1825]), 12.

11 Pascal, *The Mystery of Jesus*, 291.

12 Pascal, *The Mystery of Jesus*, 289.

13 Pascal, *The Mystery of Jesus*, 289–90.

14 Terry Eagleton, *Radical Sacrifice* (New Haven: Yale University Press, 2018), 90.

15 Pascal, *The Mystery of Jesus*, 289.

16 Goldmann, *The Hidden God*, 81.

17 Goldmann, *The Hidden God*, 81.

18 Theodor W. Adorno, *Aesthetic Theory*, trans. Robert Hullot-Kentor (London: Athlone Press, 1997), 177.

19 Shestov, 'The Conquest of the Self-Evident', 29.

20 Shestov, 'Gethsemane Night', 274.

21 Fondane, *Rencontres avec Léon Chestov*, 193.

22 See Boutcher, *Rediscovering Benjamin Fondane*, 69.

23 Shestov, 'Speculation and Apocalypse', 62.

24 Quoted in John R. Cole, *Pascal: The Man and His Two Loves* (New York: New York University Press, 1995), 239.

25 Shestov, 'Gethsemane Night', 291.

26 For the main phrases in this sentence and the previous one, see Benjamin, 'Theses on the Philosophy of History', 247. See also Jean-Paul Sartre, 'A New Mystic', in *Critical Essays*, trans. Chris Turner (Calcutta: Seagull, 2017), 221: 'There is, in my view, more than a little of Pascal in M. Bataille, particularly the feverish contempt and the desire to get his words out quickly.' Interestingly, Surya observes, albeit in a syntactically rather complicated sentence, that 'Pascal lurks within Bataille (a debauched Bataille but no more dark or desperate) for the reason – if Bataille was conscious of this – that he *also* borrowed a style from him (clearly the Pascal of the *Pensées* is the strongest detectable 'literary' influence on *Guilty* and *Inner Experience*) and that – perhaps in unconscious remembrance of Léon Chestov – Bataille's Nietzsche remains profoundly Pascalian' – see Surya, *Georges Bataille*, 331.

27 Shestov, 'Gethsemane Night', 274.

28 Shestov, 'Gethsemane Night', 275.

29 Ezra Pound, 'Three Cantos', *Poetry* 10 (June 1917): 114.

30 L. T. Hobhouse, *Questions of War and Peace* (London: T. Fisher Unwin, 1916), 129–30.

31 Shestov, 'Gethsemane Night', 274.

32 Shestov, 'Gethsemane Night', 275.

33 Shestov, 'Gethsemane Night', 281.

34 Shestov, 'Gethsemane Night', 276.

35 Benjamin, 'Theses on the Philosophy of History', 245–6.

36 Shestov, 'Gethsemane Night', 278.

37 Shestov, 'Gethsemane Night', 278. Note that in *Shakespeare and His Critic Brandes* (1898) Shestov interpreted *Macbeth* as the 'tragedy of the categorical imperative': 'Thou shalt not kill not because of the victim but because of a pending discomfort with the categorical imperative' – see Valevicius, *Lev Shestov and His Times*, 21.

38 Shestov, 'Gethsemane Night', 278.

39 Shestov, 'Gethsemane Night', 279. The Spanish religious existentialist Miguel de Unamuno was especially taken by this idea in his essay 'The Agony of Christianity' (1930) – see Miguel de Unamuno, 'The Agony of Christianity', in *The Agony of Christianity and Essays on Christ*, trans. Anthony Kerrigan, in *Selected Works of Miguel de Unamuno*, Vol. 5 (Princeton: Princeton University Press, 1974), 64–5.

40 Desmond, 'Murdering Sleep: Shestov and Macbeth', 70–1.

41 Shestov, 'Gethsemane Night', 279.

42 Shestov, 'Gethsemane Night', 279–80. For a discussion of *fides implicita* in this context, see Alexander Broadie, 'The Role of Reason in the Assent of Faith – Pascal, Shestov and the Late Medieval Background', *Lev Shestov Journal* 17 (2017): 64–6.

43 Shestov, 'Gethsemane Night', 280.

44 Shestov, 'Gethsemane Night', 281.

45 Shestov, 'Gethsemane Night', 279.

46 Shestov, 'Gethsemane Night', 283.

47 Shestov, 'Gethsemane Night', 282.

48 Shestov, 'Gethsemane Night', 284.

49 Benjamin, *The Arcades Project*, 400.

50 Shestov, 'Kierkegaard as a Religious Philosopher', 213.

51 Adorno and Horkheimer, *Dialectic of Enlightenment*, 12.

52 Shestov, 'Gethsemane Night', 285. See Pascal, *Pensées*, 63. The capitals in the upper-case quotation appear to be Shestov's.

53 Cole, *Pascal*, 72, 239.

54 Shestov, 'Gethsemane Night', 289–90.

55 Shestov, 'Gethsemane Night', 287.

56 Shestov, 'Gethsemane Night', 288.

57 Shestov, 'Gethsemane Night', 292.

58 Slavoj Žižek, *The Parallax View* (Cambridge, MA: MIT Press, 2006), 66.

59 Shestov, 'Gethsemane Night', 291. See Pascal, *Pensées*, 53. Shestov believes that 'we do not find the true Pascal and his "ideas" in the *Provinciales*', principally because 'in the *Provinciales* there is no word of the abyss' – 'Gethsemane Night', 294.

60 Shestov, 'Gethsemane Night', 291.

61 Bely, *Petersburg*, 501.

62 Shestov, 'Gethsemane Night', 292.

63 Shestov, 'Gethsemane Night', 297.

64 See Goldmann, *The Hidden God*, xxvi.

65 Shestov, 'Gethsemane Night', 313.

66 Shestov, 'Gethsemane Night', 316.

67 Shestov, *All Things Are Possible*, 134–5.

68 Shestov, 'Gethsemane Night', 317. See Pascal, *Pensées*, 120.

69 Shestov, 'Gethsemane Night', 317.

70 Walter Benjamin, 'In the Sun', trans. Rodney Livingstone, in *Selected Writings*, Vol. 2 (1927–1934), ed. Michael W. Jennings et al. (Cambridge, MA: Harvard University Press, 1999), 664.

71 Benjamin, 'Franz Kafka', 129–30.

72 Benjamin, 'Franz Kafka', 130.

73 Scholem, ed., *The Correspondence of Gershom Scholem and Walter Benjamin*, 594.

74 Benjamin, 'Theses on the Philosophy of History', 255.

75 Scholem, ed., *The Correspondence of Gershom Scholem and Walter Benjamin*, 123.

76 Theodor Adorno, *Minima Moralia: Reflections from Damaged Life*, trans. E. F. N. Jephcott (London: Verso, 1978), 247.

77 Shestov, 'Gethsemane Night', 325.

78 Shestov, 'Gethsemane Night', 326.

79 Groys, *Introduction to Antiphilosophy*, 37.

80 Shestov, 'Dostoevsky and Nietzsche', 306, 307–8.

81 Baugh, 'Private Thinkers, Untimely Thoughts', 333.

82 Shestov, 'Anton Tchekhov (Creation from the Void)', 48–9.

Conclusion

1 Shestov, 'Memento Mori', 348. Note that, in the first volume of his *Critique of Everyday Life* (1947), Henri Lefebvre quoted this sentence and attacked Shestov, whom he classified alongside Fondane as 'a contemporary "existentialist" mystic and irrationalist philosopher', in these rather unimaginative terms: 'This comparison between the soul and the earth, which is intended to discredit man's "temperate" zones, misses out a rather important fact: the polar and equatorial zones are scarcely fit for habitation, and all civilization has developed in the temperate zones – the zones of everyday life' – see Henri Lefebvre, *Critique of Everyday Life: The One-Volume Edition*, trans. Michel Trebitsch (London: Verso, 2014), 144.

2 Deleuze, *What Is Grounding?*, 85.

3 Decades later, in *What Is Philosophy?* (1991), Deleuze and Guattari repeat the point in contending that 'private thinkers' or 'idiots' are distinctive as philosophers because they want 'account to be taken of "every victim of history"' – see Deleuze and Guattari, *What Is Philosophy?*, 63.

4 On Belinsky and Dostoevsky, see Shestov, 'Dostoevsky and Nietzsche', 152–7.

5 Theodor W. Adorno, *Negative Dialectics*, trans. E. B. Ashton (London: Routledge, 1973), 365.

6 Shestov, 'The Good in the Teaching of Tolstoy and Nietzsche', 4.

7 Benjamin, 'Theses on the Philosophy of History', 352.

8 Lev Shestov, 'Kierkegaard and Dostoevsky: Instead of a Preface', in *Kierkegaard and the Existential Philosophy*, trans. Elinor Hewitt (Athens: Ohio University Press, 1969), 8–9.

9 Shestov, 'The Good in the Teaching of Tolstoy and Nietzsche', 6, 8.

10 Lev Shestov, 'On the "Regeneration of Convictions"', 153.

11 Shestov, 'The Good in the Teaching of Tolstoy and Nietzsche', 5.

12 Shestov, 'Kierkegaard and Dostoevsky', 2.

13 Shestov, 'Kierkegaard and Dostoevsky', 5.

14 Adorno and Horkheimer, *Dialectic of Enlightenment*, xi.

15 Adorno and Horkheimer, *Dialectic of Enlightenment*, 3.

16 Benjamin and Adorno, *The Complete Correspondence, 1928-1940*, 67.

17 Adorno, 'Commitment', 188. It is possible that Adorno was thinking in part of *The Hidden God*, published in French in 1956, for there Goldmann quotes Pascal's injunction that 'we must not sleep' until 'the very end of the world' on at least three occasions. But if it seems unlikely that Goldmann, who lived in Paris in the mid- and

late 1930s, was not familiar with Shestov's earlier essay on 'The Mystery of Jesus', though I have found no reference to it in his *oeuvre*, it seems unlikely that Adorno was familiar with it. See Goldmann, *The Hidden God*, 67, 79, 80.

18 Phillippe Lacoue-Labarthe, *Heidegger, Art and Politics*, trans. Chris Turner (Oxford: Blackwell, 1990), 35.

19 Camus, *The Myth of Sisyphus*, 21.

20 Benjamin Fondane, *Ulysses: Bilingual Edition*, trans. Nathaniel Rudavsky-Brody (New York: Syracuse University Press, 2017), 140. See also, for a translation of these lines that is freer than mine or that of Rudavsky-Brody in the bilingual edition, Benjamin Fondane, *Ulysses XXXVII*, trans. Nathaniel Rudavsky-Brody, in *Cinepoems and Others*, ed. Leonard Schwartz (New York: New York Review of Books, 2016), 47.

21 Quoted in Bruce Baugh, 'Introduction', in *Existential Monday*, xvii. Baugh's insistence on Fondane's political commitments, against the claim by some Anglophone guardians of his reputation that he placed himself in some sense beyond politics, is essential.

22 Shestov, 'The Conquest of the Self-Evident', 5.

23 Quoted in Baugh, 'Private Thinkers, Untimely Thoughts', 329.

24 Baugh, 'Private Thinkers, Untimely Thoughts', 318; see also 335.

25 Benjamin, 'Theses on the Philosophy of History', 248: 'The tradition of the oppressed teaches us that the "state of emergency" in which we live is not the exception but the rule'.

26 Quoted in Baugh, 'Introduction', xxix–xxx.

27 Benjamin Fondane, 'Preface for the First Moment', 39.

28 Fondane, 'Preface for the First Moment', 42–3.

29 See Piron, *Léon Chestov*, 149–53.

30 Benjamin Fondane, 'Man before History; or, The Sound and the Fury', in *Existential Monday*, 52.

31 Fondane, 'Man before History', 57–8.

32 Thomas Mann, *Doctor Faustus: The Life of the German Composer Adrian Leverkühn as Told by a Friend*, trans. John E. Woods (London: Vintage, 2015), 708.

33 Terry Eagleton, *Hope against Optimism* (New Haven: Yale University Press, 2015), 136. Eagleton goes on to discuss Mann's *Doctor Faustus* in this context.

34 Fondane, 'Man before History', 60.

35 Shestov, 'Gethsemane Night', 278.

36 Fondane, 'Man before History', 60–1.

37 Shestov, 'In Memory of a Great Philosopher: Edmund Husserl', 286.

38 Adorno, *Negative Dialectics*, 403.

39 Theodor W. Adorno, 'Education after Auschwitz', trans. Henry W. Pickford in *Can One Live After Auschwitz? A Philosophical Reader*, ed. Rolf Tiedemann (Stanford: Stanford University Press, 2003), 19.

40 Berdyaev, 'The Fundamental Ideas of the Philosophy of Lev Shestov', 3–4. This was evidently something about which Berdyaev and Shestov regularly argued. Fondane recorded a conversation he and Shestov had on 16 November 1937 in which his friend made this statement: 'Berdyaev calls himself an existentialist. But he always goes back to the same questions: "Did Kierkegaard regain Regina Olsen? Did Job recover his dead children? Has there ever been a single Christian who actually moved mountains? You know as well as I do that none of these came to be'. And I answer him: 'Don't you think that Kierkegaard was fully aware of that? But that's precisely the starting point of his philosophy – he sets out on a war against what he knows only too well. That's what makes him into an existentialist. But you can't follow him there, that's the very thing that makes you turn back – so how come you call yourself and existentialist?"' See Fondane, *Rencontres avec Léon Chestov*, 149.

41 Shestov, *Athens and Jerusalem*, 411.

42 Shestov, *Athens and Jerusalem*, 434.

43 Adorno and Horkheimer, *Dialectic of Enlightenment*, 12.

44 See Ernst Bloch, *The Principle of Hope*, 3 vols., trans. Neville Plaice, Stephen Plaice and Paul Knight (Cambridge, MA: MIT Press, 1986).

45 Adorno, *Minima Moralia*, 247.

46 Adorno, *Negative Dialectics*, 403.

47 Benjamin, 'Theses on the Philosophy of History', 249.

48 Alain Badiou, 'Jean-François Lyotard', in *Pocket Pantheon*, trans. David Macey (London: Verso, 2009), 100.

Bibliography

Adorno, Theodor W. *Aesthetic Theory*. Trans. Robert Hullot-Kentor. London: Athlone Press, 1997.

Adorno, Theodor W. 'Commitment'. Trans. Francis McDonagh. In Ernst Bloch et al., *Aesthetics and Politics*. London: Verso, 1980, 177–95.

Adorno, Theodor W. 'Education after Auschwitz'. Trans. Henry W. Pickford. In *Can One Live After Auschwitz? A Philosophical Reader*. Ed. Rolf Tiedemann. Stanford: Stanford University Press, 2003, 18–33.

Adorno, Theodor W. *Minima Moralia: Reflections from Damaged Life*. Trans. E. F. N. Jephcott. London: Verso, 1978.

Adorno, Theodor W. *Negative Dialectics*. Trans. E. B. Ashton. London: Routledge, 1973.

Adorno, Theodor W. *Prisms*. Trans. Samuel and Shierry Weber. Cambridge, MA: MIT Press, 1983.

Adorno, Theodor W. and Max Horkheimer. *Dialectic of Enlightenment*. Trans. John Cumming. London: Verso, 1986.

Alter, Robert. *Necessary Angels: Tradition and Modernity in Kafka, Benjamin, and Scholem*. Cambridge, MA: Harvard University Press, 1991.

Althusser, Louis. *Philosophy of the Encounter: Later Writings, 1978-1987*. Trans. G. M. Goshgarian. London: Verso, 2006.

Anonymous. 'Biographical Sketch'. In *Thoughts of Blaise Pascal, Translated from the French, Preceded by a Sketch of His Life*. Trans. Edward Craig. Andover: Allen, Morrill & Wardwell, 1846.

Anschuetz, Carol. 'Bely's *Petersburg* and the End of the Russian Novel'. In *The Russian Novel from Pushkin to Pasternak*. Ed. John Garrard. Yale: Yale University Press, 1983, 125–46.

Apostolos-Cappadona, Diane. *Dictionary of Christian Art*. New York: Continuum, 1994.

Badiou, Alain. *Lacan: Anti-philosophy 3*. Trans. Kenneth Reinhard and Susan Spitzer. New York: Columbia University Press, 2018.

Badiou, Alain. *Philosophy for Militants*. Trans. Bruno Bosteels. London: Verso, 2012.

Badiou, Alain. *Pocket Pantheon*. Trans. David Macey. London: Verso, 2009.

Badiou, Alain. *Saint Paul: The Foundation of Universalism*. Trans. Ray Brassier. Stanford: Stanford University Press, 2003.

Badiou, Alain. *Wittgenstein's Antiphilosophy*. Trans. Bruno Bosteels. London: Verso, 2011.

Barth, Karl. *Church Dogmatics*, Vol. 4. Ed. G. W. Bromiley and T. F. Torrance. London: T&T Clark, 2010.

Bataille, Georges. *Inner Experience*. Trans. Stuart Kendall. Albany: SUNY Press, 2014.

Bataille, Georges. *On Nietzsche*. Trans. Stuart Kendall. Albany: SUNY Press, 2015.

Baugh, Bruce. 'Introduction'. In Benjamin Fondane, *Existential Monday: Philosophical Essays*. Ed. and trans. Bruce Baugh. New York: New York Review of Books, 2016, vii–xxxv.

Baugh, Bruce. 'Private Thinkers, Untimely Thoughts: Deleuze, Shestov and Fondane'. *Continental Philosophy Review* 48, no. 2 (2015): 313–39.

Baugh, Bruce. 'Sartre, Fondane, and Kierkegaard'. In *New Perspectives on Sartre*. Ed. Adrian Mirvish and Adrian van den Hoven. Newcastle: Cambridge Scholars Press, 2010, 296–314.

Bauman, Zygmunt. 'Interview with Zygmunt Bauman'. In *JDC International Centre for Community Development* (February 2009). http://www.jdc-iccd.org/publications/int erview-with-zigmunt-bauman-2009/

Bauman, Zygmunt. *Modernity and Ambivalence*. Cambridge: Polity Press, 1991.

Bayley, John. 'Idealism and Its Critic'. *New York Review of Books* 14, no. 12 (18 June 1970): 3–5.

Beaumont, Matthew. *Nightwalking: A Nocturnal History of London*. London: Verso, 2015.

Beaumont, Matthew. 'R.S. Thomas's Poetics of Insomnia'. *Essays in Criticism* 68, no. 1 (2018): 74–107.

Bely, Andrei. *Petersburg*. Trans. David McDuff. Harmondsworth: Penguin, 2011.

Benjamin, Walter. *The Arcades Project*. Trans. Howard Eiland and Kevin McLaughlin. Cambridge, MA: Harvard University Press, 1999.

Benjamin, Walter. *The Correspondence of Walter Benjamin, 1910-1940*. Ed. Gershom Scholem and Theodor W. Adorno. Chicago: University of Chicago Press, 1994.

Benjamin, Walter. *Illuminations*. Ed. Hannah Arendt. Trans. Harry Zohn. London: Fontana Press, 1992.

Benjamin, Walter. *One-Way Street and Other Writings*. Trans. Edmund Jephcott and Kingsley Shorter. London: Verso, 1997.

Benjamin, Walter. *Reflections: Essays, Aphorisms, Autobiographical Writings*. Ed. Peter Demetz. New York: Schocken, 1986.

Benjamin, Walter. *Selected Writings*, Vol. 1 (1913–1926). Ed. Marcus Bullock and Michael W. Jennings. Harvard, MA: Harvard University Press, 1996.

Benjamin, Walter. *Selected Writings*, Vol. 2 (1927–1934). Ed. Michael W. Jennings et al. Cambridge, MA: Harvard University Press, 1999.

Benjamin, Walter. *Selected Writings*, Vol. 4 (1938–40). Trans. Edmund Jephcott et al. Cambridge, MA: Harvard University Press, 2003.

Benjamin, Walter and Theodor W. Adorno. *The Complete Correspondence, 1928-1940*. Trans. Nicholas Walker. Cambridge: Polity Press, 1999.

Berdyaev, Nikolai. *The Brightest Lights of the Silver Age: Essays on Russian Religious Thinkers*. Ed. and trans. Boris Jakim. Kettering: Semantron Press, 2015.

Berdyaev, Nikolai. 'The Fundamental Ideas of the Philosophy of Lev Shestov'. In Lev Shestov, *Speculation and Revelation*. Trans. Bernard Martin. Athens: Ohio University Press, 1982, 1–6.

Berger, John. *Portraits: John Berger on Artists*. Ed. Tom Overton. London: Verso, 2015.

Bespaloff, Rachel. *Cheminements et Carrefours*, 2nd edn. Paris: Librairie Philosophique J. Vrin, 2004.

Bloch, Ernst. *The Principle of Hope*, 3 vols. Trans. Neville Plaice, Stephen Plaice and Paul Knight. Cambridge, MA: MIT Press, 1986.

Bloch, Ernst, et al. *Aesthetics and Politics*. London: Verso, 1980.

Bosteels, Bruno. 'Radical Antiphilosophy'. *Filozofski vestnik* 19, no. 2 (2008): 155–87.

Boutcher, Arta Lucescu. *Rediscovering Benjamin Fondane*. New York: Peter Lang, 2003.

Breslin, James E. B. *Mark Rothko: A Biography*. Chicago: University of Chicago Press, 1993.

Broadie, Alexander. 'The Role of Reason in the Assent of Faith – Pascal, Shestov and the Late Medieval Background'. *Lev Shestov Journal* 17 (2017): 57–71.

Brown, Raymond E. *The Death of the Messiah: From Gethsemane to the Grave: A Commentary on the Passion Narratives in the Four Gospels*. New York: Doubleday, 1994.

Buber, Martin. *A Believing Humanism: Gleanings*. Trans. Maurice Friedman. New York: Simon & Schuster, 1967.

Bykova, Marina F. 'Lev Shestov: A Russian Existentialist'. *Russian Studies in Philosophy* 55, no. 5 (2017): 305–9.

Cahiers Léon Chestov/The Lev Shestov Journal, 1- (1997-).

Campbell, Caroline. 'The Agony in the Garden'. In *Mantegna and Bellini*. Ed. Caroline Campbell et al. London: National Gallery, 2018, 135–9.

Camus, Albert. *The Myth of Sisyphus*. Trans. Justin O'Brien. Harmondsworth: Penguin, 2000.

Carlson, Maria. 'Armchair Anarchists and Salon Supermen: Russian Occultists Read Nietzsche'. In *Nietzsche and Soviet Culture: Ally and Adversary*. Ed. Bernice Glatzer Rosenthal. Cambridge: Cambridge University Press, 1994, 107–24.

Celan, Paul. *Collected Prose*. Ed. Rosemarie Waldrop. Manchester: Carcanet Press, 1986.

Chesterton, G. K. *St. Francis of Assisi*. In *Collected Works*, Vol. 2. San Francisco: Ignatius Press, 1987.

Chestov, Léon. *La Nuit de Gethsémani: Essai sur la philosophie de Pascal*. Paris: Bernard Grasset, 1923.

Cioran, E. M. 'Reflections on Philosophy, Poetry, and Benjamin Fondane: An Interview with Leonard Schwartz'. In Benjamin Fondane, *Cinepoems and Others*. Ed. Leonard Shwartz. New York: NYRB, 2016, 209–15.

Clark, Roland. 'Lev Shestov and the Crisis of Modernity'. *Archaeus* XI–XII (2007–2008): 233–48.

Clivaz, Claire. '"Asleep by Grief" (Lk 22: 45): Reading from the Body at the Crossroads of Narratology and New Historicism'. *The Bible and Critical Theory* 2, no. 3 (2006): 29.1–29.15.

Clowes, Edith W. *Fiction's Overcoat: Russian Literary Culture and the Question of Philosophy*. Ithaca: Cornell University Press, 2004.

Coates, Ruth. 'Religious Renaissance in the Silver Age'. In *A History of Russian Thought*. Ed. William Leatherbarrow and Derek Offord. Cambridge: Cambridge University Press, 2010, 169–93.

Coetzee, J. M. 'Philip Roth, *The Plot Against America*'. In *Inner Workings: Essays 2000-2005*, ed. J. M. Coetzee. London: Vintage, 2007, 228–43.

Cole, John R. *Pascal: The Man and His Two Loves*. New York: New York University Press, 1995.

Copleston, Frederick C. *Philosophy in Russia: From Herzen to Lenin and Berdyaev*. Notre Dame: University of Notre Dame Press, 1986.

Covington, Sarah. 'The Garden of Anguish: Gethsemane in Early Modern England'. *Journal of Ecclesiastical History* 65, no. 2 (2014): 280–308.

Crone, Anna Lisa. *Eros and Creativity in Russian Religious Renewal: The Philosophers and the Freudians*. Leiden: Brill, 2010.

Davie, Donald. 'A Puritan's Empire: The Case of Kipling'. *The Sewanee Review* 87, no. 1 (1979): 34–48.

Davison, R. M. 'Lev Shestov: An Assessment'. *Journal of European Studies* 11 (1981): 279–94.

Decker, Gunnar. *Hesse: The Wanderer and His Shadow*. Trans. Peter Lewis. Cambridge, MA: Harvard University Press, 2018.

Deleuze, Gilles. *What Is Grounding?* Trans. Arjen Kleinherenbrink. Grand Rapids: &&& Publishing, 2015.

Deleuze, Gilles and Félix Guattari. *Anti-Oedipus: Capitalism and Schizophrenia*. Trans. Robert Hurley et al. London: Continuum, 2004.

Deleuze, Gilles and Félix Guattari. *A Thousand Plateaus: Capitalism and Schizophrenia*. Trans. Brian Massumi. London: Continuum, 2004.

Deleuze, Gilles and Félix Guattari. *What Is Philosophy?* Trans. Hugh Tomlinson and Graham Burchill. London: Verso, 1994.

Derrida, Jacques. *Specters of Marx: The State of the Deb, the Work of Mourning, and the New International*. Trans. Peggy Kamuf. London: Routledge, 1994.

Desmond, William. 'Between Finitude and Infinity: Hegelian Reason and the Pascalian Heart'. In *Hegel on the Modern World*. Ed. Ardis B. Collins. New York: State University of New York Press, 1995, 1–28.

Desmond, William. 'God Beyond the Whole: Between Solovëv and Shestov'. In *Is There a Sabbath for Thought?: Between Religion and Philosophy*. New York: Fordham University Press, 2005, 167–99.

Desmond, William. 'Murdering Sleep: Shestov and Macbeth'. In *The Tragic Discourse: Shestov and Fondane's Existential Thought*. Ed. Ramona Fotiade. Oxford: Peter Lang, 2006, 67–78.

Dickinson, Emily. *The Complete Poems of Emily Dickinson*. Ed. Thomas H. Johnson. London: Faber & Faber, 1975.

Diment, Galya. *A Russian Jew of Bloomsbury: The Life and Times of Samuel Koteliansky*. Montreal: McGill-Queen's University Press, 2011.

Dostoevsky, Fyodor. *The Idiot*. Trans. David McDuff. Harmondsworth: Penguin, 2004.

Duclaux, Mary. *Portrait of Pascal*. London: T. Fisher Unwin, 1927.

Eagleton, Terry. *Hope against Optimism*. New Haven: Yale University Press, 2015.

Eagleton, Terry. *Radical Sacrifice*. New Haven: Yale University Press, 2018.

Earle, Irene. *Renaissance Art: A Topical Dictionary*. New York: Greenwood Press, 1987.

Edwards, Cliff. *Van Gogh's Ghost Paintings: Art and Spirit in Gethsemane*. Oregon: Cascade Books, 2015.

Eiland, Howard and Michael W. Jennings. *Walter Benjamin: A Critical Life*. Cambridge, MA: Harvard University Press, 2014.

Eliot, T. S. *The Poems of T.S. Eliot*, Vol. 1. Ed. Christopher Ricks and Jim McCue. London: Faber & Faber, 2015.

Eliot, T. S. 'Rudyard Kipling'. In *A Choice of Kipling's Verse*. Ed. T. S. Eliot. London: Faber & Faber, 1941, 5–36.

Europe: revue littéraire mensuelle, ed. Ramona Fotiade 960 (April 2009): 3–201.

Facos, Michelle. *Symbolist Art in Context*. Berkeley: California University Press, 2009.

Falque, Emmanuel. *The Guide to Gethsemane: Anxiety, Suffering, Death*. Trans. George Hughes. New York: Fordham University Press, 2019.

Felstiner, John. *Paul Celan: Poet, Survivor, Jew*. New Haven: Yale University Press, 1995.

Field, George Wallis. *Herman Hesse*. New York: Twayne, 1970.

Finkenthal, Michael. *Lev Shestov: Existential Philosopher and Religious Thinker*. New York: Peter Lang, 2010.

Fitter, Chris. 'The Poetic Nocturne: From Ancient Motif to Renaissance Genre'. *Early Modern Literary Studies* 3, no. 2 (1997): 21–61.

Fondane, Benjamin. *Cinepoems and Others*. Ed. Leonard Shwartz. New York: NYRB, 2016.

Fondane, Benjamin. *Existential Monday: Philosophical* Essays. Ed. and trans. Bruce Baugh. New York: NYRB, 2016.

Fondane, Benjamin. *Rencontres avec Léon Chestov*. Paris: Non Lieu, 2016.

Fondane, Benjamin, *Ulysses: Bilingual Edition*. Trans. Nathaniel Rudavsky-Brody. New York: Syracuse University Press, 2017.

Fotiade, Ramona. *Conceptions of the Absurd: From Surrealism to the Existential Thought of Chestov and Fondane*. Oxford: Legenda, 2001.

Fotiade, Ramona. 'Introduction to the Second Edition: Lev Shestov – The Thought from Outside'. In Lev Shestov, *Athens and Jerusalem*, 2nd edn. Trans. Bernard Martin. Athens: Ohio University Press, 2016, 1–20.

Fotiade, Ramona. 'La pensée du dehors: posterité et interlocuteurs privilégiés'. In *Léon Chestov, 1866-1938: La pensée du dehors*. Ed. Ramona Fotiade. Paris: Société d'Études Léon Chestov, 2016, 111–31.

Fotiade, Ramona, ed. *Léon Chestov, 1866-1938: La pensée du dehors*. Paris: Société d'Études Léon Chestov, 2016.

Fotiade, Ramona, ed. *The Tragic Discourse: Shestov and Fondane's Existential Thought*. Oxford: Peter Lang, 2006.

Foucault, Michel. 'The Political Function of the Intellectual'. Trans. Colin Gordon. *Radical Philosophy* 17 (1977): 12–14.

Foucault, Michel. 'Standing Vigil for the Day to Come'. Trans. Elise Woodard and Robert Harvey. *Foucault Studies* 19 (2015): 217–23.

Frank, Joseph. *Dostoevsky: A Writer in His Time*. Ed. Mary Petrusewicz. Princeton: Princeton University Press, 2010.

Fraser, Robert. *Night Thoughts: The Surreal Life of the Poet David Gascoyne*. Oxford: Oxford University Press, 2012.

Freedman, Linda. *Emily Dickinson and the Religious Imagination*. Cambridge: Cambridge University Press, 2011.

Friedman, Maurice. 'Martin Buber and Mikhail Bakhtin: The Dialogue of Voices and the Word that Is Spoken'. *Religion and Literature* 33, no. 3 (Autumn 2001): 25–36.

Fries, Willy. *Passion*. Zurich: Orell Füssli Verlag, 1976.

Gascoyne, David. *Existential Writings*. Ed. Ramona Fotiade. Oxford: Amaté Press, 2001.

Gascoyne, David. *New Collected Poems, 1929-1995*. Ed. Roger Scott. London: Enitharmon Press, 2014.

Gish, Nancy K. *Hugh MacDiarmid: The Man and His Work*. London: Macmillan, 1984.

Gogol, Nikolai. *Village Evenings Near Dikanka and Mirgorod*. Trans. Christopher English. Oxford: Oxford World's Classics, 1994.

Goldmann, Lucien. *The Hidden God: A Study of the Tragic Vision in the Pensées of Pascal and the Tragedies of Racine*. Trans. Philip Thody. London: Verso, 2016.

Gondreau, Paul. 'St. Thomas Aquinas, the Communication of Idioms, and the Suffering of Christ in the Garden of Gethsemane'. In *Divine Impossibility and the Mystery of Human Suffering*. Ed. James F. Keating and Thomas Joseph White. Michigan: Eerdmans, 2009, 214–45.

Gray, John. *Seven Types of Atheism*. London: Allen Lane, 2018.

Greer, Joan E. 'A Modern Gethsemane: Vincent Van Gogh's *Olive Grove*'. *Van Gogh Museum Journal* (2001): 106–17.

Groys, Boris. *Introduction to Antiphilosophy*. Trans. David Fernbach. London: Verso, 2012.

Hankin, Cherry A., ed. *Letters between Katherine Mansfield and John Middleton Murry*. New York: New Amsterdam, 1991.

Harrison, Andrew. *The Life of D.H. Lawrence: A Critical Biography*. Chichester: Wiley, 2016.

Herbert, George. *The English Poems of George Herbert*. Ed. C. A. Patrides. London: J.M. Dent, 1974.

Hesse, Herman. 'Recent German Poetry'. *The Criterion* 1, no. 1 (October 1922): 89–93.

Hesse, Hermann. *In Sight of Chaos*. Trans. Stephen Hudson. Zurich: Verlag Seldwyla, 1923.

Hobhouse, L. T. *Questions of War and Peace*. London: T. Fisher Unwin, 1916.

Horowitz, Brian. 'The Demolition of Reason in Lev Shestov's Athens and Jerusalem [*sic*]'. *Poetics Today* 19, no. 2 (1998): 221–33.

Hunter, Graham. *Pascal the Philosopher: An Introduction*. Toronto: University of Toronto Press, 2013.

Hyde, John Kenneth. *Benjamin Fondane: A Presentation of His Life and Works*. Paris: Droz, 1971.

James, C. L. R. *Notes on Dialectics: Hegel, Marx, Lenin*. London: Allison & Busby, 1980.

Jaspers, Karl. *The Great Philosophers: The Disturbers*. Ed. and trans. Michael Ermarth and Leonard H. Ehrlich. New York: Harcourt Bruce, 1995.

Jones, Paul Dafydd. 'Karl Barth on Gethsemane'. *International Journal of Systematic Theology* 9, no. 2 (2007): 148–71.

Kahmen, Volker. 'Walter Benjamin and Werner Kraft'. In *For Walter Benjamin: Documentation, Essays and a Sketch*. Ed. Ingrid and Konrad Scheurmann. Trans. Timothy Nevill. Bonn: AsKI, 1993, 35–55.

Kendall, Stuart. *Georges Bataille*. London: Reaktion, 2007.

Kermode, Frank. 'Waiting for the End'. In *Apocalypse Theory and the Ends of the World*. Ed. Malcom Bull. Oxford: Blackwell, 1995, 250–63.

Kierkegaard, Søren. *Søren Kierkegaard's Journals and Papers*, Vol. 3. Ed. and trans. Howard V. Hong and Edna H. Hong. Bloomington: Indiana University Press, 1975.

Kipling, Rudyard. *The Years Between*. London: Methuen, 1919.

Kirmmse, Bruce H., ed. *Encounters with Kierkegaard: A Life as Seen by Contemporaries.* Trans. Bruce H. Kirmmse and Virginia R. Laursen. Princeton: Princeton University Press, 1996.

Kitaj, R. B. *Second Diasporist Manifesto (A New Kind of Long Poem in 615 Free Verses).* New Haven: Yale University Press, 2007.

Klingender, F. D. 'Notes on Goya's *Agony in the Garden'. The Burlington Magazine* 77, no. 448 (1940): 4–15.

Kojève, Alexandre. *The Religious Metaphysics of Vladimir Solovyov.* Trans. Ilya Merlin and Mikhail Pozdniakov. Basingstoke: Palgrave Macmillan, 2018.

Koslofsky, Craig. *Evening's Empire: A History of the Night in Early Modern Europe.* Cambridge: Cambridge University Press, 2011.

Kristeva, Julia. *Black Sun: Depression and Melancholia.* Trans. Leon S. Roudiez. New York: Columbia University Press, 1989.

Lacan, Jacques. *The Ethics of Psychoanalysis, 1959-1960: The Seminar of Jacques Lacan, Book VII.* Ed. Jacques-Alain Miller. Trans. Dennis Porter. New York: Routledge, 2008.

Lacan, Jacques. *The Four Fundamental Concepts of Psycho-Analysis.* Trans. Alan Sheridan. London: Hogarth Press, 1977.

Lacoue-Labarthe, Phillippe. *Heidegger, Art and Politics.* Trans. Chris Turner. Oxford: Blackwell, 1990.

Langton, Daniel R. *The Apostle Paul in the Jewish Imagination: A Study in Modern Jewish-Christian Relations.* Cambridge: Cambridge University Press, 2010.

Law, David R. *Kierkegaard's Kenotic Christology.* Oxford: Oxford University Press, 2013.

Lawrence, D. H. 'Foreword'. In *All Things Are Possible.* Trans. S. S. Koteliansky. London: Martin Secker, 1920, 7–12.

Lawrence, D. H. *The Letters of D.H. Lawrence*, Vol. 3. Ed. James T. Boulton and Andrew Robertson. Cambridge: Cambridge University Press, 1984.

Lefebvre, Henri. *Critique of Everyday Life: The One-Volume Edition.* Trans. Michel Trebitsch. London: Verso, 2014.

Lenin, V. I. *Imperialism: The Highest Stage of Capitalism.* Harmondsworth: Penguin, 2010.

Levinas, Emmanuel. *Existence and Existents.* Trans. Alphonso Lingis. Pittsburgh: Duquesne University Press, 2001.

Levinas, Emmanuel. *Proper Names.* Trans. Michael B. Smith. Stanford: Stanford University Press, 1996.

Levinas, Emmanuel. 'Review of Lev Shestov's *Kierkegaard and the Existential Philosophy'.* Trans. James McLachlan. *Levinas Studies* 11 (2016): 239–44.

Löwy, Michael. *Fire Alarm: Reading Walter Benjamin's 'On the Concept of History'.* Trans. Chris Turner. London: Verso, 2005.

Löwy, Michael. *Redemption and Utopia: Jewish Libertarian Though in Central Europe.* Trans. Hope Heany. London: Verso, 2017.

Lukács, Georg. *The Destruction of Reason.* Trans. Peter Palmer. London: Merlin Press, 1980.

Lukács, György. *Soul and Form.* Ed. John T. Saunders and Katie Terezakis. New York: Columbia University Press, 2010.

MacDiarmid, Hugh. *Complete Poems*, Vol. 1. Ed. Michael Grieve and W. R. Aitken. Manchester: Carcanet, 1993.

MacDiarmid, Hugh. *Complete Poems*, Vol. 2. Ed. Michael Grieve and W. R. Aitken. Manchester: Carcanet, 1994.

MacDiarmid, Hugh. *The Letters of Hugh MacDiarmid*. Ed. Alan Bold. London: Hamish Hamilton, 1984.

MacDiarmid, Hugh. *Lucky Poet: A Self-Study in Literature and Political Ideas*. London: Methuen, 1943.

Madigan, Kevin. 'Ancient and High-Medieval Interpretations of Jesus in Gethsemane: Some Reflections on Tradition and Continuity in Christian Thought'. *Harvard Theological Review* 88, no. 1 (1995): 157–73.

Mann, Thomas. *Doctor Faustus: The Life of the German Composer Adrian Leverkühn as Told by a Friend*. Trans. John E. Woods. London: Vintage, 2015.

Marchi, Andrea de. 'Mantegna/Bellini: Invention versus Poetry'. In *Mantegna and Bellini*. Ed. Caroline Campbell et al. London: National Gallery, 2018, 29–39.

Martin, Bernard. 'The Life and Thought of Lev Shestov'. In Lev Shestov, *Athens and Jerusalem*. Trans. Robert Martin. Athens: Ohio University Press, 1966, 11–44.

Masson, André. *Anatomy of My Universe*. New York: C. Valentin, 1943.

Mayer, Hans. 'Walter Benjamin and Franz Kafka: Report on a Constellation'. Trans. Gary Smith and Thomas S. Hansen. In *On Walter Benjamin: Critical Essays and Reflections*. Ed. Gary Smith. Cambridge, MA: MIT Press, 1995, 185–209.

McCabe, Alexander. 'Shifting French Perspectives on Dostoevskian Anti-Rationalism'. In *Facets of Russian Irrationalism between Art and Life*. Ed. Olga Tabachnikova. Leiden: Brill Rodopi, 2016, 241–57.

McCarey, Peter. *Hugh MacDiarmid and the Russians*. Edinburgh: Scottish Academic Press, 1987.

McColl, Donald. 'Agony in the Garden: Dürer's "Crisis of the Image"'. In *The Essential Dürer*. Ed. Larry Silver and Jeffrey Chipps Smith. Philadelphia: University of Pennsylvania Press, 2010, 166–84.

McFarland, James. *Constellations: Friedrich Nietzsche and Walter Benjamin in the Now-Time of History*. New York: Fordham University Press, 2013.

McGann, Jerome J. *The Beauty of Inflections: Literary Investigations in Historical Method and Theory*. Oxford: Clarendon Press, 1985.

Milosz, Czeslaw. *Emperor of the Earth: Modes of Eccentric Thinking*. Berkeley: University of California Press, 1977.

Moltmann, Jürgen and Elisabeth Moltmann-Wendel. *Passion for God: Theology in Two Voices*. Ed. Douglas Meeks. Louisville: Westminster John Knox Press, 2003.

Monas, Sidney. 'New Introduction'. In Lev Shestov, *Chekhov and Other Essays*. Ann Arbor: University of Michigan Press, 1966, v–xxiv.

More, Thomas. *De Tristitia Christi/The Sadness of Christ*. In *The Complete Works of St Thomas More*, Vol. 14, Part 1. Ed. and trans. Clarence H. Miller. New Haven: Yale University Press, 1976.

Murphy-O'Connor, Jerome. *Keys to Jerusalem: Collected Essays*. Oxford: Oxford University Press, 2012.

Nerval, Gérard de. *The Chimeras*. Trans. Henry Weinfield. Cincinnati: Dos Madres Press, 2019.

Nerval, Gérard de. 'Christ at Gethsemane'. Trans. Henry Weinfield. *Literary Imagination* 8, no. 2 (2006): 229–31.

Nietzsche, Friedrich. *Thus Spake Zarathustra*. Ed. R. J. Hollingdale. Harmondsworth: Penguin, 2003.

Nietzsche, Friedrich. *Untimely Meditations*. Trans. R. J. Hollingdale. Ed. J. P. Stern. Cambridge: Cambridge University Press, 1983.

Obolevitch, Teresa. *Faith and Science in Russian Religious Thought*. Oxford: Oxford University Press, 2019.

Pascal, Blaise. *Pensées*. Trans. A. J. Krailsheimer. Harmondsworth: Penguin, 1995.

Pater, Walter. *Miscellaneous Studies: A Series of Essays*. Ed. Charles L. Shadwell. London: Macmillan, 1896.

Pattison, George. 'Lev Shestov: Kierkegaard in the Ox of Phalaris'. In *Kierkegaard and Existentialism*. Ed. Jon Stewart. Farnham: Ashgate, 2011, 355–74.

Philonenko, Alexis. *Chestov et la question existentialle*. Nice: Led Editions Ovadia, 2017.

Piron, Geneviève. *Léon Chestov: Philosophe du déracinement*. Lausanne: Editions L'Age d'Homme, 2010.

Porus, Vladimir N. 'A Never-Ending Dispute over Morality (Leo Tolstoy and Lev Shestov)'. *Russian Studies in Philosophy* 55, no. 5 (2017): 320–35.

Pound, Ezra. 'Three Cantos'. *Poetry* 10 (June 1917): 113–21.

Pyman, Avril. *A History of Russian Symbolism*. Cambridge: Cambridge University Press, 1994.

Rauch, Leo, ed. *Hegel and the Human Spirit: A Translation of the Jena Lectures on the Philosophy of Spirit (1805-6), with Commentary*. Detroit: Wayne State University Press, 1983.

Ray, Gene. 'History, Sublime, Terror: Notes on the Politics of Fear'. In *The Sublime Now*. Ed. Luke White and Claire Pajaczkowska. Newcastle: Cambridge Scholars Publishing, 2009, 133–54.

Ricoeur, Paul. *Figuring the Sacred: Religion, Narrative, and Imagination*. Trans. David Pellauer. Minneapolis: Fortress Press, 1995.

Rosenblum, Robert. 'Notes on Rothko's Surrealist Years'. In *Mark Rothko*. New York: Pace Gallery, 1981.

Rosenthal, Bernice Glatzer. 'Shestov's Interpretation of Nietzsche'. In *The Tragic Discourse: Shestov and Fondane's Existential Thought*. Ed. Ramona Fotiade. Oxford: Peter Lang, 2006, 133–42.

Roth, Philip. *The Plot against America*. London: Vintage, 2016.

Rubin, Dominic. *Holy Russia, Sacred Israel: Jewish-Christian Encounters in Russian Religious Thought*. Boston: Academic Studies Press, 2010.

Ruprecht, Jr, Louis A. 'Mark's Tragic Vision: Gethsemane'. *Religion and Literature* 24, no. 3 (1992): 1–25.

Sandnes, Karl Olav. *Early Christian Discourses on Jesus' Prayer at Gethsemane: Courageous, Committed, Cowardly?* Leiden: Brill, 2015.

Sartre, Jean-Paul. *Critical Essays*. Trans. Chris Turner. Calcutta: Seagull, 2017.

Scholem, Gershom. *The Messianic Idea in Judaism and Essays on Jewish Spirituality*. New York: Schocken, 1971.

Scholem, Gershom. *Walter Benjamin: The Story of a Friendship*. Trans. Harry Zohn. New York: NYRB, 2003.

Scholem, Gershom. 'Walter Benjamin and His Angel'. In *On Walter Benjamin: Critical Essays and Reflections*. Ed. Gary Smith. Cambridge, MA: MIT Press, 1995, 51–89.

Scholem, Gershom, ed. *The Correspondence of Gershom Scholem and Walter Benjamin, 1932-1940*. Trans. Gary Smith and Andre Lefevere. New York: Schocken, 1989.

Shchedrina, Tatiana G. and Boris I. Pruzhinin. 'The Historicism of Lev Shestov and Gustav Shpet'. *Russian Studies in Philosophy* 55, no. 5 (2017): 336–49.

Shein, Louis J. *The Philosophy of Lev Shestov, 1866-1938: A Russian Religious Existentialist*. Lewiston: Edwin Mellen Press, 1991.

Shestov, Lev. *All Things Are Possible*. Trans. S. S. Koteliansky. London: Martin Secker, 1920.

Shestov, Lev. *Athens and Jerusalem*. Trans. Robert Martin. Athens: Ohio University Press, 1966.

Shestov, Lev. *Athens and Jerusalem*, 2nd edn. Trans. Bernard Martin. Athens: Ohio University Press, 2016.

Shestov, Lev. *Chekhov and Other Essays*. Ann Arbor: University of Michigan Press, 1966.

Shestov, Lev. *Dostoevsky, Tolstoy and Nietzsche*. Trans. Bernard Martin. Ohio: Ohio University Press, 1969.

Shestov, Lev. *In Job's Balances: On the Sources of the Eternal Truths*. Trans. Camilla Coventry and C. A. Macartney. Athens: Ohio University Press, 1975.

Shestov, Lev. *Kierkegaard and the Existential Philosophy*. Trans. Elinor Hewitt. Athens: Ohio University Press, 1969.

Shestov, Lev. *Potestas Clavium*. Trans. Bernard Martin. Athens: Ohio University Press, 1968.

Shestov, Lev. *Speculation and Revelation*. Trans. Bernard Martin. Athens: Ohio University Press, 1982.

Sineokaya, Julia V. 'In the Circle of Non-Vengeance: Lev Shestov and Friedrich Nietzsche'. *Russian Studies in Philosophy* 55, no. 5 (2017): 350–63.

Sineokaya, Julia V. and Anton M. Khokhlov. 'Lev Shestov's Philosophy of Freedom'. *Studies in Eastern European Thought* 68 (2016): 213–27.

Small, Robin. *Time and Becoming in Nietzsche's Thought*. London: Continuum, 2010.

Sotiris, Panagiotis. 'From the "Hidden God" to the Materialism of the Encounter: Althusser and Pascal'. In *Althusser and Theology: Religion, Politics, and Philosophy*. Ed. Agon Hamza. Leiden: Brill, 2016, 152–67.

Stacy, Robert H. *Russian Literary Criticism: A Short History*. New York: Syracuse University Press, 1974.

Stein, Louis J. *The Philosophy of Lev Shestov (1866-1938): A Russian Religious Existentialist*. Lewiston: Edwin Mellen Press, 1991.

Steiner, George. *Lessons of the Masters*. Cambridge, MA: Harvard University Press, 2003.

Surya, Michael. *Georges Bataille: An Intellectual Biography*. Trans. Krzysztof Fijalkowski and Michael Richardson. London: Verso, 2002.

Sutcliffe, Adam. *Judaism and Enlightenment*. Cambridge: Cambridge University Press, 2003.

Tabachnikova, Olga. *Anton Chekhov through the Eyes of Russian Thinkers: Vasilii Rozanov, Dimitrii Merezhkovskii and Lev Shestov*. London: Anthem Press, 2010.

Tabachnikova, Olga. 'Between Literature and Religion: Silver Age Ideas Applied to Modernity – Poetic Outlook as a Type of Religiosity?' *Societal Studies* 10, no. 1 (2018): 32–47.

Tabachnikova, Olga. 'Cultural Anxieties of Russian-Jewish Émigrés: Max Eitingon and Lev Shestov'. In *The Russian Jewish Diaspora and European Culture, 1917-1937*. Ed. Jörg Schulte, Olga Tabachnikova and Peter Wagstaff. Leiden: Brill, 2012, 127–45.

Tabachnikova, Olga. 'Patterns of European Irrationalism, from Source to Estuary: Johann Georg Hamann, Lev Shestov Anton Chekhov'. In *Facets of Russian Irrationalism between Art and Life*. Ed. Olga Tabachnikova. Leiden: Brill Rodopi, 2016, 258–312.

Tongeren, Paul Van. 'Kant, Nietzsche and the Idealization of Friendship into Nihilism'. *Kriterion: Revista de Filosofia* 54, no. 128 (2013): 401–17.

Toscano, Alberto. 'Everybody Thinks: Deleuze, Descartes and Rationalism'. *Radical Philosophy* 162 (2010): 8–17.

Tsvetayeva, Marina. *A Captive Spirit: Selected Prose*. Ed. and trans. J. Marin King. Ann Arbor: Ardis, 1994.

Unamuno, Miguel de. *The Agony of Christianity and Essays on Christ*. Trans. Anthony Kerrigan. In *Selected Works of Miguel de Unamuno*, Vol. 5. Princeton: Princeton University Press, 1974.

Valevicius, Andrius. *Lev Shestov and His Times*. New York: Peter Lang, 1993.

Van Gogh, Vincent. *The Complete Letters of Vincent Van Gogh*, Vol. 1. London: Thames & Hudson, 1978.

Van Gogh, Vincent. *The Complete Letters of Vincent Van Gogh*, Vol. 3. London: Thames & Hudson, 1978.

Vigny, Alfred de. *Poèmes*. Ed. Louis Roinet. Paris: Librairie A. Hatier, 1961.

Vorozhikhina, Ksenia V. 'Lev Shestov's Ideas in the French Philosophical and Cultural Context'. *Russian Studies in Philosophy* 55, no. 5 (2017): 364–75.

Weingrad, Michael. 'New Encounters with Shestov'. *The Journal of Jewish Thought and Philosophy* 11: 1 (2002): 49–62.

Werckmeister, Otto Karl. *Icons of the Left: Benjamin and Einstein, Picasso and Kafka after the Fall of Communism*. Chicago: University of Chicago Press, 1999.

Williams, Rowan. *Meeting God in Mark*. London: SPCK, 2014.

Williams, Rowan. *Poems of Rowan Williams*. Manchester: Carcanet, 2014.

Wilmers, Mary-Kay. *The Eitingons: A Twentieth-Century Family*. London: Faber & Faber, 2017.

Wohl, Robert. *The Generation of 1914*. Harvard, MA: Harvard University Press, 1979.

Yarbro Collins, Adela. *Mark: A Commentary*. Ed. Harold W. Attridge. Minneapolis: Fortress Press, 2007.

Zenkovsky, V. V. *A History of Russian Philosophy*, 2 Vols. London: Routledge, 2003.

Žižek, Slavoj. *The Parallax View*. Cambridge, MA: MIT Press, 2006.

Žižek, Slavoj. 'Psychoanalysis and the Lacanian Real'. In *A Concise Companion to Realism*. Ed. Matthew Beaumont. Oxford: Wiley-Blackwell, 2010, 225–41.

Index

Made in United States
North Haven, CT
12 August 2023

40235918R00117

Lev Shestov

ALSO AVAILABLE FROM BLOOMSBURY